Alcoholism, Attachments & Spirituality

A Transpersonal Approach

By Charles L. Whitfield, M.D.

Medical Director, *The Resource Group,* Baltimore

Clinical Associate Professor of Medicine & Family Medicine,
Clinical Assistant Professor of Psychiatry,
University of Maryland School of Medicine

Faculty, *Rutgers Summer School on Alcohol Studies.*

Distributed for the Author
by
THOMAS W. PERRIN, INC.
East Rutherford, New Jersey

About the Author

Dr. Charles L. Whitfield was born in 1938 and spent his childhood and youth in Atlanta, Georgia. He earned a Bachelor of Arts in English and his medical degree at the University of North Carolina at Chapel Hill. His residency training is in internal medicine, with a subspecialty in hematology, for which he is board certified. He is also certified in the field of chemical dependence by the American Medical Society on Alcoholism & Other Drug Dependencies.

Always sensing that there was something special about alcoholics, other chemically dependent people, their families and others who grew up in dysfunctional families, he began a subspecialty in chemical dependence in 1974. In 1981 he completed a three-year Career Teaching Fellowship with the National Institute of Alcoholism and Alcohol Abuse/National Institute of Drug Abuse. Dr. Whitfield's private practice is devoted to the treatment of persons with chemical dependence, their families, and adult children of dysfunctional families.

Dr. Whitfield also teaches about alcohol and drug problems at the Rutgers Summer School on Alcohol Studies, and at the University of Maryland School of Medicine, where he is Clinical Associate Professor of Medicine and Family Medicine as well as Clinical Assistant Professor of Psychiatry. He specializes in treating professionals and their family members. He has given numerous lectures on these topics across the country. He is the author of *The Patient With Alcoholism* (out of print), and of *Healing the Child Within*.

Dr. Whitfield is available to give talks and workshops on these topics, as well as on spirituality during recovery.

Grateful acknowledgement is given to copyright holders of the cartoons to publish them in this limited pre-print edition. Dr. Whitfield may be reached at 7402 York Road, Suite 101, Baltimore, MD 21204. (301) 337-7772.

The author thanks Ms Lori McDonald, Ms Cheryl Bruchalski, and Ms Amelia Adams for their helpful work typing this book. He also thanks his colleagues and the staff of The Resource Group for their encouragement and suggestions. Finally, he thanks his patients and their family members, who are a continuing inspiration.

To purchase a copy of this book, write to

Thomas W. Perrin, Inc.
POB 190
Rutherford, NJ 07070
1-800-321-7912
or to
Perrin & Treggett, Booksellers
One Madison Street
East Rutherford, NJ 07073
(201) 777-2277

 Formerly published under the title *Alcoholism, Other Drug Problems & Other Attachments & Spirituality: Stress Management & Serenity in Recovery — A Transpersonal Approach*.

ISBN 0-933825-12-9

Table of Contents

Part I - BECOMING

Introduction

On the surface, this book is about a major part of people's recovery from alcoholism, other chemical dependence, and co-dependence. Below the surface, it is about a major part of anyone's recovery from dependence upon or attachment to anything, with recovery from alcoholism being but a model.

Indeed, there are numerous conditions that cause suffering in our daily lives. Handling them can be viewed in a helpful way through the physical, mental and spiritual approach described throughout this book. To help relieve our suffering, we can begin to view this suffering as related to our addictions - as the Western world often calls them, or our attachments - as the Eastern world tends to describe them. We become addicted or attached to the way we think things should be. This includes not only our physical posessions, but our relationships and even our personalities. Some examples of that to which we can become attached, and thereby frequently cause us suffering, are the following.

Some Examples of Attachments or Addictions

Relationships

- Close friends
- Lovers
- Family
- Other intimate relationships

Psychological

- Needing attention
- Needing to be right
  - be rational
  - be intellectual
  - be in control
  - be perfect
  - be a victim
  - please others
  - change others
- Other unrealistic expectations and belief systems
- Needing to alter our state of consciousness

Emotional

- Needing to suffer
- Wanting not to suffer

Behavioral

- Risk taking ("adrenalin junkies")
  - eg Gambling
    - Other excitement

Life style

General
Money
Material posessions

Substance intake

Eating
Chemicals

Our ego/mind or equivalent

Our body

We are each attached and addicted to many things. Using a unified approach that is a part of several modern and ancient psychological and spiritual disciplines, the principles enumerated in this book describe a way out of our dis-ease and our suffering, almost no matter what the cause. Nearly all of these principles will be useful for any form that our suffering may take.

The Zen story is told of the peasant who was crossing a river with only his begging bowl in hand. As he was stepping across the stones, he slipped, lost his grip on his begging bowl, and it was smashed on a stone and was quickly washed away by the river. As he picked himself up and reaached the other side of the river, he said to himself: "Well, there goes my last addiction."

Since alcoholism and other chemical dependence can be seen as a charicature or an exaggeration of our other addictions, attachments, and the resultant suffering therefrom, it can be used as amodel for other forms of our dis-ease and suffering. Whether one is hurting from a broken relationship, has a debilitating, chronic medical or psychological illness, or at times feels the pain and emptiness of the "human condition", this approach can be helpful.

Many clinicians in the field of alcoholism and other chemical dependence (CD), as well as the founders and countless members of self-help groups, describe alcoholism/CD as a three dimensional illness, which includes physical, mental and spiritual dimensions. Other diseases and conditions that cause human suffering have also been similarly described. The wholistic health movement also addresses these three components of our lives in its approach to healing and to prevention. Many disciplines are involved in this movement, ranging from traditional Western medicine to therapy of all sorts. Otherwise conservative physicians, therapists, and practitioners have begun to explore some of the healing possibilities of using such an approach (Simonton et al 1978; Engel 1977; Moss 1981; Joy 1979; Dossey 1982; Peck 1978; Small 1982; Capra 1982; Walsh & Vaughan 1980; Ornish et al 1983; Welwood 1983; Friedman et al 1982; de la Pena 1983; Weil 1984; Cousins 1983; Locke 1983; Benson et al 1984).

A thesis of this book is that effectively handling and preventing stress involves and includes far more than most books about stress management suggest. Using alcoholism, other CD and co-alcoholism as a model is a " natural " to illustrate advanced management of stress in general, since many stress-causing conditions also may have roots in the physical - mental - spiritual dimension.

In this book I describe an approach to the successful recovery from alcoholism/CD that extends beyond abstinence. This approach is also helpful for the stress and suffering of the family of the alcoholic/CD.

After briefly describing the effects of alcohol and alcoholism on the stress response and how conventional stress management techniques can be helpful, I describe an approach that can compliment and transcend conventional psychotherapeutic and stress management techniques. That approach is one that can be called spirituality, as described in the field of alcoholism/CD, or of transpersonal psychology, as described elsewhere (Walsh & Vaughan 1980; Boorstein 1980; Tart 1975).

To keep this book brief I have condensed most of this material. It is thus a summary of some of what is available, both for us to contemplate and to be. For a more expanded and in-depth discussion of these areas one may consult some of the references. For the beginning reader in spirituality and transpersonal psychology I recommend several references (Walsh & Vaughan 1980; Wilber 1979; Peck 1978; Alcoholics Anonymous 1976; James 1982; Jampolsky 1984). There are many other excellent ones.

This book is not meant to be a critique of individual people's thoughts, but rather is an ongoing synthesis of my own discovery of useful transpersonal and spiritual psychology as it applies to the recovery process. I would appreciate feedback from readers.

For those who are not familiar with clinical aspects of alcoholism and other chemical dependence, or with how the illness affects the person's family members, I will outline some of the essentials of recognition and treatment.

Chapter 1. Overview

Recognition

Alcoholism or other chemical dependence can be defined most simply as recurring "trouble", problems, or difficulties associated with drinking alcohol or using other drugs (Whitfield 1982). The areas of dysfunction include, in rough order of occurrence: relationships - especially family, education, legal, health, job and financial. Interference with the person's spirituality tends to occur throughout the illness and extends well into early recovery. Recurring trouble in any <u>one</u> of these areas indicates the presence of alcoholism or chemical dependence. Each of these areas can be measured by administering a diagnostic survey, such as the Michigan Alcoholism Screening Test (MAST) (Selzer 1971). The MAST is simple, relatively non-threatening, and has been validated as a reliable diagnostic survey instrument. Most people tend to answer it truthfully. The clinical interview, the blood alcohol level, the physical and laboratory examinations, and any other available data complete the intake.

Alcoholism is a protean disease, ranking among the most common "great masqueraders" today. It should be looked for in every person who is seeking help in any life area, and should be searched for in more detail in any person with any high-risk complaint, such as depression, trauma, or sexual dysfunction.

The family member of the alcoholic also suffers, and frequently develops physical, mental and spiritual illness. Their condition has been called co-alcoholism or co-dependence. A co-alcoholic is a person who experiences ill health, or maladaptive or problematic behavior that is associated with living, working with or otherwise being close to a person with alcoholism. Co-alcoholism is manifested by a spectrum of symptoms, signs or problems that span from no symptoms at all to headaches to suicide. It affects not only individuals, but families, communities, businesses and other institutions, and states and countries (Johnson 1981; Whitfield 1984). While there are differences between alcoholism and co-alcoholism, there are many similarities (Wegsheider 1981; Cermak 1984; Whitfield 1984). Like alcoholism/CD, co-alcoholism is a highly treatable condition.

Early diagnosis is one of the best ways to reach successful treatment. This is because the early alcoholic has more support systems intact and because denial is often less than in advanced alcoholism. Nearly all of the statments about alcoholism in this book also apply to the person with other drug problems and dependence.

Etiology and Genesis

Although the etiology of alcoholism is unknown, enough is known about it to postulate that it is probably multifactorial (Ewing & Rouse 1978; Whitfield 1983). Health workers view several other chronic illnesses in this way, with hypertension and diabetes mellitus being but two examples.

One can find at least eight categories of possible contributory factors or etiologies for alcoholism (Figure 1). Probably the most convincing is a parental history of problem drinking. The children of alcoholics are at higher risk for developing alcoholism than are those in the general population (Goodwin 1971). If both of one's parents are alcoholic, the risk of becoming alcoholic probably exceeds 50 percent. At times, the illness will skip one generation, usually when people choose to abstain from using alcohol or other drugs, often because their own parent was alcoholic. However, most children of alcoholics deny that their parent was so, although some my use terms like "My mother drank too much," or "My father had an occasional problem with drinking."

Figure 1

MOSAIC THEORY OF THE ETIOLOGY OF ALCOHOLISM AND OTHER CHEMICAL DEPENDENCE

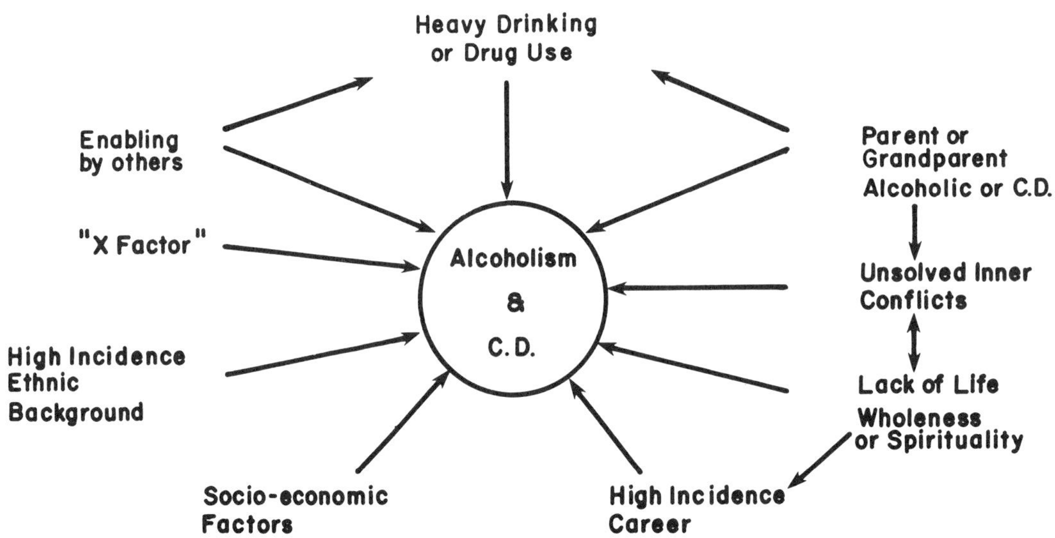

Perhaps an equally convincing cause is heavy drinking or drug use. At least 5% of heavy drinkers become alcoholic every year. One can estimate that from 25 to 75% of persons dependent upon other drugs, excluding caffeine and tobacco, either are or become alcoholic at some time during their lives.

Probably the third strongest causal factor is the phenomenon known as enabling. Enabling means reacting to symptoms of alcoholism in another person in such a way as to shield the alcoholic from experiencing the full impact of the harmful consequences of the disease. Gradually, those enablers who are close to the alcoholic develop a condition called co-alcoholism, described above (Whitfield 1984). A helping professional may become an enabler by not recognizing or making the diagnosis of either alcoholism or co-alcoholism, by treating the alcoholism solely as a symptom of "underlying psychopathology", or by not referring the person for an evaluation or for treatment. Because they received little training in professional school on alcoholism as a primary illness, and because it is now such a treatable condition, many helping professsionals are seeking such skills through books and workshops that address this area.

The "X factor" may be related to inheritance, and may even be acquired. It includes such biological phenomena that are common among alcoholics, such as loss of control, memory blackouts, a lack of hangovers early in alcoholism (Whitfield 1985), a more marked P and alpha brain wave response to alcohol, abnormal acetaldehyde metabolism, and less intoxication and body sway on drinking (Goodwin 1971 & 1982). Over half of alcoholics appear to manifest at least three of these involuntary phenomena.

Ethnic background and career are also factors. For example, second and third generation Irish Catholics and Scandanavian Americans have a higher prevalence of alcoholism than do Italians and Orientals. High incidence careers include, in roughly estimated decreasing prevalence: liquor industry workers and bartenders, entertainers, writers, military personnel, physicians and possibly other health professionals. Socio-economic factors are also influential, as well as are cultural factors such as the media, which pushes alcohol and other substances upon the public many times each day. Also important is a lack of meaning or spirituality in the person's life. I describe this lack of life meaning or spirituality throughout this book.

Unsolved inner conflicts may be due to growing up in an alcoholic and co-alcoholic family, or may result from other causes, including life in general. Interestingly, "psychological problems" are often considered by the general public and by many mental health workers as being the most common cause of alcoholism. However, if one treats the patient from this approach alone, it is unlikely that a successful recovery will be achieved. These remarks are not to discount the importance of treating unsolved internal conflicts that usually develop during and from the person's addiction, and often from growing up in an alcoholic home.

Because alcoholics often suffer as a result of using other drugs, and vice versa, and for other reasons, we now view this condition as one illness, which we call chemical dependence. The principles of treatment are the same for each, whether it be alcoholism or another drug problem.

An Overview of Treatment

Alcoholism is a highly treatable illness. Successful treatment depends on a positively motivated helping professional who is armed with specific diagnostic and treatment skills. Treatment success can be defined as the achievement of abstinence from alcohol and other drugs, or longer and longer periods of abstinence, with improved life-functioning for the person and his or her family. Using this definition, when appropriate treatment is initiated and maintained for a minimum of two years, 70 percent will successfully recover from alcoholism.

The "spontaneous" recovery rate from alcoholism is in the range of from 5 to 8 percent. If a person is motivated into accepting treatment, about 40 to 50 percent will recover. If, in addition, a treatment plan is initiated and regular followup is maintained, about 70 percent will recover. Most alcoholic and other chemical dependent people have to be therapeutically coerced into treatment and to stay in treatment. The appropriate terms for describing an alcoholic in recovery are "recovered" (a public or polite term) alcoholic or "recovering" (a personal or clinical term) alcoholic. The terms "ex-, "reformed", "former", or "cured" alcoholic are misnomers and are inappropriate.

It has been repeatedly shown that treating alcoholics as though their abnormal drinking behavior were secondary to underlying psychopathology is not only usually unsuccessful, but often couter-therapeutic. Insight-oriented or in-depth psychotherapy early in the treatment of alcoholism is contraindicated. By contrast, general supportive and directive psychotherapy, using modern treatment methods and focusing on the alcoholism as a primary illness, is usually eventually effective in helping the alcoholic person reach a successful recovery. Treatment consists of motivating the person into treatment, initiating a treatment plan, and providing regular followup treatment for at least two years.

Alcoholics and other chemically dependent people seem to recover best in group therapy settings. Groups effectively break down the denial process through a combination of identification, confrontation, feedback and support. Every alcoholic should be strongly encouraged to regularly attend Alcoholics Anonymous. Many specialists consider it the single most important aspect of treatment. Formal alcoholism group therapy is also successful. In concert, AA and group therapy are highly successful, constituting one of the strongest forms of treatment available. For the basic principles of assessing and treating alcoholism/CD in the early stages of recovery, i.e. the first one or two years, the reader may consult standard sources (Gitlow & Peyser 1980; Pattison & Kaufman 1982; Whitfield 1981 & 1982; Whitfield et al in press).

Chapter 2. Alcohol & Stress

Stress is a non-specific arousal response which occurs when any demand is made upon a person (Selye 1974; Pelletier 1977). It may be felt strongly or subtly. Some workers in the area of stress say that stress occurs when there is an imbalance between the demand perceived and the person's assessment of his capability to meet that demand (Cox 1979). Stress has also been described as occurring "When you don't get what you want, or when you get what you don't want" (Blaike 1980).

Stress is neither " good " nor " bad ". However, depending on how we chose to use it, stress may be positive or negative in our life. It can thus be growth-inducing, or it can cause illness and suffering, or both.

Transient stress is usually short-lived, especially if it is dissipated with muscle action or with a fairly quick resolution, and thus itself is not damaging. Such a response has been called eustress (Selye 1974; Pelletier 1977; Cox 1979; Nuernberger 1981; Girdano & Everly 1979). However, chronic stress, also called distress (Selye 1974), occurs when the person has an incomplete and thus unhealthy response to a demand, and tension remains and accumulates. Distress is a prolongation and continuation of acute stress and may accumulate and linger indefinitely. When stress is prolonged in this manner, it can fatigue and damage the body, often targeting certain organs. These target organs vary among individuals. Chronic stress can continue for months or years without the person knowing or feeling it.

Physiologically, the stress response consists of a non-specific arousal due to stimulation of the adrenergic or sympathetic nervous system. Often erroneously called " stress ", the stimulus that causes the arousal reaction is more accurately called a stressor (Girdano & Everly 1979). The pituitary gland releases adrenocorticotrophic hormone, and the adrenal gland releases corticosteroids, aldosterone, and the catecholamines norepinephrine and, especially, epinephrine into the bloodstream. The blood glucose rises, as do serum triglycerides and free fatty acids. Other changes also occur (see Figure 2).

All of these hormones and chemicals serve a useful purpose when we are in a physical emergency situation, wherein we need to fight or to flee. But when we do not need to fight or flee, they serve no apparent purpose, and indeed are toxic to our body and often to our psyche. If they continue to be elevated, we can become ill. These elevations of some of the body's toxic though necessary chemicals are either rapidly dissipated with muscle action, or are less rapidly dissipated by slow absorption by the body. However, when elevated chronically, they are toxic to the body and the psyche, and reflect a chronic stress state.

Stressors may be psychosocial (adaptation, frustration, overload, or deprivations), bioecological (nutrition, toxins, noise or biorhythms), or personality related (self-perception, anxiety or behavioral patterns) (Girdano & Everly 1979). Heavy alcohol drinking or other drug using tends to distort and to exaggerate each of these stressors, and thus tends to help bring about a chronic distress state.

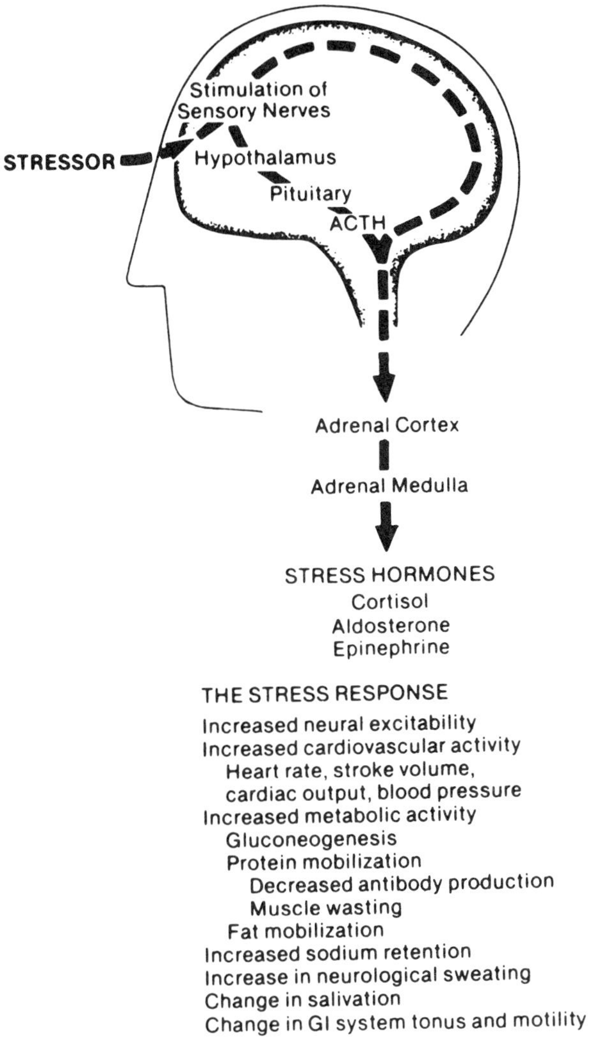

FIGURE 2. The Stress Response Pathway (from Girdano & Everly 1979)

Table 1.
Known Relationships between
Alcohol Intoxication and Stress
(Compiled in part from Pohorecky 1981)

Intoxication

- Can decrease stress in low doses
- Increases stress in high doses

Stress

- No evidence that is a major factor in causing alcoholism
- Often temporarily "sobers up" user

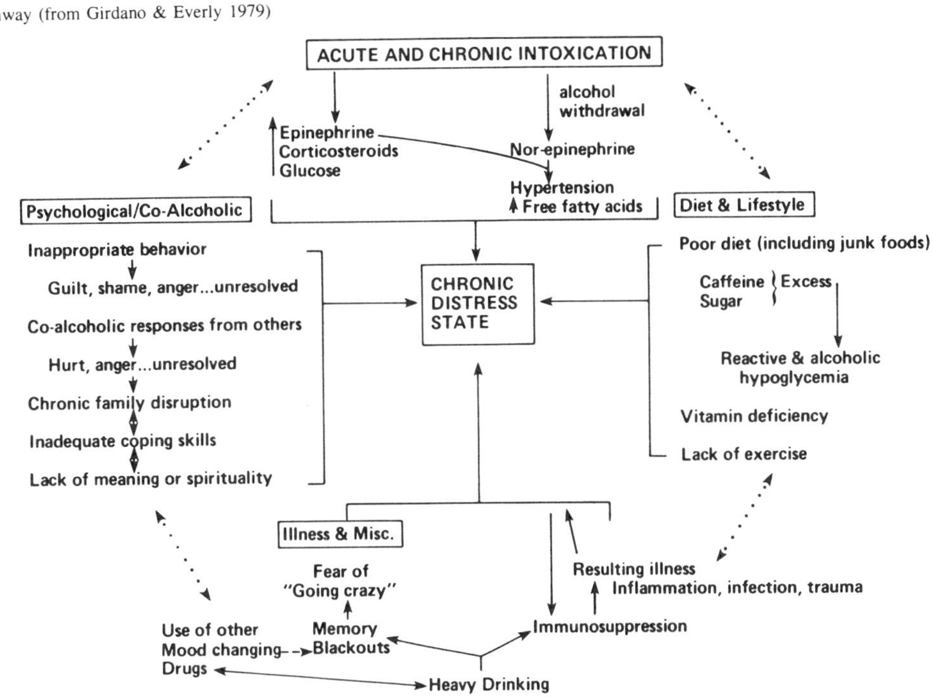

Figure 3. Scheme of Heavy Alcohol Use and an Alcoholic Lifestyle Contributing to a Chronic Distress Reaction

Stress related illness is a major medical, psychological and spiritual problem in the world (Girdano & Everly 1979; Pelletier 1977; Sehnert 1981; Litvak 1980; Schwartz 1982). For example, in the U.S.A. from 60 to 80% of people seeking help in physicians offices are estimated to have stress related conditions. The chronic stress state is estimated to be a major cause of many psychosomatic illnesses and may contribute to many other chronic medical and psychological conditions.

The Role of Alcohol and Other Drugs

Alcohol and other psychoactive drugs may be either stress producers or stress relievers, depending on the dose, frequency, duration and conditions of use, as well as on the physical and emotional condition of the user (Gitlow 1980; Barry 1977). Used acutely and at low doses, alcohol and other depressants are often considered to be stress relievers (Table 1). However, part of the physiological response that depressant drugs produce in humans and in other animals is nearly identical to the acute stress state (Barry 1977). Upon stopping a depressant drug and after the drug effect has abated, a hyperarousal stress state ensues, the severity of which depends upon the dose of alcohol or drug used (Gitlow 1980). But at heavy doses of alcohol or another depressant drug the resulting stress is sizeable, thus exaggerating any pre-existing stress that may be present. By contrast, one alcoholic drink consumed with a meal will cause negligible, if any, stress. Figure 3 shows how continued heavy drinking can initiate a chronic stress state. Combined with an "alcoholic lifestyle" (described below), such heavy drinking assures such a state of chronic distress.

Many alcoholics/CD's believe that they became alcoholic/CD because of stress. However, this illness has a life apart from stress. Many, if not most alcoholics did not have an abnormally stressful life before their alcoholism began (Savada et al 1978; Whitfield, in press). Actually most alcoholics begin as normal drinkers and gradually begin to manifest alcoholic drinking due to unknown factors, and not specifically due to stress (Vaillant 1983). Generally, as the amount of alcohol or other drug intake increases, the more stress is produced.

Alcoholics/CD's, and often their co-alcoholic family members or other close people, usually want stress to be the alleged cause of their alcoholism/CD for two general reasons: so they can continue to drink or to use drugs, while at the same time try to control the excess stress they are feeling. The problem is that since they cannot consistently control their intake, the <u>drinking or using other drugs generates</u> even more stress.

Using alcohol or drugs is not the most efficient way to reduce stress. The disadvantages of using these chemicals are: 1) the helpful effect is transitory, lasting but a few minutes or hours, 2) it usually leaves a hangover or unpleasant after effect, 3) the mind may be clouded while using, preventing judgement and logical thinking, 4) the person may become so accustomed to the drug's effectiveness at temporarily allieviating stress that s/he becomes dependent upon it, and 5) as described above, alcohol and drugs themselves cause stress.

There have been few articles written on alcohol, drugs and stress (Savada 1978; Litman 1974; Bell et al 1976; Pohorecky 1981; Pohorecky & Brick 1983). A study of 370 adults' life stress experience and drinking produced data that were not consistent with a " learned, intentional escapist " model (Savada 1978). Stress-related misuse of alcohol or drugs appeared to be impulsive, possibly reflecting conflict, learned helplessness or an attempt to reduce cognitive dissonance. Another study supported the role of stress in the possible formation of alcoholism (Bell et al 1976). Most articles and monographs refer to people's using alcohol or other drugs to ameliorate stress. Few have mentioned the important and sometimes damaging role of alcohol or alcoholism in causing stress.

Chronic Stress During Recovery

Once stress is maintained through repeated heavy drinking, a vicious cycle is in place (Figure 3). This vicious cycle is magnified and further maintained by what can be called an "alcoholic lifestyle", which may consist of the following additional stressors: inappropriate behavior, inadequate coping skills, co-alcoholic (enabling) or angry responses from others, heavy smoking, lack of sleep, a poor diet, and a generally " overdoing-it " lifestyle. While stopping the alcohol and drugs is the most crucial action, much, if not most of the alcoholic lifestyle may continue during abstinence, maintaining a chronic disstress state. Even though this stress state is usually less than when drinking, it is often enough to cause the person to feel dysphoric - to feel physical, mental, emotional, or spiritual discomfort. One problem is that it may be difficult to convince the person that these - for example, a poor diet - are important factors in their continuing to feel bad.

However, such unnecessary or excess stress can be alleviated. To do so, and thus help make recovery go more smoothly, the person can begin to change some of the factors listed above and in Figure 3. Some of these can be changed fairly quickly (although not always easily), such as altering a poor diet, correcting vitamin deficiency, discontinuing the use of other mood changing drugs, and getting regular physical exercise. The poor diet consumed by alcoholics often consists of "junk" or fast foods, which include refined (white) flour products, caffeine, sugar, sweets, and is lacking in grains, fresh vegetables and fruits. A principle of the healthy diet recommended by many nutritionists and by Overeaters Anonymous is to eat a balanced diet with natural or whole grain flour products and no sugar.

Other stressors can be changed only gradually, over a period from months to years. Some of these are inappropriate behaviors, inadequate coping skills, and chronic family disruption. Probably one of the most effective ways to help bring about a lasting change in these problems for the chemical dependent is through long term group treatment (AA and group therapy), especially by working the Twelve Steps of AA. I discuss the usefulness of these important treatment aids throughout this book. Depending on the degree of severity, individual psychotherapy that is insight-oriented may be of help if indicated, but usually is most effective after from one to three years of abstinence and recovery. Co-alcoholic stress responses from others can aggravate the recovery of the alcoholic/CD, and vice versa (Gorski & Miller 1983 & 84). These common and important stressors can be changed by the family members' regular attendance at Al-Anon, working the Al-Anon program,and by participating in group therapy. Family or individual therapy may be helpful subsequently.

Early recovery itself is usually especially stressful. For one or two hours each time while intoxicated during active drinking or drug using the person at least experiences some peace or relief from stress. As the alcoholism/CD advances, this time duration shortens, so that during advanced stages the relief may last only a few minutes. However, especially during the first 30 days of abstaining from chronic, heavy use of alcohol or drugs, the person often feels no relief from feeling stressed. (Frequently, other people feel good, with increased energy). This is where group therapy and especially AA can be helpful in their provision of warmth, caring and support. Individual supportive and directive psychotherapy is helpful, as long as it does not detract from group therapy and AA. Also, taking disulfiram (Antabuse) can help relieve stress, since taking it tends to remove the frequent and at times nearly constant obsessive thinking and worrying about drinking. This concept of higher stress tending to occur early in recovery also supports the helpfulness of a one month inpatient treatment program.

Another stressor in early recovery is the normal grief reaction that occurs on stopping drinking (Friedman 1984) (discussed further below). This has to be recognized and worked through with patience. Other behavioral addictions can also occur that can contribute to the stress of both active drinking and recovery. Some of these are work addiction (workaholism), pathologic gambling (compulsive gambling) and compulsive overeating or other eating disorders. These must be addressed by both the patient and the therapist.

One stressor - cigarette smoking - should not usually be eliminated until the person has reached a comfortable sobriety. Reaching a comfortable sobriety often takes two to three years or more. At that time it can be useful as a stress reduction method to stop smoking. However, since heavy smoking can aggravate stress, it can be of benefit for people who are in a 30 day or longer inpatient treatment program to stop smoking at the start of the inpatient stay, since there may be support to do so at that time.

Other Stress Reduction Methods

Other methods of reducing stress are available (Girdano & Everly 1979; Pelletier 1977; Sehnert 1981; Schwartz 1982; Mills 1982; Khalsa & Briggs 1979; Brown 1984; B. Brown 1984). Some of these are exercise, meditation, yoga, assertiveness training, strategies to enhance self esteem, social engineering strategies, visualization techniques, biofeedback, self-improvement training and adopting a positive attitude about life. While they are not generally so described, many of these techniques have components that can be called spiritual, which I will be describe in some detail below.

An Approach to Reducing Chronic Distress

If unrelieved, chronic distress eventually causes gradual deterioration and often dysfunction in one or more of our body's organ systems, including our psyche. Just which organ systems are most damaged by chronic distress varies among individuals. For example, some people tend to have headaches, while others have backaches or other musculoskeletal problems, and still others tend to become depressed. We can call each of these affected organ systems " target " organs, feelings, problems, or behaviors. When the chronic distress state becomes severe enough in a given person, the symptoms or signs tend to occur in the same target organs or areas each time. This concept is important in training ourself to begin to recognize the chronic distress state in us. When the target organ or problem flares up, it is time to re-assess how we are caring for ourself. At that time we can ask some of the following questions.

1) Am I overdoing it in any area in my life?
2) Am I getting enough rest and sleep?
3) Am I eating a nutritious diet regularly?
4) Am I consuming too much caffeine, sugar, sweets, or other " junk foods "?
5) Am I drinking alcohol or using any other psychoactive drugs? (This question is for the recovering alcoholic/CD; for the non-alcoholic/CD this question can be modified to ask: Am I drinking alcohol or using other drugs too heavily and/or too often?)
6) Am I exercising regularly?
7) Am I ventillating my feelings in a healthy way to one or more trusted friends?
8) Am I being assertive when and where I need to be?
9) Am I meditating or praying each day?
10) Am I regularly using a sharing and support system? (For the alcoholic/CD, this

can often mean a self-help group and/or, especially in the first two years of recovery, a therapy group)

11) Am I resolving my life's conflicts in a healthy manner?
12) Am I using the powers of my intuition and my imagination?
13) Am I helping others?
14) Am I letting go of my struggle against life (including my expectations and "shoulds")?
15) Am I turning my life's negatives into positives?
16) Am I periodically relaxing and having fun?

These questions address our physical-mental-spiritual dimensions, and thus our wholeness. I will discuss healthy approaches to answering questions six through sixteen throughout the remainder of this book.

To prevent a chronic distress state, we can practice basic stress reducing methods, such as eating nutritional foods, exercising regularly, healthily ventillating our feelings, and turning the negatives in our life into positives. We can also select one or more individual specific stress reducing practices, such as meditation, and practice them regularly. As I suggest throughout this book, I believe that spiritual practices are the most effective long term stress-relievers that are known to humankind. For many people, these practices are easily learned and experienced. And for others they are difficult. Learning to take care of ourself, to nurture ourself, and actually doing it - including asking others, when appropriate, the help nuture us - may be the greatest gift we can give to ourselves and to humankind.

Stress Management & Spirtuality during Recovery

The first effective treatment for alcoholism - Alcoholics Anonymous - involved spirituality in an important way. We may take this observation seriously, and not pass it off as an historical or a mere coincidence.

Of the many books and articles written on stress management, few address the practice of spirtuality. Yet spirituality is a vast area for consideration by both the alcoholic in recovery and by the clinician. It is an effective stress reliever, both short and long term. Because of this, and since there is so much literature available on stress management (see above references) and so little available on spirituality during recovery from alcoholism/CD that is useful or concise, I will devote the remainder of this book to spirituality. Indeed, spirituality subsumes, includes and supports both stress management and psychotherapy. I will discuss some of the ways that it does so.

In a broader and deeper sense, spirituality has a worthy and powerful part to play for everyone, beyond handling the stress in our lives. It adds a richness, dimension and depth to living that celebrates our entire being.

Although the focus of this discussion of spirituality is upon alcoholism/CD recovery and the recovery of the family members, these principles described can be applied for any illness and any suffering. Indeed, alcoholism/CD can be viewed as an advanced or extreme example of many other conditions in which issues such as control, dependence and suffering are an important part. In addition to alcoholism/CD, we can be addicted to relationships, lifestyles, money, work, and more. Addiction nearly always brings about suffering. Spirituality is a way through and a way out of the suffering.

At this point, the reader may wish to take the Spirituality Self Assessment survey as an exercise (Appendix A). It may then be helpful to take it periodically afterwards, to explore any changes that may be occurring in one's life.

Appendix A:

Spirituality Self Assessment Scale

Name ______________________________ Date ____________________

Please make a check mark about where you feel you are regarding the following areas.

	Never	Sometimes		Often	Nearly Always
1) I live in the Here & Now.	1	2	3	4	5
2) I know there is a power greater than I.	1	2	3	4	5
3) I turn the negative things in my life into the positive.	1	2	3	4	5
4) I regularly practice some form of meditation or prayer.	1	2	3	4	5
5) I feel very open to learning about myself from others.	1	2	3	4	5
	Never	Sometimes		Often	Nearly Always
6) I exercise regularly.	1	2	3	4	5
7) I am able to detach from my frustrations by viewing my life as a "game" or melodrama.	1	2	3	4	5
8) I am amused about or laugh at myself.	1	2	3	4	5
9) I am able to concentrate or focus on what I am doing.	1	2	3	4	5
10) I accept "what is".	1	2	3	4	5
11) I regularly take time off for myself for relaxation and recreation.	1	2	3	4	5
	Never	Sometimes		Often	Nearly Always
12) I see the pradoxes in my life, i.e. life's opposites as compatible with each other.	1	2	3	4	5
13) I regularly work a self help program (eg. AA, Al-Anon, other).	1	2	3	4	5
14) Even though I do not always get what I want, I see everything that happens to me as "perfect", i.e. just the way it should be.	1	2	3	4	5
15) I love someone and feel loved by someone important to me.	1	2	3	4	5
16) I have a sense of being able to differentiate my mind (or ego) from my spirit (or higher self).	1	2	3	4	5

17) Regarding my death, I feel prepared and unafraid.	1	2	3	4	5
	Never	Sometimes		Often	Nearly Always
18) I feel an emptiness or void.	1	2	3	4	5
19) I have a meaning, purpose or mission in my life.	1	2	3	4	5
20) I am honest with others.	1	2	3	4	5
21) I am honest with myself.	1	2	3	4	5
22) I practice forgiveness.	1	2	3	4	5
23) I feel unconditional love for another.	1	2	3	4	5
	Never	Sometimes		Often	Nearly Always
24) I choose to have peace of mind	1	2	3	4	5
25) I feel connected to others and to the universe.	1	2	3	4	5
26) I feel sexually fulfilled.	1	2	3	4	5
27) I trust most people.	1	2	3	4	5
28) I am gentle.	1	2	3	4	5
	Never	Sometimes		Often	Nearly Always
29) I enjoy even my most menial tasks, such as cleaning the toilet.	1	2	3	4	5
30) I accept others' choices for themselves, even when they differ from what I would chose for them.	1	2	3	4	5
31) I feel firmly balanced and grounded.	1	2	3	4	5
32) I feel accepting and accepted	1	2	3	4	5
33) I feel unconditionally loved.	1	2	3	4	5
34) I have had the feeling of being close to a powerful spiritual force that seemed to lift me out of myself.	Yes ____			No ____	
35) Other (please write in) ____________ ____________	1	2	3	4	5

Any comments about yourself? ____

____

I and most of my colleagues and many other clinicians in the field of the addictions have observed repeatedly that abstinence alone, whether it be from alcohol, other drugs, or trying to control another's use, is associated with a low likelihood of a successful ongoing recovery. The AA/NA saying that "The same person will drink or use again" is a powerful statement. To realize a successful ongoing recovery, the person first becomes aware of the need for change, then little by little works to change mentally-emotionally and spiritually. Once changed, they will no longer be "the same person," but a new one, more fully conscious and actualized. It is not that they won't want to drink or will be able to drink normally, but that they will now have an effective way of handling life's daily stresses, including not drinking/using/controlling.

But it is also easy to slide back, to regress, to forget. When such a regression continues, the person can unconsciously and easily return to being their former self. However, much of this backsliding can be prevented by daily spiritual practice and, when appropriate, continued work on self-improvement and growth. Some examples of daily spiritual practice are: meditation, prayer, attending self-help meetings, spiritual study groups, and reading spiritual literature. And there are numerous other spiritual practices that on first glance might not appear to be so, such as dream analysis and physical exercise.

We can thus summarize these important principles of recovery as follows.

Recovery Technique	Likelihood of Successful Ongoing Recovery
1) Abstinence alone	Low
2) . . . plus Mental-Emotional change	Moderate
3) . . . plus Spiritual change	Good
4) . . . plus Daily Spiritual Practice	Excellent

Throughout this book I will describe some ways to realize these approaches to growth and to serenity.

By being aware of spirituality in active illness and in recovery, both the recovering person and the counselor or therapist discover that its use provides several advantages over not using it. Some of these are the following.

1) Spirituality is there anyway and many clinicians and recovering people use it well.

2) It is inclusive, not exclusive. Rather than reject other recovery methods, it includes and nurtures them.

3) It is relatively easy to integrate into standard treatments.

4) It offers a wider and deeper perspective than psychological approaches alone.

5) It is more effective clinically than psychological approaches alone.

6) It tends to fill emptiness, forgive shame and guilt, and remove fear. (Organized religion can begin filling emptiness and forgiving shame, though it may also increase shame, guilt and fear.)

7) It is in part based upon a body of knowledge and experience that is both ancient and modern.

8) It helps the person understand successful self-help use of the three fold recovery model, especially including the usefulness of the Twelve Steps of AA/NA/Al-Anon.

9) It helps in understanding important recovery concepts, such as

Trust	Abandonment	Acceptance & Love	Forgiving
Feelings	Hitting Bottom	Patience	Assertiveness
Honesty	Paradox	Risking	Surrender

10) It helps in pacing issues for discussion and work in group or individual therapy.

11) It encourages more risking and self-disclosure, and thus more potential for mental and emotional growth.

12) It is useful in sorting out and in resolving transference and relationship issues.

Becoming aware of our spirituality can help us to answer several important human questions and dillemas. These include:

1) Who am I? (Identity confusion)

2) Can I enjoy my life?
. . . with meaning and purpose?
(i.e. is it all worth it?)

3) Can I experience inner peace? (Attaining serenity)

While these and the above 12 advantages may appear to some readers to be innaccurate and even somewhat grandiose, I invite you at least to consider them as possibilities as you read this book and as you reflect upon your own life and that of others' lives as they unfold. By contrast, other readers may want to actualize these advantages of spirituality immediately - or at least as soon as possible. However, to do so usually takes time and practice, which may thus test an important spiritual challenge - that of patience.

While the addictions are perhaps the clearest examples of illnesses being effectively treated through spirituality, there are several others in which it can be of a major help. Some of these include: psychosomatic and stress related illness, some "psychoses" that are in actuality spiritual emergencies (Grof & Grof 1984 & 85), suicidal ideation, and existential and transpersonal or spiritual conflicts and issues. Frankl (1985) and others go even further, believing that spirituality is helpful in all conditions that befall mankind.

Chapter 3. The Nature of Spirituality

The human spirit can be defined as the principle of conscious and vital life, that which animates the body and the mind (Random House Dictionary 1967; Muktananda 1981). And it is much more. Closely related to humanistic and transpersonal psychology, spirituality has to do with one's relationships in three areas: 1) with one's self 2) with other people, and 3) with the universe, (Schreder 1982; McKeon 1983). It concerns both positive and negative aspects of our lives, ranging from trust, gentleness and love, to confusion, suffering and death. It involves not only the higher realms of our consciousness, but our practical everyday life.

A symbol of freedom of recovery in self-help groups has appropriately been the butterfly. This delicate creature is also a metaphor for spirituality. If we try to grasp it, we can crush it. We have to let it go to experience, appreciate, and enjoy it.

While spirituality is subtle, it is also powerful. Indeed, it appears to be so vast and so powerful that it is often called " the indescribable ". And even when we attempt to describe it through the most intellectual and perceptive of our minds, we know that our description is incomplete. In fact, the mind can begin to understand the spirit only through seeming contradiction and through paradox. Yet all humans have a spirit, and at some time in our lives we have each experienced that part of us. Although people have described it in words, it has to be experienced to know it. Thus, our spirit is not knowable by our intellect. It is only " be-able ".

From the beginning of human kind, we have used metaphors, symbols and stories to create mental concepts and pictures (Metzner 1980). We map with both words and images (Hampden-Turner 1982). But our maps are limited. For example, they are usually two dimensional. Consider different shadows cast by a cylinder, one shadow being circular and another shadow being square. And a cylinder, a sphere and a cone can all cast the same circular shadow, yet that is not what they are. Maps also vary as to the experiences, values, and points of view of the map maker (Hampden-Turner 1982). Superimposed upon these are the experiences, values and points of view of the map reader. A map is like a finger pointing to the moon; it is not the moon. We thus know that " the map is not the territory " (Korzybski 1948), meaning that our description is not the same as our experience. With these reservations in mind, I will attempt to describe and map what may be some clinically useful parameters of the human mind and spirit, and then relate them to the process of recovery from alcoholism, other chemical dependence, and co-dependence. These principles will also be similar for recovery from any debilitating illness or suffering.

Introduction to the Spirit (Self) and the Mind

There is a part of each one of us that is a sanctuary from stress. It can be described by many names, including our spirit, essence, true nature, soul and higher self (Wilber 77; Muktananda 1981). For simplicity, and to emphasize the very personal nature of this part of us all, many have called it " the Self ".

The Self is not the mind. The mind is the ego, the linear-rational thinker, the computer, the busy thought producer.* By contrast, the Self is the wisest part of us, and

---

* I here use the term ego in the more popular sense, and not in a strict psychoanalytic sense, to include the Freudian super ego and part of the id (the remainder of which can be included in the lower two levels of consciousness, described under " Levels of Consciousness " below). The ego is discussed further under " Psychology, Science, Religion and Spirituality " below, and is described throughout this book.

is at peace with itself, the mind, others and with the universe. It is also androgynous, i.e. it has both "masculine" and "feminine" qualities. Our thoughts and ideas are most often a manifestation of our mind, as is our suffering. Some further characteristics of the mind and the Self are listed in Table 2 and Appendix B.

Table 2. Some Characteristics of the Mind and the Self (compiled from Muktananda 1981 and Ram Dass & Levine 1976)

Mind	Self
Ego, id, superego, etc.	Positivity
Other " maps "	Creativity
Survival tool	Boundless Love
Uses defenses	Inner Bliss
Defensive	Drive to contribute
Controlling	All powerful
Righteous	Wisest part
Wants to " win "	Consciousness
Attached	Compassionate
Addicted	Natural or direct knowing
Worse enemy/best friend	Knows the Collective Unconscious
Bondage/liberation	Enlightenment
Hides the Self	Child Within
The way to the Self	Detached
The " body " of the Self	Choice
Contracted consciousness	Humble
Somebody special	Nobody special

None of the traditional Western psychological frameworks or theories adequately relates the mind/ego and the Self. However, Jungian psychology and other psychologies speak of the Self as an archytypal structure of the psyche (Jung 1965; Hall & Nordby 1973; Assagioli 1976; Ferrucci 1982; Walsh & Vaughan 1980). Until the recent interest in Eastern philosophy, Eastern and Western esoteric religions, and in the study of consciousness with techniques such as meditation, yoga and psychedelic substances, Western psychological experiences related to spirituality were usually relegated to the realm of psychopathology. Most psychotherapists learned about " spirituality " from their own and others' religious upbringing and then later often in the context of psychotic symptoms reported by their patients. However, as I will describe thoughout this book, spirituality is far deeper and more vast, and it reflects opportunities for us to reach higher levels of health than normal, whether we are alcoholic or not (James 1982; Maslow 1971; Roberts 1978; Walsh & Vaughan 1980).

A dictionary definition of self is one's own person, identity, individuality, the individual consciousness (Random House 1967). This self can be divided into two parts, which can be called a Higher Self and a lower self. These two parts of us are our more loving, trusting, peaceful, compassionate and understanding nature in the Higher Self, and our competitive ego or mind and our passionate and survival-oriented nature in the lower self. These two can be each further subdivided into three levels, as shown in Table 3. I will discuss these concepts further under " Levels of Consciousness " below.

Some readers may find some difficulty relating to words like " spirituality ", " consciousness ", " Self ", " heart ", or " God ". Part of this difficulty may be related to our personal upbringing and our professional training. For many years my own upbringing and training made them difficult for me to understand. In this book I attempt to clarify and expand upon these words and ideas.

Appendix B: Further Characteristics Ascribed to the Mind & Self (compiled in part from Hampden-Turner 1982)

Reference	Mind	Self
Neuro-anatomical	" Left hemisphere "	" Right hemisphere "
General	Rational, Linear	Intuitive, Creative
	Verbal	Quiet
	Understandable	Paradoxical
	Obvious	Subtle
	Knowledge	Wisdom
	Doing	Non-doing
	Controlling	Letting go
	Fear*	Love
	Chaos*	Peace
	Causal	Acausal
	Hard	Soft
	Form	Formless
	Microcosm	Macrocosm
	Closed	Open
	Many	One
Psychology theory	Psychoanalytic	Transpersonal
(see also below)	Behavioral	Humanistic
I Ching	Yang	Yin
	Time	Space
	Day	Night, etc.
Lao Tsu	Matter	Energy
	Content	Process
	Structure	Design
Homer	Scylla	Charybdis
Greek Tragedy	Hubris	Nemesis
Genesis	Human Purpose	Unified Eden
Descartes	Mind	Body
Bakan	Agency	Community
Freud	Conscious	Unconscious
	Ego	Id
	Secondary process	Primary process
Jung	Thinking	Feeling
	Sensation	Intuition
	Persona	Shadow
Camus	Solitary	Solidary
May	Positivist	Existential
Laing	False self	True self
Becker	Denial of death	Death
Blake	Natural religion	Fourfold vision
Koestler	Commissar	Yogi
	Robot	Lotus
	Outlook	Insight
	Sauter	Reculer
Getzels, Jackson	Convergent	Divergent
deBono	Vertical thinking	Lateral thinking
Buber	I-it	I-thou
Russell	Object-level	Meta-level
Chomsky	Surface Structure	Deep Structure
Salk	Ego	Being
Kuhn	Normal Science	Paradigm Change
Varela	Tree	Net
Levi-Strauss	Positive	Mythic
Williams	Skepticism	Faith
	Reason	Imagination
	Finite	Infinite
	Objective	Subjective
	Active	Contemplative
	Autonomy	Dependence
	Determinism	Freedom
Bohm	Explicate	Implicate
	Unfolded	Enfolded

*Note - in a conventional view these would be reversed, i.e. fear & chaos would be associated with the mystical.

Alcoholism has been described as being a three-fold illness: physical, mental and spiritual. The alcoholic in recovery tends to recover in that order. These components can be illustrated by three circles, either interlocking or separate. To those people who have recovered along a spiritual path, and to those clinicians who work " from their heart ", it is clear that alcoholism/CD and co-alcoholism are spiritual illnesss, diseases of the soul (Martin 1982; Roessler 1982; Royce 1981). They are thus diseases of the whole person.

Relationship of the Self to a Universal Consciousness

A major block to recovery from alcoholism - and often from co-alcoholism - is the person's grandiosity, wanting to control life and others, and not listening to what others offer. Yet their life gradually deteriorates, in spite of attempts at control. The way out of this dilemma is through surrender. What one surrenders to is a power, existence, or consciousness greater than oneself. The higher power can be the group, a universal consciousness, or a light bulb - it does not matter. This surrendering helps the person to listen more constructively and to begin the work of recovery.

Many people with alcoholism, chemical dependence and co-dependence have difficulty with organized religion and often cnfuse it with spirituality. They have frequently experienced barriers from organized religion and their own views of it that have slowed or prevented their acceptance of surrendering to a higher power. Some may believe that organized religion is irrelevant and isolated. Some may have found that praying doesn't work. Others may not nurture their faith, i.e. practice spiritual practices in a disciplined way (Rudd 1983).

Some people have had a conflict over a good versus a powerful and punishing concept of god. Others rely on their own will only, and not on a higher will. Still others tend to intellectualize about a god. They have difficulty experiencing or feeling a higher power. Some have never known love or fellowship from others. Finally, some feel so shameful and unworthy of love from anyone, including a higher power, that they are unable to experience feelings of loving and being loved.

Thus, many active alcoholics and those close to them, for many possible reasons, have become so discouraged with their lives that they have lost their values and meaning. They have lost their spirit for life, they have lost their Self. Many are either agnostic or atheistic. Their higher power has become alcohol, other drugs, and their ego. Thus, for them to surrender to anything is difficult, and to surrender to a Higher Power or a God is even more difficult, if not seemingly impossible. In an unpublished survey of 20 recovering alcoholics attending AA, 12 (60%) said that they did not believe in a Higher Power during their active alcoholism. However, all of them believed in a Higher Power after their recovery (Whitfield 1982).

The Western conception of a popular and perhaps an orthodox spiritual reality is that humankind and God are separated in this life and that heaven and hell come after our life on earth (Wilber 1981). God has often been viewed as being rigid, with a lack of trust and faith in us, and as kingly rather than positive and nurturing (Watts 1975; Kung 1978). It is also viewed as a father, often a punitive one. While this is an overly simplistic, incomplete, and limited view, it is nonetheless a major part of the view that nearly everyone, including most alcoholics in the USA, have grown up hearing, and thus it is the view they so commonly reject.

However, there is a more expansive view of our relationship to a universal higher power. This is a view held in whole or part by many theologians, philosophers, sages, mystics and even scientists, ranging from Spinoza to Einstein, from Schopenhauer to Jung, and from Plato to William James. It is the " perennial philosophy " or psychology

(Huxley 1945; Wilber 1975, 1977, 1981; Quinn 1979; Smith 1976). The two most striking features of the perennial philosophy are that 1) a part of the universal Higher Power or God exists in the consciousness of each human being, and 2) that consciousness exists as a hierarchy of dimensional-levels, moving from the lowest, densest, and most fragmentary realms to the highest, subtlest and most unitary ones (Wilber 1977, 1982). The perennial philosophy has also been called the " primordial tradition " by Smith (1976), " primordial " to emphasize its existing from " the beginning " or its fundamental nature. It has also been given other names (Quinn 1979).

In its purest form, the perennial philosophy is not at all anti-science, but is trans-science or even ante-science, so that it can comfortably co-exist with and complement the hard data of the pure sciences. Einstein expressed this view of reality when he said:

> The most beautiful emotion we can experience is the mystical. It is the sower of all true art and science. He to whom this emotion is a stranger . . . is as good as dead. To know that what is impenetrable to us really exists, manifesting itself as the highest wisdom and the most radiant beauty, which our dull faculties can comprehend only in the most primitive forms - this knowledge, this feeling, is at the center to true religiousness. In this sense, and in this sense only I belong to the ranks of devoutly religious men.

The " religion " of the perennial philosophy is quite different from the salvation of traditional, organized, Western religions. The aim is not to be saved by some external force, but to discover the wholeness within each of us (Huxley 1945; Smith 1976; Wilber 1981). Furthermore, there is no final judgment in which an ultimate evaluation is made on our quality of life by a higher power. We create our own "heaven " and " hell " daily, moment by moment, and thus our own self judgment.

The divine consciousness within each of us is our spirit or our Self. On the hierarchy of consciousness it can be represented by the final three levels, or the Higher Self (Table 3). Moving from bottom to top, the levels of consciousness are: 1) Survival, such as securing food, shelter and warding off illness. 2) Passion, including emotions and lusty sexuality, 3) Power, represented by mind or ego. These three constitute what can be called the lower self. The next level links the lower with the Higher Self. It is 4) Acceptance, represented by the human heart, and reflects acceptance of both our lower and our higher selves. The next levels of the Higher Self, or Self, include: 5) Understanding, natural knowing or intuition, 6) Compassion and love for our fellow men, women and children, and 7) Unity consciousness or being at one with the consciousness of the universe* (Campbell 1975; Small 1982; Ram Dass 1974-83; Motoyama 1981; Keyes 1975). This hierarchy has also been called the Great Chain of Being (Wilber 1981). It is also similar or identical to the ancient Eastern chakra system, also called " spiritual energy centers " or centers of consciusness (Ram Dass 1975; Motoyama 1981; Joy 1979). This system of thinking and being has been refined pragmatically over thousands of years, and while "the map is not the territory", these seven levels of consciousness are a simplified way of beginning to express its knowledge and its wisdom. Smith (1976) said:

> Twenty years ago I wrote a book, The Religious of Man, which presented the world's enduring traditions in their individuality and variety. It has taken me until now to see how they converge. The outlooks of inidividual men and women . . . are too varied even to classify, but when they gather in collectivities - the outlook of tribes, socieities, civilizations, and at the deepest level of the world's great religions - these collective outlooks admit of overview. What then

---

* Our levels of conscious may be divided into from as few as two to as many as thirty two levels, depending on the needs of the individual. I have selected seven levels and have used these names for them for ease of understanding and effectiveness, and because many others have so used them. Perhaps the two most useful categorizations of these levels that I have found are lower self - Higher Self (Small 1982) and gross, subtle and causal (Free John 1977; Wilber 1980).

Table 3. Similar Hierarchies of Human Development, Functioning and Consciousness*: Comparison with Recovery in Self-Help Group Programs and Stress Management/Spiritual Practices

Maslow's Needs		Levels of Consciousness	AA/Al-Anon/NA Program	Corresponding Stress Management/Spiritual Practices in Recovery
	Higher Self	Unity		
Trancendence			Serenity	Letting go
		Compassion		Helping others
		Understanding (Natural knowing)	Helping others	Imaging, visualizing, intuiting
Self actualization		Acceptance (Heart)	Improved relationships	Healthy conflict resolution
	Lower Self			Using sharing & support system
Self-esteem		Power (mind, ego identity)	Self examination, catharsis & personality change	Meditating, playing
				Being assertive & ventillating healthily
Belonging-love		Passion (emotions, sexuality)	Changing isolation to sharing & Higher Power	Exercising regularly
Safety			Admission	Right nutrition
Physiological		Survival (food, shelter, illness)	Active alcoholism/CD	Abstaining from alcohol & drugs

*Note: See text & references for many other similar descriptions of this hierarchy.

emerges is a remarkable unity underlying the surface variety.

It is not surprising that self-help groups such as Alcoholics Anonymous have tapped into and spread this universal knowledge and wisdom.

The wisdom of AA is much of the same universal knowledge that is reflected in the perennial philosophy. It is also found in parts of the world's organized religions. Once could even consider the possibility that the world's organized religions have some commonalities - a common core (Figure 4). A great historian of religion devoted 40 years to determining what the world religions have in common. He found two principles: belief in a Higher Power - if there be one, and that life is worth living - sometimes (Smith 1958). I and others believe that there are more commonalities, such as the direct experiencing of a universal consciousness in our being and in our lives, and the power of forgiveness and unconditional love, as described by the great mystical religious traditions. In this book I further describe these commonalities and other spiritual and psychological principles and relate them to the illnesses of alcoholism, chemical dependence and co-dependence - and other attachments.

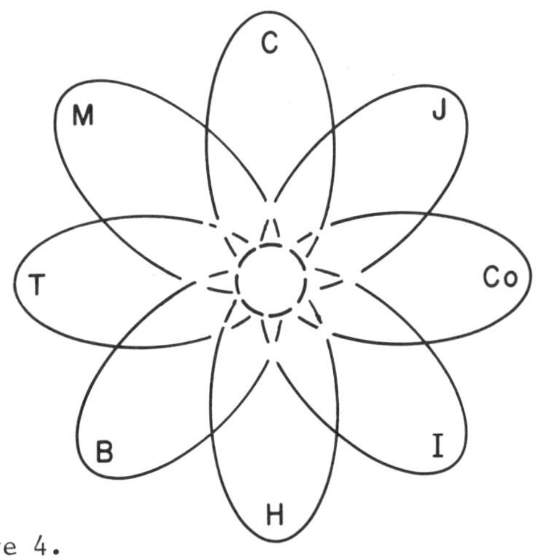

Figure 4.
The Common Core of Religious Systems
(C=Christian, J=Judaism, Co=Confucianism I=Islam, H=Hinduism, B=Buddhism, T=Taoism, M=miscellaneous religions)

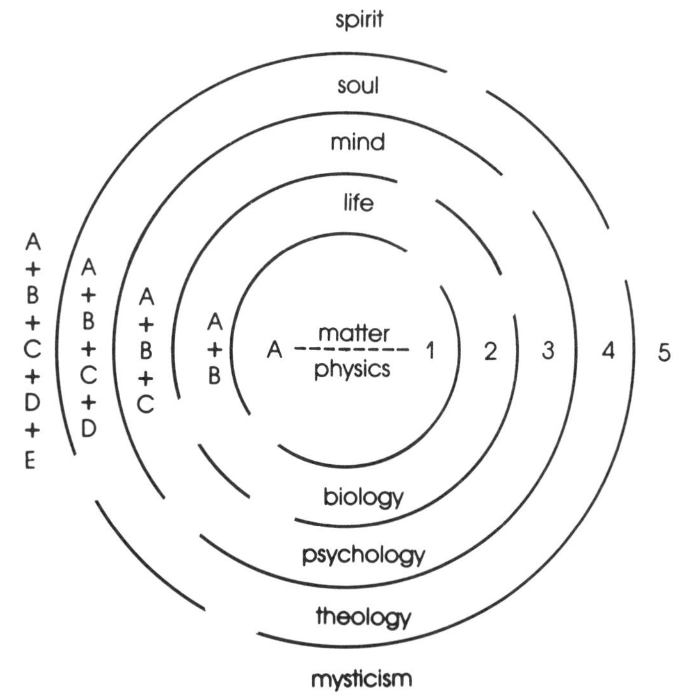

Figure 4-A. The Great Chain of Being. Demonstrating the Inclusiveness, Support, Nurturance and Interconnectedness of Domains of Existence (from Wilber 1984).

Similarity of the Steps of Self-Help Groups and Others to the Hierarchy of Consciousness

Each of us can thus be viewed as becoming, experiencing and being an existence that spans these seven levels of consciousness. These levels are similar to the Twelve Steps of the fellowships of Alcoholics Anonymous, Al-Anon, Narcotics Anonymous, Overeaters Anonymous and other self-help groups. These programs are based on the same Twelve Steps of recovery. These can be simplified as follows: 1) a problem drinking or addicted person, 2) admits powerlessness and unmanageability and begins, 3) changing isolation to sharing and yielding to a Higher Power, and eventually 4) makes a self examination, catharsis & personality change, which can lead to 5) improved relationships and 6) helping others, and thereby likely 7) experiencing serenity. The Twelve Steps of AA are reproduced in Appendix C.

These Twelve Steps are also similar to the hierarchical views of many other cultures and the work of students of consciousness and psychology throughout recorded history. Among the many available, four examples follow. Maslow's hierarchy of needs are: 1) physiological, 2) safety, 3) belonging and love, 4) esteem, 5) self actualization, and 6) transcendence (Maslow 1962, 1968, 1971; Roberts 1978). Glasser views a hierarchy as: 1) being negatively addicted, 2) being symptomatic, 3) giving up, 4) feeling secure, and 5) feeling fulfilled (Glasser 1976, 1980). The top two levels of each of these are actually a bit below the top level of the perennial psychology/levels of consciousness hierarchy, as is the serenity of the AA program (Table 3). Although not included in Table 3, the following two hierarchies are also similar to these examples.

Kaplowitz has extended Piaget's four stages of cognitive development and conventional scientific thinking by two additional stages. All of these also parallel the hierarchy of consciousness. These are: 1) sensori-motor, 2) pre-operational thinking, 3) concrete operational thinking, 4) formal operational thinking, 5) systems thinking, and 6) unitary operational thought (cited in Ferguson 1980). Systems thinking introduces often simultaneous causes that cannot be separated. Unitary operational thinking brings in paradox, meditation, experience, interconnectedness and unity, as opposed to separateness, and the view that it is not a rejection of reason and science, but a transcendence of it. Other examples of similar human hierarchical structure and development can be cited, ranging from organized religions to theoretical psychologists (Erickson 1963; Werner 1964; Kohlberg 1969; Grof 1973; Loevinger 1976; Lacoursiere 1980; Houston 1980; Keyes 1975; Smith 1976; Schuon 1984, Wilber 1977, 1981a & b; Green & Green 1971; Free John 1983; Keen 1983; Branden 1983; Smith 1984 and others).

In an example from 12th century China, the path to " direct knowing " was described as being sevenfold: 1) glimpsing the true nature of reality, 2) encountering the dangers of early experience, 3) needing to train one's attention, 4) dissociating from the individual self or ego, 5) becoming enlightened or discovering that the light was there all along, 6) connecting with the source that generates the world of appearances, and 7) reuniting with all living things (Ferguson 1980).

The similarity among these hierarachies of human development and consciousness may provide a type of conceptual bridge between Eastern and Western psychologies (Roberts 1978). They can also be expanded and made more dynamic by viewing them as a spiral (Houston 1980) or a continuum, rather than separate or distinct stages.

A simplified view of all these levels consists of struggle, confusion, surrender, and seeing the light. This history of our relationship to our consciousness recapitulates these levels, just as ontogeny recapitulates phylogeny. For example, the earliest and lowest of living organisms function at the survival level, whereas the later and higher animals, such as dogs, cats and non-human primates, function as well at an emotional level and at a mind level. I and others believe that most humans function most often at the first three levels, and often as they get older are able to function at progressively higher levels. Many people function up to and at about levels 3 1/2, i.e. barely and occasionally reaching into the Acceptance or heart level. Thus, most of us are only half evolved to our potential. The actively addicted person tends to remain stuck at the first 2 1/2 levels, at times reaching higher. Both the addicted and non- addicted person can at times reach into higher levels, perhaps most commonly during non-drug " peak-experiences " (Maslow 1964) and sometimes during intoxication with psychoactive drugs (discussed under Drugs and Spirituality in Part III). Some alcoholics/CDs/co-alcoholics reach higher levels, or serenity, during advanced stages of their recovery.

Appendix C:

The Twelve Steps of AA (with some key words underlined Showing How Each Addresses the Seven Levels of Consciousness, Practices For Being Our Self, and Mature Ego Defenses)

Step	Survival	Passion	Mind/Ego	Acceptance	Understanding	Compassion	Unity	Surrender	Here & Now	Watching, Witnessing	Meditating	Accepting Paradox	Thinking Positively	Communicating	Being Patient	Forgiving	Telling Story Ventilating	Being Humble	Suspending Beliefs	Accepting Our Shadow	Unconditional Love	Sublimation	Humor	Altruism	Anticipation	Suppression
1. We admitted we were powerless over alcohol - that our lives had become unmanageable.	+		+	+	+	+		+	+	+		+		+			+	+	+	+	+		+		+	
2. Came to believe that a Power greater than ourselves could restore us to sanity.		+	+	+	+	+		+		+		+	+		+			+	+	+		+			+	
3. Made a decision to turn our will and our lives over to the care of God as we understood Him.	+		+	+	+	+	+	+		+		+	+	+		+			+	+	+	+			+	
4. Made a searching and fearless moral inventory of ourselves.			+	+	+	+		+		+		+	+	+		+	+	+	+	+			+		+	
5. Admitted to God, to ourselves and to another human being the exact nature of our wrongs.		+	+	+	+	+	+	+		+				+		+	+	+	+	+	+		+	+		
6. Were entirely ready to have God remove all these defects of character.			+	+	+	+	+	+	+	+			+		+	+		+		+			+			+
7. Humbly asked Him to remove our shortcomings..		+	+	+	+	+	+	+	+		+		+	+				+		+			+		+	
8. Made a list of all persons we had harmed, and became willing to make amends to them all.		+	+	+	+	+	+	+					+	+		+	+	+	+	+	+		+	+	+	
9. Made direct amends to such people wherever possible, except when to do so would injure them or others.		+	+	+	+	+	+	+					+	+		+	+	+	+	+	+		+	+	+	
10. Continued to take personal inventory, and when we were wrong promptly admitted it.		+	+	+	+	+	+	+	+	+			+	+	+	+	+	+		+			+			+
11. Sought through prayer and meditation to improve our conscious contact with God, as we understood Him, praying only for knowledge of His will for us and the power to carry that out.			+	+	+	+	+	+	+		+		+	+	+	+		+	+	+	+	+				
12. Having had a spiritual awakening as the result of these steps, we tried to carry this message to alcoholics, and to practice these principles in all our affairs.*			+	+	+	+	+	+	+		+	+	+	+		+	+	+	+	+	+	+		+	+	
	Levels of Consciousness							Being Our Self														Mature Defenses				

24

Chapter 4. Levels of Consciousness

Defining Consciousness

Defining consciousness is complex. Perhaps its simplest definition is one's degree of alertness or awareness. It is the awareness of what passes not only in our intellectual mind, but in our feelings. In this sense, consciousness is our experience in the now. It is also the process or context (as opposed to content), of where we " come from " in our relating to ourself, to others and to the universe.

Depending on our point of view (itself a form of consciousness), and more academically, we can further define consciousness by our 1) focus of attention, 2) structure, i.e. foreground, background, and overview, 3) attributes, and 4) flow (Marsh 1977). We can also view it from our 5) sensing of our external or our internal world, our body, and our identity, 6) emotions, 7) memory, 8) sense of time, e.g. here and now, 9) evaluating and cognitive processing, 10) motor output, and 11) interaction with our environment (Tart 1975). Many of these attributes have been called "representational systems" by some psychotheorists.

We are most used to our ordinary waking consciousness. Some call our non-ordinary states " alternate " or " altered " states of consciousness. Some examples of these are daydreaming, sleep dreaming, meditation, hypnosis, deja vu experiences, psychoactive drug intoxication, drug withdrawal states, trance states, psychosis, delirium, ecstasy and peak-experiences (Tart 1975; Ferguson 1980; Zinberg 1977).

Consciousness is thus our awareness that is modulated by our knowledge, beliefs, values and priorities. We are in this sense in control of our consciousness. Our consciousness is also continually changing, as a moving stream, never the same from moment to moment (James 1982). The higher we become on the levels of consciousness, the more we become consciousness itself, which is what we are in our truest essence anyway. The specific levels of consciousness can be described in more detail (Wilber 1977). Table 4 describes some characteristics and examples of experiencing each level of consciousness. A brief description of each follows.

Survival

Survival represents our most primitive level of consciousness. Coming out of the will to live, it is an instinctual drive for self-preservation and reproduction. It concerns obtaining food and shelter, bodily functions and metabolism, and the prevention of disease. During human evolution the earliest humanoid beings, from at least three million to as recently as 200,000 years ago, functioned on this level, which has also been called the reptilian or uroboric level (Neumann 1971; Wilber 1981). The being appeared to operate out of fear, and the solution was to find food, shelter and to survive (Small 1982).

Today the pitfall to functioning too much at this level is isolation, which is an end stage of being overly addicted or attached to anything. The person who is stuck at this level may be fearful, paranoid, mistrustful, alienated, hopeless and negatively childish, using primitive ego defenses such as splitting (viewing things as either all positive or all negative) or acting out. Physical illness is usual (Small 1982). To survive, the alcoholic person often stops drinking and temporarily may also enter treatment. Taking the First Step of AA is precisely survival oriented: " We admitted we were powerless over alcohol - that our lives had become unmanageable. "

The treatment of the alcoholic stuck at this level is helping the person achieve 1) abstinence from alcohol and other drugs, and 2) healthy nutrition, which includes minimizing or stopping caffeine, sugar and white flour in the diet, and eating regular, nutritious meals (see Table 3 and Figure 3). 3) Exercising regularly is also helpful, discussed further below.

Table 4. Some Characteristics and Examples of Experiencing Each Way of Being or Level of Consciousness

	Characteristics	Examples
7)	Cannot be described accurately with words	Perfect contentment, fulfillment, serenity and bliss. Experienced in advanced meditation and other peak experiences. Another example is unitive components of experiencing an intimate, prolonged, intense, letting go, loving orgasm. No longer separated from Experience, we become It. Beyond such experiences as these, Unity consciousness is a Divine Mystery.
6)	Unconditional Love and Letting Be	A component of "tough love". Gratifying 12th Step work. Advanced detachment. Non-judgementally and totally forgiving, eg of a new born. Continued serenity and inner peace.
5)	Intuitive or Natural Knowing	Pure creativity and intuitive understanding. Knowing truth without any rational-linear reason. Listening to wisdom, eg correct hunches. Relaxed productive choice. More advanced detachment. A major part of our observer Self, and serenity and inner peace.
4)	Acceptance through Conflict	Resolving conflict. Acute grieving. Cathected struggle. Becoming aware of and resolving conflict in the now. Pain felt from sensing pain in another. The beginning of detachment. The gateway to the Higher Self and to serenity.
3)	"Small-s "self, Ego/Mind	Being rational, intellectual, "right", and separate. Competing. Winning. Thinking (anything passing through the mind in words). Psychoanalytic "secondary process thinking". In AA, "stinking thinking" originates here.
2)	Animal Emotions	Emotions and feelings: mild to intense, gratifying to painful. Psychoanalytic "primary need gratification" (also part of level 1).
1)	Physical	Basic survival. Fight or flight, stress response. Primitive fear. Intense pain. Simple orgasm.

Passion

Emerging out of the will to feel, passion represents the next level. It is alive with feelings and emotions, ranging from pain to pleasure, and from sensuality to devotion to anger. Whereas survival is self-preservation, passion is related to self-gratification (Small 1982). During human evolution, it appears to have gradually come into our beings around 200,000 years ago, and part of it can be called the typhonic or magical level of consciousness development. Now the men, women and children could operate out of several feelings more than out of simple fear. At this stage and level magic was used to ward off death, which is the major threat to survival at level one (Wilber 1981).

To master this level, one needs to experience, i.e. identify, ventilate and process one's feelings in a healthy manner, without too prolonged a delay.* Like caring for our physical needs, constructively handling our most primitive feelings is a spiritual act that pushes us into higher, more functional, and more mature realms.

A major pitfall of this and the next level is a feeling of separateness or duality. The person who becomes stuck here views feelings as a great bother, or worse, as an enemy. Many men and some women experience such a block. The person may not only be out of touch with feelings, but may misuse them to manipulate or to hurt others. There may be a greater than normal lability of mood, and rigidity (Small 1982) and splitting. Both the actively addicted and the person in early recovery usually manifest such a block.

Treatment of the person blocked at this level includes helping the person learn how to 1) experience, handle and use feelings constructively. Especially for the recovering alcoholic, part of this includes 2) learning to be assertive. It also includes 3) letting go of those feelings, e.g. anger and grief, that are blocking the inner peace of the Self. For most people these are life-long tasks that improve in a step wise fashion, and they involve the use of the mind and letting go or opening it to higher levels.

Mind/Ego

Coming out of the will to know and the drive for self definition, the mind is concerned with individual power and identity** (Small 1982; Ram Dass 1974-83). When people are asked " Who are you? ", they usually respond in a mind-oriented and linear-rational manner. They most often answer that they are their job, role, gender or ego in some way. The mind usually stays busy both producing thoughts and ideas, and analyzing them. And above all, it wants to be right. Competition is important to it. Indeed, the mind is a very useful and fairly efficient survival kit for living. However, the mind also rejects parts or extensions of itself, usually those that it believes are not acceptable or " right ", called the " shadow " (discussed further in Part II below). Some other characteristics of the mind are listed in Table 2 and Appendix B.

The mind has studied itself over the ages and has produced hundreds of views or maps of itself (Hampden-Turner 1982). Scientists and psychologists still do not know just what the mind is. In human evolution it appears to have come into being in the majority of the human populaton at least by around 2500 B.C., after the verbal or membership stage of developing language and communication, and has been called the mental or egoic level of consciousness (Wilber 1981). Now a person could operate out of thinking, reasoning, and communicating, in addition to passion and survival.

Mastering this level of consciousness appears to be more difficult than mastering the lower two levels. Here one needs to produce and practice constructive and healthy thoughts and thinking. In large part because it operates in a linear-rational manner, to understand and accept itself the mind has to view both itself and the Higher Self through confusion and paradox. While the mind is busy producing difficulties and often misery for itself and others, it also can produce positivity and joy for itself and others. It is thus both a place of bondage and of liberation from suffering (Muktananda 1981).

---

* I use the term "master" not to imply domination and control, but rather to mean a letting go into the experience or level of consciousness, and an acceptance of them; by doing so, one gains a higher level of control.

**Here and throughout this book I use the term mind with a small-m. The "large M" Mind is used by some as being synonymous with the Self.

The person who is blocked or stuck at this level is attached to status, separateness, competition, seeking material goods, being right, and is overly defensive and righteous. Many active and early recovering alcoholics and their family members are stuck in negative parts of this level. It plays a major role in the powerful denial process of both dependence and co-dependence (Whitfield 1981, 1982, 1984 b&c). Indeed, the mind or ego level may be our greatest block to ultimately attaining inner peace or serenity. Both clinicians and patients who try to handle suffering rationally, i.e. through the mind alone, often become so frustrated that they develop an illness or they "burn out".

Treatment of the person stuck here is complex and has many approaches, ranging from psychoanalysis and other ego psychologies to gestalt therapy and meditation (Wilber 1979). The clinician may find the discussion throughout this book to be helpful in sorting out what approach or treatment is most appropriate for each individual. A great advantage of meditation as a part of treatment lies in its ability to quiet the mind. And when the mind is quiet, the person becomes more open to transcending to the heart level of acceptance and to its Higher Self.

In a frequently quoted passage, William James (1982) said,

> Our normal waking consciousness is but one special type of consciousness, while all about it parted from it by the filmiest of screens there lie potential forms of consciousness entirely different. We may go through life without suspecting their existence, but apply the requisite stimulus and at a touch they are there in all their completeness. . . . No account of the universe in its totality can be final which leaves these other forms of consciusness quite disregarded. How to regard them is the question. . . . At any rate, they forbid our premature closing of accounts with reality.

These realms can be called the higher levels of consciousness, which I will now describe briefly.

Acceptance

Driven by a desire for self creation and represented by the human heart, this level concerns awakening and acceptance. Awakening occurs when we get the first glimpses that " things " or " reality " are not the way we thought they were (Ram Dass & Levine 1976) and is an ongoing process of further awakening toward enlightenment throughout our lives. Acceptance occurs when we accept and forgive ourselves and our pasts, as well as our loved ones and fellow humans as we and they are, with all their strengths and their weaknesses, discussed further under " Forgiving "in part II.

To accept, we usually go through conflict with ourselves, others and with the universe. Thus, this level is often described as that of " acceptance through conflict ". The business end of " Tough Love " takes place here, in combination with level five. The Acceptance/heart level is the gateway to experiencing the Higher Self. During human evolution this level may have first begun emerging into our consciousness after that for the mind, and continues to emerge and develop in many of us. Some writers on the subject of consciousness do not describe this level as being a distinct one, but generally describe it under the previous ego level (Wilber 1977, 1981).

This is probably the most tumultous of the seven levels of consciousness. The heart level lies between the lower self and Higher Self, and thereby brings about harmony through conflict (Small 1982). It is difficult to live here, since the mind and passion keep pulling us back, and the conflict can become so painful that we block it all out (Ram Dass 1974-83). Paradoxically, our pain can at times force us to reconsider our approaches to life and to open to new and possibly more useful and serene approaches.

Thus, our heart has another strength, for it is from here that we can really listen and hear what people say, including their joy and their suffering. This includes listening to and hearing our loved ones, our friends and our patients and clients. And listening allows us to transcend to higher levels.

Mastery of this level is by self creation through constructive conflict, living in the now, and caring for and helping our fellow sufferers. Living and working from the heart can be a great therapeutic advantage for the helping professional. If the clinician is open, accepting and caring, the patient usually intuits that and can feel more free to rise into his or her own heart and Higher Self, which is then physically and emotionally healing for both. Accepting and living from the heart is one of our greatest tests and is also one of our greatest opportunities to live to our highest potential as a complete person.

The danger of being stuck here is becoming attached or addicted to conflict. While few active alcoholics live regularly at this level, many do so in an unhealthy way during their recovery. The attachment is in large part to the emotional ups and downs of the conflict, and the person frequently regresses to the Passion level. There may be indiscriminate infatuation, and the ego defense of splitting is common.

Treatment of the person blocked at this level is by helping him or her with the healthy use of sharing and support systems, and by continuing the spiritual practices for lower levels regularly, including meditation. Regular attendance at a self-help group and working its program is very helpful at this level and all of the other six levels. By doing so the recovering person will have an opportunity to experience his or her Higher Self, the three parts of which are described below.

The clinician who becomes overly attached at this level can also suffer. By observing so much suffering and " injustice, " we can become repeatedly angry, and with no release of it, can tune ourselves out and become cold and uncaring, or we may reject our helping role outright, which is often called burn-out (Ram Dass 1974-83; Edelwich & Brodsky 1980). Many, if not most of us have forgotten or deny our heart, which is our gateway to our Self.

In making the transition into understanding the Higher Self, it may be helpful to remember that, because of its " distorted lens " view of reality, the only way that the mind can comprehend the Self is through confusion, paradox, and letting go.

Understanding

Coming out of the love of truth, this level is that of universal comprehension and expression. It can be viewed as being the mirror image of the mind, as the other two levels of the Higher Self can be viewed as being mirror images of their counterparts in the lower self (Small 1981). It thus complements the mind, so that when the two are experienced together, the person's knowledge and understanding are whole. Here paradox is no longer necessary for understanding. Everything is as it is, perfect and undisguished.

Probably a minority of people become this level of their consciousness very regularly, even today. In human evolution, it may have just begun to emerge strongly in some people (Wilber 1981). Although it is difficult to attain, more of us are becoming aware of this and higher realms. This level has also been called " natural knowing ", " intuition in its broadest sense ", and " knowing from the inside. " It is the major level used in contemplative practices. When one experiences consciousness here, one knows by a pure sense of truth, without requiring any material, rational, or scientific evidence that is bound by either space or time (Goldberg 1983). Paradoxically to our mind, this is the part of us that is most creative, and from which it is likely that most of the great discoveries - both scientific and otherwise - and creations of humankind have come. Einstein said, " The mind can proceed only so far upon what it knows and can prove. There comes a point where the mind takes a leap - call it intuition or what you will - and comes out on a higher plane of knowledge " (Wilber & Hayward 1984). Combined with discipline and persistence, periodically functioning at this level is vital to the scientist and the clinician.

Thinking interferes with intuitive discovery and knowing. Our intuition comes when we stop thinking and struggling intellectually. We can awaken our intuition by 1) paying attention to it, wanting and valuing it, 2) learning to quiet our mind, e.g. through meditation, 3) focusing our attention on what we want to attend to (Assagioli 1976), and 4) being quietly and openly receptive to whatever comes (Vaughan 1983).

Thus, mastering this level consists of letting go of our mind or ego enough to experience and become natural knowing. A paradox involved in " getting there " is the same one for becoming the other two levels of the Higher Self, in that it is both simple and complex. For those who have experienced or been universal understanding, no explanation of what characterizes it is usually needed. And for those who have not experienced it , almost no amount of words, symbols, or pictures will be enough to allow experiencing and being it. Yet we each have and are this level (Vaughan 1983). Developing an openness to experiencing it comes from all the spiritual practices mentioned thus far, and especially from meditating, and by living and working " from the heart ".

The person stuck at this level may manifest a " letting go " to such an extent that he or she neglects taking care of the lower self. An example is the recovering alcoholic who turns it all over to a Higher Power, neglecting to be his or her own life's co-creator. There may be loss of concern or discrimination necessary for self care and creativity (Small 1982). Treatment of the person blocked at this level is by working toward a healthy integration of all levels. The AA sayings " First things first " and " Keep it simple, stupid " can apply here.

Compassion

Emerging out of the love of life, this level is represented by compassion, the complementary and mirror image of Passion (Weber 1981; Small 1982). Being compassion, as opposed to compassionate, is concerned with empathy, altruism, love for our fellow sufferer, and wisdom. When we look into the eyes of our patients or clients and see ourselves, we are compassion in one of its highest senses. Being compassion also involves letting the person be, letting them go where they need to go in their own way (Ram Dass 1974-83). Compassion is a major component in the " tough love " talked about in Al-Anon and elsewhere (Table 4).

Starratt (1979) said,

> The compassionate person knows the pain that rises out of our flawed human nature. He doesn't expect people to be always truthful, always brave, always understanding, always kind, always pure, always faithful, always competent, always successful, always right - always in conformity with any ideal you can imagine. The truly compassionate person sees and responds to the limited, dark side of human existence. He looks upon our universal human imperfection with profound pity and an urge to be helpful where he can. He cares for you because you are human, and being human he knows that you suffer at some time or other, in one way or another, and he wants to help . . . (He is also) able to feel

	Staying Sober	Working the Program	Making Self-Change
Stage 4 6 months to One Year	Be grateful. Share your happiness. Count your blessings. Cherish your recovery.	Take a searching and fearless moral inventory. Share your inventory with someone else. Carry the mesage of AA. When you are shaky work with another alcoholic. Seek God's will for you and the power to carry it out.	Accept work to eliminate self-deception. Watch out for anger and resentments. Let go of old ideas. Accept life as it comes. Get out of the " if " trip. Develop the habit of gratitude. Try to heal yourself by helping others. Share your experience, strength, hope. Find the courage to change yourself. Avoid using the truth to injure others. Avoid gossip.
Stage 5 Over 1 Year	Maintain a spiritual condition.	Continue to take a personal inventory. Promptly admit when you are wrong. Meditate. Make a list of those you have harmed. Make amends to them when possible. Practice these principles in all your affairs. Practice rigorous honesty. Admit and correct your errors today. Seek God's will for you and the power to carry it out.	Watch out for complacency. Avoid self-righteousness. Find your own way. Try not to dwell on the faults of others. See adversity as opportunity. Don't fear needed change. Try to do a good mental house-cleaning. Try to become a part of the world you have rejected. Develop self-restraint. Suspend judgment of yourself and others. Find the serenity to accept others. Beware of phony pride. Avoid using the truth to injure others. Be good to yourself. Cherish your recovery.

Since its founding in 1935, AA has helped to make the word "spiritual" more acceptable, no small feat in this modern world. It presents alcoholism as a threefold illness. As described by Kurtz (1979): "The pinch of alienation AA suggests comes less from man's separation from the product of his labor than from modernity's claim and attempt to separate three aspects of human life and experience that are in reality essentially conjoined - the physical, the mental, and the spiritual. The AA insight insists first that body, mind, and spirit are so intimately related within each individual that what affects one influences the others."

Failure to recognize our three essential parts contributes to our suffering in a major way, in that it leaves us feeling empty, incomplete, and, at times, sick. Participation in AA heals that suffering.

However, many people reject the spirituality of AA, often because they have been hurt by their experiences with organized or other religion. But the Spirit is not a prisoner of religion. Every day thousands of people enter self-help group meetings feeling the pain of sadness, fear, guilt, shame, and anger, and leave the meeting feeling good, feeling renewed and whole. The spirituality attained through sharing their own stories and through listening, through honesty and trust, and through surrender and more, opens the heart, and thus the channel to the Self and serenity.

Appendix D

The Twelve Steps of AA Paraphrased in a Transpersonal View

1) Honestly admitting hopelessness, and ego deflation at depth. Insight. Beginning of physical recovery. Oriented to survival. Initial step to being humble.

2) Possibility of surrendering to a higher consciousness. Viewing our life optimistically. Beginning of ego strengthening through another.

3) Deciding to surrender to a higher consciousness. Starting to transcend isolation. Beginning of active spiritual recovery.

4) Self-examination in anticipation of transcendence (positive change). Introspection. Self objectivity as the basis for honesty.

5) Honest self-revelation to another. Continuing to transcend our isolation.

6) Chosing transcendence by being a co-creator with a higher consciousness.

7) Asking our higher consciousness to help us accept and transcend our shadow and our ego. Being humble.

8) Preparing to transcend our isolation through relationships by asking possible forgiveness.

9) Carrying out #8 above. Restitution.

10) Continued self-examination, experiencing, surrender, and ego transcendence. Continued reorganization.

11) Continued transcendence through meditation or prayer. Communicating with a higher consciousness. Faith as an answer to fear.

12) Awakening, leading to altruism and continued spiritual practice.

Appendix G

JUST FOR TODAY

1. **Just for today** I will try to live through this day only, and not tackle my whole life problem at once. I can do things for 12 hours that would appall me if I had to keep them up for a lifetime.

2. **Just for Today** I will be happy. This assumes that what Abraham Lincoln said is true that "most folks are about as happy as they make up their minds to be." Happiness is from within, it is not a matter of externals.

3. **Just for Today** I will try to adjust myself to what is, and not try to adjust everything to my own desires. I will take my family, my business and my licks as they come and fit myself to them.

4. **Just for Today** I will take care of my body. I will exercise it, care for it, nourish it, not abuse or neglect it, so that it will be a perfect machine for my bidding.

5. **Just for Today** I will try to strengthen my mind. I will learn something useful. I will not be a mental loafer. I will read something that requires effort, thought and concentration.

6. **Just for Today** I will exercise my soul in three ways. I will do somebody a good turn and not get found out. I will do at least two things I don't want to do, as William James suggests, just for exercise.

7. **Just for Today** I will be agreeable. I will look as well as I can, dress as becomingly as possible, talk low, act courteously, be liberal with praise, criticize not at all, nor find fault with anything and not try to regulate or improve anyone.

8. **Just for Today** I will have a program. I will write down what I expect to do every hour. I may not follow it exactly, but I will have it. It will eliminate two pests: hurry and indecision.

9. **Just for Today** I will have a quiet half hour all by myself and relax. In this half hour sometimes I will thank God, so as to get a better perspective of my life.

10. **Just for Today** I will be unafraid, specially I will not be afraid to be happy,to enjoy what is beautiful, to love, and to believe that those I love, love me.

THE TWELVE PROMISES OF AA

1. **We will attain** and maintain sobriety.
2. **We are going to know** a new freedom and a new happiness.
3. **We will not regret** the past nor wish to shut the door on it.
4. **We will comprehend** the word "serenity" and we will know peace.
5. **No matter** how far down the scale we have gone, we will see how our experiences can benefit others.
6. **That feeling** of uselessness and self-pity will disappear.
7. **We will lose** interest in selfish things and gain interest in our fellows.
8. **Self-seeking** will slip away.
9. **Our whole attitude** and outlook on life will change.
10. **Fear of people** and economic insecurity will leave us.
11. **We will intuitively know** how to handle situations which used to baffle us.
12. **We will suddenly realize** that God is doing for us what we could not do for ourselves.

Human Will and God's Will

A central stumbling block and opportunity during recovery is surrendering to God's will for us. Thurston (1984) and others describe various stages of human will and its growth and development. This growth and development parallels our seven levels of consciousness. I have summarized these stages of our will in Table 9-A.

The will of the active alcoholic/CD or co-dependent is at stage zero - it is non-existent. Between this stage and stage 4 (God's will) are three important stages or steps. These include the re-building, or at times building from scratch, 1) a new "masculine" or assertive will, 2) a new adult, flexible or "feminine" will, and 3) then discovering an empowering or creative will. In early recovery it can be difficult to jump from no will to God's will very quickly. This is why Steps Two and Three can be so difficult to work through (Two = Came to believe that a Power greater than ourselves could restore us to sanity; Three = Made a decision to turn our will and our lives over to the care of God as we understood Him). Thus, in recovery we have to keep coming back to these two and each of the other Steps, over and over, as Step Twelve describes.

Before we can surrender our will totally to the Will of the Universe, we have to construct or re-construct a strong, yet flexible and creative will of our own to surrender. This is equivalent to building a healthy, i.e. assertive yet flexible ego (e.g. as depicted in Figure 9). When we are ultimately able to surrender our will to God's will, we discover a powerful insight: God's will is also our will. It was ours all along! "There is no strain in doing God's will as soon as you recognize that it is also your own" (Course 1975).

Discovering that God's will is our will is a powerful and freeing insight and experience, thus liberating our soul to higher realms of creativity. Thurston (1984) defines our soul as having three parts: spirit, mind and will. Spirit is already and always free. Our mind or ego, while very useful, is not as free, as described throughout this book. And our will is in a developing state in recovery. Thus, by the energy of our spirit, the survival and achievement orientation of our ego/mind, and the motivational aspect of our will, we grow toward wholeness, each in our own unique way. What a creative and wonderful gift Higher Power has bestowed upon us and upon Itself!

MISS PEACH

Since God created us, a central part of Its will for us is that we become and be who we are as individuals, i.e. "for me to be me" as a unique, complete and whole being. This wholeness includes our being in community with other men, women and children. A key to stress management thus lies our celebrating who we are as a total human being. However, it can be risky to be fully ourself. Perhaps some major meanings of the Twelve Steps are described in AA's "Just for Today" and "Twelve Promises" (see Appendix G). These describe who we already are and how we can live in our wholeness (AA 1976). Indeed, not limited to alcoholics, the physical, mental and spiritual recovery program of AA/Al-Anon is a "way out" of needless suffering for all of humankind.

compassion toward himself. He can be well acquainted with his personal failings and limitations without such knowledge causing him to feel contempt for himself.

Mastering this level consists both of letting go of Passion and at the same time of balancing the two, Passion and Compassion, in an awareness that we are all part of a whole that is both suffering and joyous. (Christ's suffering was called His Passion.) Sharing, belonging and supporting with our friends and loved ones helps us in mastering compassion.

A pitfall is in so over-identifying with the suffering of humanity that one is unable to function and to help others. Treatment of the person stuck at this level involves helping him or her to work toward becoming all levels of consciusness. Other aspects of treatment are described below.

Unity Consciousness

Coming out of the love of the Higher Power, who is also Self, this level concerns self mastery (Small 1982). Students of spirituality and sages often use capital letters in describing this level. It is pure Being, Void, Godhead, samadhi, radical absorption in the Uncreate (Wilber 1981). It is our causal insight and our ultimate identity. It is pure enlightenment and consciousness, the source and nature of all other levels. And it is Indescribale. We are Divinely Ignorant about this level (Free John 1984), yet it is what we seek.

Reaching Unity Consciousness has been a goal of most spiritual people and religions (Kung 1978; Smith 1976; Wilber 1983 a). Many names have been used to describe the Higher Power, some of which are listed in Table 5. In human evolution it is the Creator, having always been and will always be. A paradox is that while it is the Source or the Ground, it is also the Goal, which we each are striving to become (Wilber 1981).

Table 5. Other Names Given for the Self

Higher Self	Nature
Soul	Universe
Intuition	Unity or Universal Consciousness
Natural knowing	Transpersonal Consciousness
Direct knowing	Superconsciousness
Inner voice	The Supreme Identity
Is-ness	The Suchness of the universe
Spirit	Seamless coat of the universe
Ultimate Reality	Buddah Nature (Buddhist)
Reality	Atman (Hindu)
the Absolute	Brahma/Vishnu/Shiva (Hindu)
the One	Allah (Islam)
the Whole	G-d, the Name, Hashem, Adonai (Orthodox Jewish)
the Ultimate	Holy Spirit (Christian, Catholic)
the Unanalyzable	Great Spirit (American Indian)
the Source	God (Judeo - Christian, other)
the Void	Ram
Omega Point	Tao (Chinese, other Eastern)
Oneness	Higher Power (self-help groups)

Mastering this level is total transformation into the One. Few people achieve this until their death. Some get a glimpse of Unity Consciousness through a near death experience, discussed below, or through another powerful peak-experience, and others may get a glimpse of it by using a psychedelic drug. Yet these are not necessary to reach it. Being our Self, possibly including Unity Consciousness, is within us all right now, attained in a split second, if we can open ourself to being it. A Course in Miracles suggests that while on this earth,Unity Consciousness is pure Unconditional Love.

When we use the term "the One" to describe unity consciousness, we have to remember the limitations of doing so. Using such a term may imply finiteness, which is not a characteristic of It, since It has no limitations or boundaries.

Starratt (1979) said " . . . you are a limited variation of the activity of the creating power. The one is you, the knower, as well as all that you know, for there is no line of demarcation anywhere in the universe where the Creating Power ends and something else begins. There is no way that you can separate youself from the ground of your being and thus make it an object of knowledge".

The pitfall is relying on a Higher Power alone, without being one's own co-creator, as is true with all levels of the Self. Treatment of being stuck at this level includes helping the person to work to integrate all the levels into his or her consciousness. Other aspects of Unity Consciousness are described throughout the remainder of this book.

Three Vignette Examples

The following vignettes may be helpful as a further introuduction illustrating some of the clinical and everyday usefulness of the levels of consciousness.

Joan

Joan is a 30 year old social worker, mother of two, and an alcoholic since about age 27. She joined our weekly therapy group six months ago, stopped drinking, and began attending Alcoholics Anonymous meetings several times weekly. As one would expect, her mood swings improved during these first six months of her recovery, and her life became more organized.

One afternoon in group therapy she told of a recent feeling of confusion. She was feeling like there were at least three different parts of herself: 1) a logical or rational self, that knew she was getting better and that she should not drink, one day at a time, and that she should continue going to meetings, 2) a somewhat grandiose self that believed that even though she was the most junior member at the agency where she had just started to work, that she could run the agency better than anyone presently doing so, and 3) a masochistic self, one that wanted to say "to hell with it all" and stop working, explode and curse her bosses. She said he couldn't decide exactly where her alcoholism related to these three "selves".

She had recently stopped taking disulfiram (Antabuse). Over the past few days she had wanted to drink, and she had been scared about it. A part of her wanted to stay healthy and not relapse back into alcoholic drinking. She had then decided to attend an AA meeting every day, to call one of her therapy group members, and to meditate on it all. She soon thereafter decided to resume taking the Antabuse, and returned to trusting in the positive aspects of her recovery.

At the end of the group therapy meeting I pointed out that Joan's confusion over her "three selves" might be clarified by looking at which of these might be a part of her lower self and her Higher Self. Her "logical" self that sounded healthier was probably her Higher Self. Her grandiose self was her Ego/mind level, and her masochistic self was a part of her ego combined with her Passion level. The alcoholism was what locked her into her lower self - and, paradoxically, through her suffering, what allowed her eventually to realize and be her Higher Self. These relationships can be illustrated as follows.

Level		
	7	
	6	
	5	healthier self
	4	working-to-get-well self
	3	grandiose, ego/mind
	2	masochistic self
	1	frightened self

And her Level 4 was the "part" of her that helped handle the urge to drink and that worked on the confusion and on getting well in and outside of the group. At the next few weeks' group meetings she spoke of how helpful thinking about these selves or levels was. At the same time, she felt frightened working on her new job in a lower socio-economic and sometimes dangerous neighborhood. She cried several times while discussing this. Part of this fear was coming from her Survival level. I pointed out that when she can be aware of and confront these parts of herself, she can begin to get free of their stress-inducing effects.

Joan demonstrates a healthy, gradual strengthening and integration of her lèvels of consciousness. She is on her way to wholeness and to serenity.

The next two vignettes are examples of how some people, in their search for serenity, can get "stuck" in their lower self and in their Higher Self.

Harry

Harry was a 34-year-old accountant who was an active alcoholic and chemical dependent since his mid twenties. He was caught by police buying illicit drugs, which forced him into treatment. Treatment consisted of regular attendance at three AA meetings and a weekly group therapy meeting. He remained alcohol and drug free for nine months (to the present). During this time he was tried in court for his drug related arrest, and was given a suspended sentence and placed on probation. Shortly after the trial he required major surgery, the morning of which he experienced a dramatic feeling of inner peace, just before having the surgery. When he got out of the hospital he became very active in a protestant church.

Over the next three months in the group he was relatively quiet, although he looked fine. One day a group member asked him why he had been so quiet. He responded by saying he had found inner peace through Jesus, and spoke in a somewhat preaching way for nearly half an hour on how finding Jesus was the "only way" to recovery and to God.

The group reacted at first with quietness, and then some anger. Two members identified with his getting inner peace through a higher power, but were uneasy about his rigidity of insisting that the only way was through Jesus. One member commented that Harry looked tired, and he replied that he had felt stressed all week, in part related to losing an important customer. The group leader commented that Harry had shared his enthusiasm for his religious feelings for one half hour, but had not used the group to work on his feelings of stress and fatigue.

Harry illustrates a person who is "stuck" in his Higher Self, and is not taking care of the chronic distress affecting his lower self. The group helped him to realize his position. The sages say "Seek Allah, but tether your camel first." To be our Higher Self authentically, we have to be totally aware of our lower self - and take care of it. Harry was not authentically his Higher Self, because he was denying his lower self. More accurately, he was stuck in the self-righteous part of his ego-mind level. I disucss this concept throughout this book, and especially in Chapter 15, Accepting Our Shadow.

Joe and Barbara

Joe was a 62-year-old dentist who was an episodic alcoholic for most of his adult life. He went on drinking binges every few weeks until he lost two jobs and was forced into treatment by the State Dental Association. He became a regular member of AA and his drinking episodes decreased to one every few months. After three years in AA, he voluntarily joined a therapy group to work further on his recovery.

For the first few weeks in the group he was often angry, and attacked the group leaders and group members. Over the next several months he began to participate more constructively in the group. At one group he disagreed with the statm ents about spirituality that another member made. When challenged by other group members, he became angry, saying "Alcoholism is not a supernatural or spiritual disease, any more than cancer or stroke is. All you have to do is not drink, and you'll do O.K. You can't prove to me that there is a higher power. I can't see one. It can't be proved scientifically. 'Turning it over' is a waste!"

These statements set the group into much activity. Several members identified with his statements. Some identified the source of their disbelief in a higher power as their experience with organized religion. Others challenged his statements: "What have you got to lose by pretending that there is something greater than you are?" "Have you ever met people who were serene? Happy?" "It helps. It works. It is successful in gaining a comfortable sobriety." "Joe, it seems like you're looking at spirituality from the outside."

Barbara was another therapy group member, and a 43 year old chemical dependent lawyer, alcohol and drug free for four months. She said "When I was a child I tried to use religion to make my life better and it didn't work. I'm still angry about that. I'm more angry about being an alcoholic. Although I found going to AA meetings helpful early in my recovery, I still do not believe in a higher power."

Joe and Barbara are both "stuck" in their lower selves. They deny the usefulness of spirituality in recovery. This is a denial of their wholeness, their connection with a higher power, their own divine nature. It is a kind of self denial. Self-help groups say that "the same person will drink or use drugs again." At the same time they are fearful and running away from spirituality, by their very denial and anger they are actively seeking it. For lasting recovery in a comfortable sobriety, it is useful for the person to work on his or her mental-emotional and spiritual growth. Since group treatment, which consists of self-help groups and group therapy, are the most helpful long term recovery aid, Joe and Barbara are certainly in the right place. With continued participation, they will likely grow to realize their wholeness.

About three weeks later Joe relapsed on a two week drinking spree. He returned angry at himself, the group and the world. The group encouraged him to enter inpatient treatment for a month, and he refused. Sometimes a group has to let go of trying to help one of its members who won't accept any help. Nonetheless, they were still aware of his needs, and did not ignore him. After two years in the group and five years in AA, Joe has slowly opened up to the possibility that it can be enlivening and freeing to conceive of a higher power. His attitude toward life and toward himself are improved, and the frequency of his drinking binges has decreased so that his last drink was 18 months ago (his previous pattern was binge about every three months).

Progress in recovery is usually slow, coming in fits and starts over a two to five year period of a comprehensive recovery program. Joe and Barbara are both becoming more aware of their lives and are growing little by little. By not drinking or using other drugs, one day at a time, and by continuing in group treatment, and by using spiritual practices, including working the Twelve Steps of AA (discussed later), they will continue to grow to realize their wholeness.

Some Interrelationships of the Higher and Lower Self

Viewed from our human existence, the Higher Self and lower self are interconnected and necessary parts of each of us. Each progressive level of our consciousness not only includes, but subsumes, transcends and nurtures all prece ding levels in the hierarchy (Wilber 1976, 1979, 1981). Thus, for example, the Acceptance/heart level does not ignore the three levels below. It transcends them, and at the same time it includes them and nurtures them. This principle of transcendence yet inclusion, support and nurturing is further illustrated in Figure 4-A(page 22).

The Self, which is the Higher Self, knows no time or space, because it is not in time or space, i.e. it is not limited to time or space. If this part of us were asked " Who are you? " it would not answer as the mind would, with a job, role, or other ego-related answer. Its answer is simply " I am ", needing no limits or boundaries. Edinger (1974) describes the Self as "... the ordering and unifying center of the total psyche (conscious and unconscious) just as the ego is the center of the conscious personality.... The Self is the supreme psychic authority and subordinates the ego to it. The Self is most simply described as the inner empirical deity...."

Ferrucci (1982) said, " Identification with the Transpersonal Self is a rare occurrence - for some individuals, the culmination of years of discipline; for others, a spontaneous extraordinary experience. It was described in ancient times with the Sanskrit words sat-chit-ananda: being-consciousness-bliss. The Transpersonal Self, while retaining a sense of individuality, lives at the level of universality, in a realm where personal plans and concerns are overshadowed by the wider vision of the whole. The realization of the Transpersonal Self is the mark of spiritual fulfillment.

"... The personal self [ego/mind] is a reflection or an outpost of the Transpersonal Self - enough to give us a sense of centeredness and identity. It lives at the level of individuality, where it can learn to regulate and direct the various elements of the personality. Awareness of the personal self is a precondition for psychological health.... Personal and Transpersonal self are in fact the same reality experienced at different levels: our true essence beyond all masks and conditions. "

The mind or personal self has been called " a terrible master and a wonderful servant ". The only way the mind can view the Self is through confusion and as a paradox. While we use our mind to get to our Self, we have to give up our mind to experience and become our Self. We cannot intellectualize or think ourself into spirituality.

Like a whisper, the Self is subtle, and it is also powerful. The Self provides the energy that runs the lower self. Muktananda (1976) said, "... the Self ... works through all your senses. Your eyes can't see, ... your ears can't hear, ... your tongue can't speak without it. The Self is in all senses and without senses ... is all forms and without form. The mind turned outward takes the form of the objects in the world. The mind turned within merges with consciousness and becomes consciousness."

The lower self, represented by the mind, sees us as separate, the two or the many, while the Self sees us, and it all, as one. For the fully realized person to function on earth, he or she continually cycles between seeing the many and being the One, discussed in Part II under " Thinking Positively " and elsewhere.

While we have to give up our ego/mind/personal self to grow to wholeness, we cannot reject this important part of us. Not only an impeccable survival mechanism, the self is the way to the Higher Self. We must honor our self (Branden 1983). With their low self-esteem, alcoholics/CD's and their family members early in recovery generally need to build a healthy and strong ego and self-esteem. Some suggestions for doing so are briefly described in this book and in more detail elsewhere (Jourard 1971; Vaillant 1977; Branden 1983; Simonton 1984).

Chapter 5. Psychology, Science, Religion, and Spirituality

In many ways the fields of psychology, science, and organized religion have assisted us in denying our Self. And paradoxically, in other ways, they have assisted us in being our Self.

Up until the late 1960's, with some few exceptions, traditional psychology and psychiatry did not delve into or concern itself with spirituality and the transpersonal to any serious degree. And few scientists, except for those of the likes of Bohr and Einstein, consciously or publicly related it to their work. However, similar to the history of humankind, the history of science and of healers' views of helping people through the ages has followed a course that is nearly identical to that of the hierarchy of consciousness. In dawn-men and -women there were apparently no healers. Then somewhere around 200,000 years ago, when the Passion level of consciousness is estimated to have begun developing strongly, magic and ritual came into use, represented by the shaman or witch doctor. Over the millenia, demons and evil spirits were used to explain suffering and illness, and then later, more formal and multiple gods were used. Probably around 3,000 B.C. the concept of a single god began to be used by many people (Wilber 1981). After Christ, most people remained bewildered for several centuries, and then gradually, organized religions as we know them today began to emerge. By this time, if a Higher Power were to heal, it was said to work through a representative of organized religion. Eventually, and gradually, mixed with the above, Western medicine began to become a strong force, culminating in the view that scientists and physicians were absolute. In this sense, science and technology can be viewed as being a kind organized religion (Fromm 1967).

In the mid to late 1800's the first two "forces" or "waves" of psychology theory emerged, with the behavioral and the psychoanalytic view of mental development and illness (Sutich 1969). These first two forces tend still to dominate much of psychology theory. But we do not remain the same; we evolve and grow. From at least 1951 until the 1970's, humanistic psychology became the " third force ." It acknowledged humans as more than the sum of their physical reflexes (behaviorism) or their unconscious sources of neurosis and psychosis (Freudianism or psychoanalysis). It introduced a philosophy or way of being in which many useful therapeutic approaches share commonalities to foster choice, creativity, and dignity. It affirmed a view that was new and bold: that experience and meaning are the primary realities in human psychology, thus affirming our existential and the spiritual dimensions (AHP 1982). This set the stage for the "fourth force " - transpersonal psychology - which began around 1969, and which is concerned with the transpersonal and spirituality as a major factor in human development, health, illness and its treatment (Sutich 1969, 1973, 1976).

The spiritual or transpersonal therapy approach helps people with their problems and their lives on all levels of consciousness (Meadow et al 1979). It is thus concerned with attaining levels of psychological health that surpass what is commonly accepted as normal (Walsh & Vaughn 1980). In a practical way it addresses blocks within the lower self and transcendence to higher realms. Its approach is wholistic, eclectic, cross cultural and multidisciplinary. It is concerned with one's belief systems, one's true identity, one's relationship with self, others and the universe, and with growth of and through consciousness. Thus, one's consciousness itself is both the object and the instrument of change (Vaughan 1982). The therapy is limited by the personal fears and beliefs of the therapist as well as by the readiness of the patient or client to explore these realms. The transpersonal therapist generally works " from the heart " as well as the head. The therapy is concerned with both the content and the context or process of one's life. In addition to using any number of therapeutic techniques, it may use dream work, guided imagery and other inward focusing. However, the techniques themselves do not define either the content or the context as transpersonal. It helps the person learn an effective approach to handling life's developments and problems as they arise, rather than resolving a particular one alone (Vaughan 1982).

Vaughan (1984) writes: "The transpersonal perspective is a meta-perspective, an attempt to learn from all different perspectives. It does not attempt to impose a new belief system or a new metaphysics, but rather to see the relationship between existing world views, in order to create something that can be truly transformational in our world. The transpersonal perspective is what has been emerging from the needed integration of ancient wisdom and modern science. Science without wisdom can destroy the world; wisdom without science remains ineffectual. The transpersonal perspective sees the eastern and western approaches as complementary, and recognizes the transcendental mystical unity of all religions. Mystical teachings all agree that the source of wisdom is within. We need to have access to this source of wisdom if we are going to turn the tide of destruction in this time and age. Each tradition has a different way of saying this. In Christianity, it is: 'The Kingdom of God is within.' In Buddhism, enlightenment is the discovery of our own true nature. In Hinduism, the inner search culminates in Self-realization as Atman. In psychology, we speak of the Transpersonal Self as that part of us which has access to the perennial wisdom."

The discussion in this book emphasizes a transpersonal, i.e. a spiritual, psychologic and therapeutic approach to helping both the person and the family with alcoholism/CD. It may also be useful for people with other attachments.

Recognizing a Void

Conventional psychology and psychiatry arose out of the vision that we must change ourselves and not depend on an imaginary God for help (Needleman 1981). Part of that vision was that science, which brought undreamt - of power over external nature, could explain and control our human inner world. Realizing that we can go only so far through them in our journey to find and to actualize ourselves, many of the hopes of both psychology and science are slowly dissolving (Needleman 1981).

Whether voiced by psychiatrists, psychologists, philosophers, scientists or others, humankind has long felt a void, that there was something missing in its life. Einstein said, " The world we have made as a result of the level of thinking we have done thus far creates problems we cannot solve at the same level at which we created them" (cited in Orman 1982). That level, that which is missing, has been with us all along, although we are only now turning to it in a serious way. It is our spirit, our Self. While their desire was to explore the psyche and to strengthen the ego, Freud and others also knew that something crucial was missing (Fromm 1967; Bettelheim 1983), and called at least part of it the unconscious; they kept it at bay by often viewing it as negative or undersirable, and/or the cause of our mental illness. At that time, they may have been unaware of, afraid or reluctant to let go fully into their higher realms (Wilber 1980a; DiLeo 1984). Jung, along with James, Adler, Horney, Assagioli, Maslow and many others, discovered the importance of experiencing the search for self-fulfillment through our higher consciousness, and thus helped set the groundwork for studying and for being the Self.

Many psycho-theorists and psychotherapists today may remain uncertain about the nature and relationship of our two selves. While they are clear about our mind, they are unclear about our Self, and indeed, most do not even call it our Self. As their search continues, they have removed demons and gods from things that can prey upon us, and are currently replacing them with diagnostic categories, pharmacology, and drugs - all of which are useful at our lower levels of consciousness. However, while such a medical model of psychiatry has been developing, a potentially confusing concept to those learning about transpersonal psychology has emerged from within psychiatry theory called " self psychology ". This self, with a "small s", generally represents a part of us that is developing in our psyche, which is within our lower self (Mahler 1975; Kohut 1981;

Kernberg 1982; Mahler & McDevitt 1982; Rangell 1982). An analogy may be made of the developmental points along our life's journey as being the rungs of a ladder and of the climber as being our "self-sense", including its needs, functions and development, in a climb destined to release or detach the self from its former self (Wilber 1981), as it grows and develops. Others describe our self from somewhat different viewpoints (Jourard 1971; Branden 1971, 1983). Another departure has been the work upon and the description of our " right brain " (Hampden-Turner 1982). While this left - right brain concept has important similarities to our ego/mind and our Self (Appendix B), a pitfall to so categorizing our Self as being the same as our right brain lies in its being reductionistic and incomplete. Just as we are more than our psyche, we are much more than the two hemispheres of our anatomical brain.

Whether we call it the Self, the spirit, or the " right brain ", it is not easy to explain, and scientists and psycho-theorists find it difficult to describe or even to imagine. It is not simply the antithesis of the mind. It has been called " the room in which things happen" (Sun 1979). Lao Tsu said that what is useful in a lump of clay is the hole in it, the space in the middle that allows a form. Yet we Westerners continue to have difficulty understanding our " right brain " and being our Self. Our so called " left brain ", which some describe as analogous with our mind, through its " distorted lens " tends to block out our right brain's vision. We thus continue to lock ourselves up, for example, by looking for linear (cause-effect) conclusions. All the while, however, our Self keeps on working and talking to us, through dreams, hunches, flashes of insight, and other ways. We cannot forget it for long.

Organized Religion and Spirituality

Organized religion is important in the evolution of our consciousness. Its rules and rituals often serve a positive purpose. It comes from and is part of spirituality. Much of it can be viewed as being a rational-linear or ego-oriented interpretation and execution of a large part of spirituality. Its organization and its limitations may have resulted in part because of its fear of what might happen if it let go. Letting go might mean that it and the people it serves would then accept rather than reject their dark side, their shadow (discussed in Part II). And each type of religion would then have to accept all other religions.

The traditional, conservative, and organized forms of religion may be called exoteric, and this is the kind of religion that most people have come to understand as being "religion". However, since the beginning of religious existence there has been a less traditional, generally less organized, and more flexible and expansive form called esoteric religion. This type is found within all religions, although it is less exposed, less talked about, and therefore relatively hidden (Figure 4). A simplified view is that it is part of the perennial philosophy.

In the above two paragraphs, and in numerous similar statements throughout this book, I do not at all mean to reject the importance of organized religion in our life's journey. Indeed, organized religion has been a major repository of spiritual concerns and values throughout the ages. It has been concerned with such crucial issues and practices as community, hope, peace, prayer, and the essence of what human life is about. While it has been a major causal factor in the suffering of many, it has also been a major source of release from suffering for many. And like any ego-involved organization, it has had its diversions, difficulties, and distortions; anything that is powerful can be used to help or to harm. It has appropriately corrected itself little by little as it learned from these and from the people it served and the Power that it worshiped. Just as we can make peace with our parents and other close or important people, for those of us who have resentments toward organized religion, we can begin to make peace with it if we choose.

With some few exceptions, there are today only two places that are readily available to many people where they can gather to explore and share spiritual concerns and practics: the meeting places of organized religion and the fellowship of Alcoholics Anonymous. And AA (including NA, Al-Anon, etc.) is generally only available to people who are concerned about alcohol and other drugs in their lives. At first glance these latter groups may appear small in number. On further examination, one finds that there are probably some 15 million alcoholic and chemical dependent people and conservatively an additional 45 million family or concerned others, totalling 60 million people in the USA, or about one third of our population who are suffering from a preoccupation with alcohol or other drugs. However, only an estimated ten percent or less of these attends self-help group meetings with any regularity. Thus, the potential for using these powerful self-help groups as vehicles for the individual suffering person's discovery, growth and enlightenment is enormous. Besides organized religion and AA there are a growing number of diverse groups, ranging from those in spiritual retreats and ashrams, to metaphysical societies, to study groups on various teachings such as A Course in Miracles. Later in their recovery many AA members are participating in the growth-inducing activities of these varied groups as a part of their continued pursuit for spiritual knowledge and serenity.

From a spiritual perspective, there is no competition to help ourselves and others. As Neem Karoli said "The best form in which to worship God is every form". There is slowly a merging of parts of organized religion with these diverse groups. For example, most AA meetings are held in the physical buildings of organized religion. Esoteric and exoteric religious theory are re-merging. An examples, in modern Christian theology a link between these two has been called "Process Theology" (Pittenger 1959). And Teilhard (1945) explored both a dynamic and a scientific link, and his writings continue to influence postively a growing number of theorists, practitioners and scientists (King & Salmon 1983). There are many other links.

The Methods of Science and Spirituality

The interface between and merging of science and consciousness/spirituality has been the subject of several books (Capra 1975; Zukav 1979; LeShan 1975; Wilber 1982; 1983b; Sheldrake 1982; Loye 1983; Comfort 1984; Wilber and Hayward 1984). Science means forming a theory and then checking its accuracy against evidence, ideally more than once. In its purest form it studys the lowest part, matter and its function, of the lowest level of consciousness, Survival. Its information is obtained through the senses, often via machines, and is usually translated into numbers. It is empirical, analytical and reductionistic (Wilber 1979b, 1982, 1983b). Science has and continues to serve us well, although we do not always use it well. However, I believe that the scientific paradigm as we know it is unlikely to solve the problem of stress and suffering - i.e. help us find relief from it without our becoming addicted to or dependent upon damaging chemicals or practices.

The higher the level that one tries to study on the spectrum of consciousness, the more difficult it becomes for our rational - linear mind to apply this scientific method. Thus, to study the mind one needs a different system of observation and verification. Whereas the verification test for the pure science of matter is empiric, sensory and physical, that for the mind is rational, descriptive, phenomenological, linguistic, and involves the meaning and interpretation of symbols (hermeneutics). It also involves using historical data, analyzing and synthesizing concepts, and using introspective psychology and intersubjective communication (Wilber 1979b, 1982, 1983b). The fields of psychology, psychiatry, philosophy and others use these techniques to study the mind and its many aspects.

The study of the Self requires an even different model. Just as we cannot study the mind with the same pure science with which we study its lower level counterpart, the brain and nervous system, likewise we cannot accurately study the Spirit with the rational-phenomenological model that we use for the mind and for behavior. A " category error " occurs if we attempt to reduce one realm to another, or if we attempt to interpret the findings of one level of knowledge in terms of another (Wilber 1979b, 1983b). The study of the Self, which can in part be called ontology, rapidly falls away from what has been called observation, and appears to require an experiential approach for its verification. The experiences involve life itself, with our relationship to our self, others and the universe. The meaning and results of transpersonal and spiritual practices, such as living in the now and meditating, are shared and verified in an ongoing manner with a teacher, such as a Zen master or a transpersonal therapist, or with a spiritual community or a community of intersubjective interpreters (Wilber 1982).

At first, these areas and their methods of study and verification may appear to be irreconcilable. However, they are closely linked by at least two important connections. First, the Self not only transcends science and psychology, but it also subsumes and includes them. This is a principle for each level of consciousness in its relationship to each level below it. Science and traditional Western medicine study and treat the Survival level, and has even been viewed by some as the " religion " of that level. Traditional psychology and other related disciplines study the Passion and the Mind levels. Spirituality and transpersonal psychology address all other levels above, and thus are not a rejection of science, medicine and psychology (Grof 1983). Rather, with their energy, positivity and creativity, they are nurturing and enfolding to all of them.

A second connection is that a major branch of psychology - psychoanalysis - without acknowledging doing so, uses or involves the Spirit in a major way as part of its healing techniques. In its study and use of the human unconscious, it taps into both the shadow, or the unwanted parts of the lower self, and into intuition, which comes from the Understanding level. Through such techniques as dream analysis and free association, it analyzes the individual or personal unconscious (Fromm 1967; Fine 1979). In Jungian analysis the process extends into the collective unconscious. It appears that some psychotherapists, such as Jung and others, recognized this close link between the unconscious and spirituality. Peck (1978) goes so far as to postulate that the collective unconscious is universal consciousness: " If you desire wisdom greater than your own, you can find it inside you. What this suggests is that the interface between God and man is at least in part an interface between our unconscious and our conscious. To put it plainly, our unconscious is God. God within us. We were part of God all the time. . . . In my vision the collective unconscious is God; the conscious is man as individual; and the personal unconscious is the interface between them. " Most thinkers in psychoanalytically oriented psychology believe that the individual or personal unconscious is the seat of mental illness. Peck suggests the opposite: " I believe that the conscious is the seat of psychopathology . . . It is because our conscious self resists our collective unconscious wisdom that we become ill. "

To develop further and to help illustrate these areas, one can create a map (Fig 5), (realizing that " the map is not the territory. ") The collective unconscious might represent a large part of the knowledge and the wisdom of Universal Consciousness. Each of us has and is an essence, which we call our Self, evolving from Universal Consciousness. Our mind, ego or "personal or individual self" can thus be viewed as being a contraction of the energy of our Self (Muktananda 1981). Usually viewed as negative, our personal unconscious is, rather, a major part of us that forces us each to evolve and to celebrate our oneness and our love. It thus has both a dark and a light side.

Peck's (1978) view of the collective unconscious, as well as many Judeo-Christian views of God, may be equated with the half of the collective or transpersonal unconscious that is positive and good. However, there may be an expanded view (Figure 5). It may not be accurate to blame ourselves totally when we get into trouble in our lives, because there are also "negative" factors (sometimes called "karmic factors") in our collective unconscious which may determine the kinds of circumstances that we get into. The ego/mind thinks it is in total control, and when anything "bad" happens, it often blames itself. Or often, as with many active alcoholics, it projects blame onto others. But according to transpersonal psychology, the issues are more complex: the ego/mind is a co-creator with a higher, wiser and more powerful Creator. It is difficult for the ego to let go, to ask and to listen to a Higher Power. The ego keeps wanting the "right answer" or a "magic bullet". The simple answer is that it must <u>deal</u> with this Higher Power, whatever It is. To do so, it has to communicate with It by experiencing, resisting, struggling, surrendering, becoming, and finally <u>being</u> its Higher Power.

Figure 5.

A Possible Relationship Among the Personal Self, the Self, and the Collective Unconscious

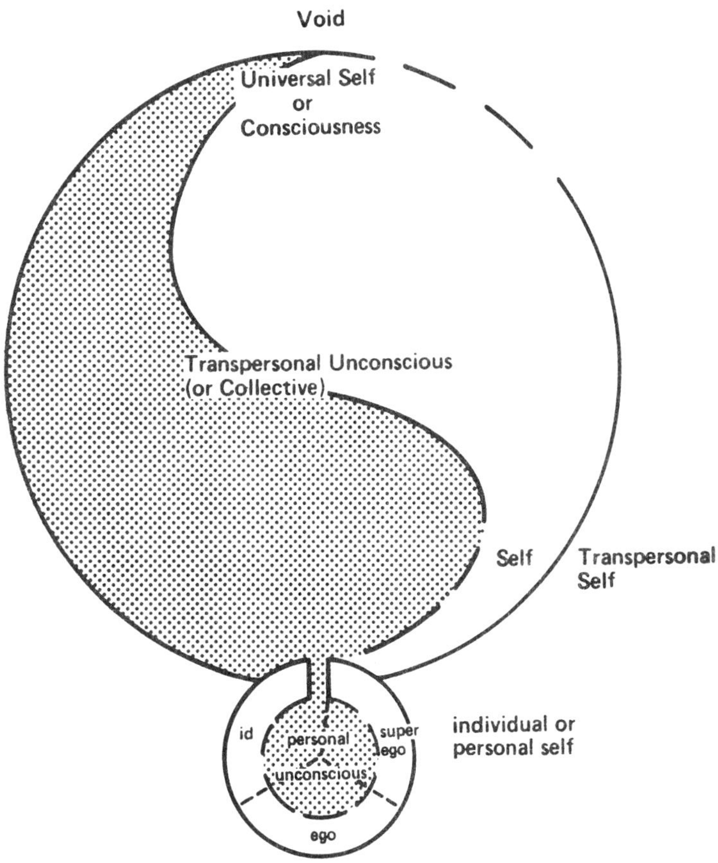

A dichotomy between God and human may be our seeing God as all good and humans (ego/mind) as the sole cause of problems. However, the negative or dark side of the collective unconscious collaborates in the creation of problems that provide us with the experience of painful feelings needed for the completion of our Soul's journey (DiLeo, 1983). It is from this vantage point that we view alcoholism and co-alcoholism as a disease. And then later, some time after we have been in recovery, we can also begin to see and accept our own roles as co-creators of this illness, as well as the alcoholism being viewed as a gift (discussed below). By so doing, we can achieve a greater understanding of our human condition, have a deeper knowledge and experience of ourselves and become more free of our attachments and our suffering. (I will discuss these concepts further under "Being Positive" in Part II.)

Traditional psychology, psychiatry and science do not recognize or accept the existence of realms such as a collective unconscious or even any concepts that extend beyond standard biology and the current limited view of the psyche (lower part of Figure 5). In fact, the belief systems of traditional psychology and psychiatry tend to reduce transpersonal experiences to the escapist imaginations and fantasies of a child or of a person with mental illness. This is paradoxical, because while at the same time they so reduce these forms of imagination, they also seek scientific and phenomenologic truth by the strength of their own creative imagination, which is a major part of their Higher Self.

We can call our lower levels of consciousness our content, the " melodrama " or "soap opera" of our ego and unconscious. At higher levels we can desribe our being and the activity of our Self, our personal unconscious and our collective unconscious by the term context or process. Just as each higher level of consciousness subsumes all lower levels, our context subsumes our content. We might say that our context is that we are all one, loving and forever celebrating ourself. As a prelude to our celebration, we forget our oneness-loving-forever, through the " distorted lens " of our ego, and thus believe that we are separate, which Buddhists and Hindus call " maya ", which means an illusion. They maintain that we each work through our maya or illusion through karma, not just in this lifetime, but in repeated lifetimes in cycles (Ram Dass 1974-83). Karma is the work we do to grow, develop and evolve, and we not only inherit karma, but we also can create it. However, karma and reincarnation can themselves be seen to be illusions or paradoxes. For example, how can a being that is forever, then die and be reborn? And how can many psychologists view the personal unconscious as dark and negative, and how can many organized religions view it as evil or sin, when we can and do use it to grow physically, mentally and spiritually? I will discuss these questions and ideas further under " Alcoholism as a Gift ", " Being Positive ", and "Love + the Human Unconscious".

The Merging of Science and Spirituality

Science and consciousness are merging in several addtional ways. The first is that consciousness, in its continuing evolution, has created science; the insights and creativity of scientific discovery tend to come from our Understanding level of consciousness. For example, many scientists have recently grasped concepts such as serendipity as being a valid part of their work, and some are beginning to understand and accept paradox. The high technology that we have developed from science has created problems that force us to use our higher levels. For example, Naisbitt (1982) describes how " high tech " is leading us into more isolation, which then forces us into "high touch", which is physical, mental and spiritual intimacy. Another area is the discovery of the similarity of quantum - relativistic physics to higher levels of consciousness (Capra 1975; Zukav 1979; LeShan 1975; Wilber 1982; Sheldrake 1982, Comfort 1984). Some observers are even saying that by that observation science is " proving " the existence of consciousness, for example, through its holographic theory. However, even though these similarities are almost uncanny, it appears that they may be no more than similarities, since the scientific method can study generally only the Survival level of consciousness (Wilber 1979b, 1982, 1983b).

Thinkers are also describing other scientific and cosmologic relationships to our personal and our universal consciousness (Bateson 1979; Bohm 1980; Jantsch 1980; Jeans 1930; Penfield 1976; Prigogine 1980; Young 1976). Finally, Tofler (1980) has described the current, dramatic coming together of technology and consciousness as the great "third wave " of human history, the first two having been the agricultural revolution that evolved about eight thousand years before Christ, and the industrial revolution. The rapidity with which the third wave has followed the second, combined with the changes beginning in the 1960's, and other rapid and profound developments, are leading some to say that we are in perhaps the greatest period of change in consciousness thus far in the history of humankind. And it is possible that the apocalyptic changes that are occurring - war, famine, great suffering and death - are forcing us to face and eventually to accept our shadow and thereby to transcend to our Higher Self.

A Need for Training

Most helping professional schools pay little or no attention to humanistic and transpersonal psychology, and thus to spirituality, in training their students. Many of their faculty members tend to view spirituality as being the same as religion, an area with which they are admittedly only partially familiar. Or they tend to view it as so " soft " or ethereal that they see it as having little or no relevance to the work they do. Others may view it as indicating psychopathology, as did Freud. Such beliefs and lack of training may be related to why many of their patients and clients are able to go only so far in their recovery and their growth. However, some professional school faculty members and many students are beginning to take an interest in the relationship of spirituality to their profession.

Many, if not most psychologists, psychiatrists and other mental health workers still use a psychoanalytic, behavioral, or a biologic approach, and some are using a humanistic approach. Some use a combination of these. A few use transpersonal techniques in addition. However, as people rise higher on their levels of consciousness and as the transcending process of spirituality spreads, more and more therapists are becoming aware of the growth inducing potential of transpersonal techniques, and many are using them - and many more will likely soon to be using them. To initiate a transpersonal approach, the already skilled clinician begins to work from level four, the level of the heart, acceptance and caring.

"In strictest confidence, there are times when even I cannot tell yin from yang."

Chapter 6. Alcoholism/CD as a Gift

Sometimes poeple seem to need an illness or great suffering to help them move deeper into themselves (Moss 1981). However, when the suffering active alcoholic, other CD person, or their family member first encounters recovery, he or she is often so angry and depressed about having the disease, or is busy denying it, that the notion that it might be a point from which to grow is not even remotely considered. Such a view is normal and appropriate in early recovery, since there is usually a great deal of anger, guilt, shame, fear and grief to work through. However, the first part of the gift lies exactly here, in the pain and suffering during the active addiction and early recovery. Therapists (Peck 1978; Forest 1983) and sages (Ram Dass & Levine 1976; Bancroft 1976) have described suffering in this sense as grace, i.e. through pain and not getting what I want and expect, I learn the most about my attachments and about myself, and thus I can grow.

Suffering may force a new perspective and perception about what is reality. It can weaken the ego through repeated frustration just enough to allow a giving up or surrendering, which opens the person to the possibility of transcending his or her previous belief systems and levels of consciousness. While the pain hurts, the wound will heal, and it can become a point of access to our greatest gifts. Although suffering can be grace, i.e. a way to transcendence and growth, it is not always so, and thus the apparent need for continued relapses and suffering for many.

A next stage in the gift process is getting the opportunity, often through being forced, to work through a recovery program in a self-help group and/or in a therapy group. The person may also work in individual psychotherapy or counselling. Already mentioned, to do so promotes a usually gradual growth or transcendence often far beyond that which would have been reached through abstinence without treatment. This work is best accomplished both with others and in the silence of our aloneness. By working thus, we can re-examine our relationships in the three areas of spirituality: self, others and universe.

Another part of the gift can be seen in the frequent observation that many alcoholics in early recovery are clearer, less defensive and use less intellectualization and denial of feelings than is seen during psychotherapy with many neurotic patients. Because feelings often can flow more easily, their release helped by removal of the drug, the person has a chance to grow more rapidly than otherwise.

An additional part of the gift lies in helping others, exemplified by the Twelfth Step of AA: " Having had a spiritual awakening as the result of these steps, we tried to carry this message to alcoholics and to practice these principles in all our affairs. " Throughout the ages the admonition " We get to keep what we give away " has helped many people along their life's journey. It is also seen in mythology as the return of the hero who has been wounded, who returns with the gift to the community, and it thereby becomes his own (Hillman 1981). A final component of the gift is in the observation that through working a recovery program the alcoholic often becomes healthier, with more serenity, than he or she was before becoming alcoholic.

In AA, using the term gratitude implies that one is grateful for the opportunity to awaken, to grow and to begin to experience inner peace. The many times that one hears this word, and its companion term grateful, further supports the power and reality of using and experiencing alcoholism as a gift. They are "grateful alcoholics" because in the process of being alcoholics they found their authentic self and a Higher Power (Roessler 1982).

Even with all these views about how the disease can be a gift, most alcoholic and other chemical dependent people do not recover from their illness, not only because of something within them, but commonly because of the enabling behavior of others, with their own concomitent suffering. And of those who do recover, many do not reach a state of serenity, i.e. learn to be their Self, a process that is often associated with their lack of surrender. Thus the paradox of the gift is that it can also be a curse (Hillman 1981). With the peace of viewing it as a gift can come a sometimes agonizing responsibility, discussed further under " Transforming " and " Loving " in Parts III & IV. Suffering from other causes can also be viewed as being a gift, including that of the family or a close friend of an alcoholic or CD person. Much or even all of the above can apply to their suffering.

With all the above discussion, the ultimate requirement for it all to be a true gift is for the person to experience it as a gift. And this can be accomplished only through experiencing the Self or a Higher Power. For this to happen, the difficult process of surrender is required.

Surrender and Control

Control is perhaps the most dominant issue in early recovery. Whether the person is alcoholic/CD or co-alcoholic, keeping "control" of alcohol or drug use or of another's use becomes more and more important. Early, the person may be drinking or using drugs normally, without experiencing related difficulties, problems or trouble. Eventually - and usually subtly - he or she drinks or uses drugs to fill a growing emptiness, and then finally does so to survive. The co-alcoholic develops and progresses in the same way, only instead of alcohol or drugs, their need is to control another's drinking or drug using behavior. Trying to "control" becomes the same as surviving, and thus they feel deep inside that to survive is to "control". They fear that if they are not always in control, they will dissolve, disintegrate or die. By now they are caught in a vi cious cycle of progressively losing control, and reacting to it by wanting, needing, and acting more and more to be in control, while their spirit and their life are disintegrating before them.

Another word for control is attachment. Sages teach that attachment, or needing to be in control, is the basis for suffering. We each may have to suffer to such an extent that we will then begin to consider our alternatives. The one alternative that nearly consistently relieves our suffering is to surrender. But surrendering does not come easily.

In this context, I and others do not use the word "surrender" to mean "give up" or "lie down" in the military sense, wherein one will have "lost" the war. Rather, we mean that when one surrenders, he or she wins the struggle of trying to control and ammeliorates most the needless suffering that results therefrom.

Needing to be in "control" is intimately related to and includes several major life issues. Some of these are the issues of willpower, fear of losing control, dependence/independence, trust, experiencing feelings, self-esteem and shame, being spontaneous, self-nurturing, splitting (viewing things or others as all-or-none), and expectations of self, others and Higher Power. Most alcoholics/CD's, co-dependents and many others have not worked through these important life issues. Indeed, most of the time they believe they can overcome, i.e. control, these issues and all their other life problems. They even believe they can control life itself.

It is a hard lession to learn. Life cannot be controlled. Its powerful and mysterious Process goes on, no matter what we seem to do. Life cannot be controlled because it is far too rich, spontaneous and rambunctious to be fully understood, much less controlled, by our thinking, controlling minds. Only a person who is attached to his or her ego/mind would persist in trying to control something so powerful. And the charicature of such attachment is the active dependent and co-dependent. Continued attempts at control, whether it be of alcohol, other drugs, someone else's use of them, or of Life itself, only further frustrates us. Indeed, we may feel we are "going crazy", and we may even contemplate suicide.

It is at this point that we can discover that there is a way out, a way to get free. Countless people have found that the way out is to surrender and then to become, gradually, a co-creator of their life. This book - and many others - begin to describe how to become and to be a co-creator, in harmony with Life, i.e. with our Higher Power. And by so doing, we discover that our life becomes more free, creative and serene.

When the person surrenders trying to control their alcohol or drug use - or another person - they make a surprizing discovery - nothing happens (Cermack 1984, 1985). They do not disintegrate or die, and neither do others. Life goes on as usual. Eventually, their life even gets better, especially if they participate in an appropriate recovery program. They learn that their need to control is but an illusion, since it has usually caused them only suffering. Through the crucial life issue of control - as well as numerous other issues - this illness can be a charicature of and thereby a model for becoming aware of and solving the physical, mental and spiritual issues of other illnesses and parts of people's lives.

Indeed, surrender is probably the most difficult part of the entire recovery process. Until the alcoholic/CD or co-dependent person surrenders by admitting and eventually accepting the illness, it is likely that he or she will drink or use drugs again and thereby continue to suffer, or will suffer from trying to control another's use. Or they may become abstinent from alcohol and other drugs, yet not surrender into an effective recovery program, and thus suffer nearly as much as before.

The surrender is nearly impossible for the person who is stuck or blocked at the lower levels of consciousness, the usual position of the actively addicted person, unless the person experiences " ego deflation at depth ", hopelessness, and hits a " bottom ", (James 1982; Jung 1965; 1969; Kurtz 1979) discussed in Part III. At the Survival level, not drinking is difficult, since the body's neurochemical " thermostat " is set for a relatively high blood alcohol or drug level. At the level of Passion there may be so much anxiety or depression when not drinking that, since drinking relieves the painful emotions, the person drinks for relief. Thus, the person is now drinking to feel normal. However, at the level of the Mind the person can avoid drinking without treatment and/or spirituality for a time, ranging from a few minutes to a few months, and at times even years. However, there is no known long term effective mental or ego-oriented help against taking a drink, a drug, or trying to control another, other than surrender. This is why it is often said in AA that " The same man or woman will drink again ", i.e. if the person does not change through the mental and spiritual part of the AA program, they will not experience serenity, and therefore will continue to drink.

Surrender often comes about when the alcoholic's ego defenses, ranging from denial to grandiosity, are so confused and frustrated that the person lets go of them all. The defenses are rendered completely powerless by the force of circumstance or reality (Thiebout 1944, 1954). When the person surrenders, he or she can immediately transcend to the highest heart level, which is Acceptance. Such a change may last for from a few seconds to a lifetime. Nonetheless, it opens the channel of consciousness to our Self, our Spirit. The more we can be our heart level, by working through conflicts around drinking, using drugs, relationships, self and the universe, the more likely we will be able to transcend to our Self, and able to keep open a more permanent channel to it.

The act of surrender initiates the switch from negative to positive. The positive change is inseparable from the surrendering, and one can say that if there is no change there has been no surrender. The positive change of recovery is actually a continuation of the surrender on a moment by moment and day by day basis (Thiebout 1944, 1954).

However, many people, and especially alcoholics and their family members, have difficulty surrendering to anything or anyone. This is commonly related to overdeveloped and unhealthy ego defense mechanisms of denial and gradiosity (Whitfield 1984b). Especially difficult for them to surrender to are authority figures, such as employers, the courts and helping professionals. Perhaps the ultimate authority figure is a universal Higher Power. Until they so surrender, it is unlikely that they can experience a lasting serenity.

When the alcoholic totally surrenders to a Higher Power, the comfort and peace that is derived therefrom is related to the ability to live in the sanctuary of the Self, which is a part of the Higher Power. When that happens, the person feels whole and complete. And he or she can also begin to view and accept the alcoholism as a gift. The paradox of surrender is that by so giving up control, one rises to the Self, where one is control.

Death - Our Ultimate Detachment

Crucial to spirituality and to serenity is making peace with our own inevitable death - our ultimate detachment and letting go. However, most of us go through life so attached to being "alive" that we have difficulty letting go of anything, especially our mind's wanting to be right and the struggles that ensue therefrom. That part of our lives which we experience at levels one through four, whether it be pleasure, boredom or turmoil, can be called parts of our individual storyline, melodrama, or "soap opera". What usually causes suffering in life is our attachment to what goes on at these levels, attachment to our melodrama. And another word for attachment is addiction. The sages have said: To the extent that we identify with that which is in time and space, we will suffer (Ram Dass 1974-83).

I have raised the question under Mind above, " Who are you?" However, I am probably not who or what I think I am. And what I own is not what I think I own. I am not, and I do not own my mind or ego, my pride, my emotions, my suffering, my melodrama, my body, my relationships, or any of my material possessions. I simply am, and I am my Self, my Spirit (Assagioli 1976; Muktananda 1981; Ferrucci 1982). And I, my Spirit, am a child of Universal Consciousness, God, or whatever I choose to call it or not call it (Figure 5 & Table 5). Wilber (1981) said, " Man's prior Nature is Spirit, the ultimate Whole, but until he discovers that wholeness, he remains an alienated fragment, a separate self, and that separate self necessarily is faced with an awareness of death and the terror of death. It is not a circumstantial terror. It is existential, given, inherent, and it remains so until Spirit is resurrected and the self is one with all possible others. " However, for many, if not most people, resurrecting their Spirit is too frightening, for to do so would mean letting go of who they think they are, which would

"The schizophrenic is drowning in the same waters in which the mystic is swimming with delight." (Joseph Campbell)

Grof '82

and the alcoholic is frantically thrashing about in it.

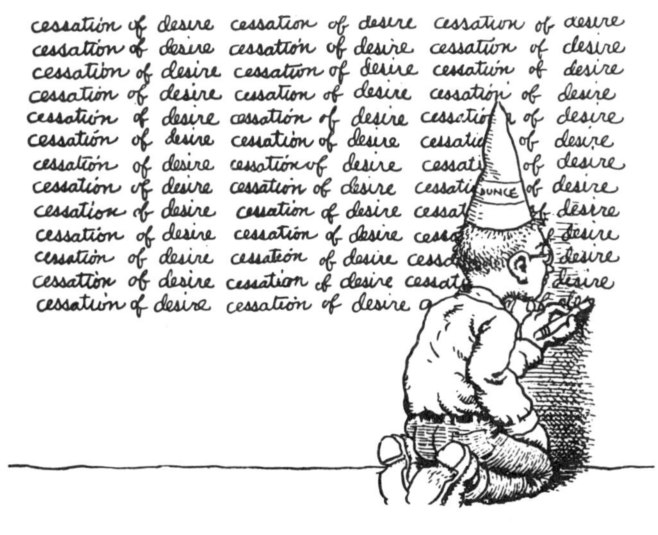

mean that they would have to give up "control", and dissolve or die. Therefore, a part of them, perhaps from their unconscious, screens out or represses anything that threatens with death or with transcendence. And a part of them searches out all sorts of substitute gratifications that pretend to fulfill its desire for Unity, wholeness, immortality and cosmocentricity (Wilber 1981). In some alcoholics and chemical dependent people their drinking and drug using can be viewed as representing a kind of substitute gratification. Or perhaps more commonly it may, after heavy and eventually addictive drinking, develop into a substitute gratification. Thus the illness reduces them to functioning at only lower levels of consciousness, blocking their ability to be their whole person. This is a partial explanation of why alcoholism is a spiritual illness, as well as being a physical and mental one.

Many of my alcoholic patients and others have told me that they felt an emptiness or a void, nearly always when they were actively addicted, and commonly well into their recovery. I believe that a large part of that void, if not often all of it, is related to a blocked channel to their Self, to their Spirit. When I ask them where they felt the void, they usually point to an area between their umbilicus and their mid chest, about where the heart chakra is located, i.e. the " physical location " of level four (Motoyama 1981; Joy 1979). Alcoholism has been described as a slow form of suicide, a kind of death wish. Could it be that the person is thereby somehow seeking transcendence, seeking a fulfillment of the emptiness (Leech 1973; Westermeyer & Walzer 1975; Galanter 1983)? Is death a transcendence? And can talking about death, dying and near-death experiences help us with transcendence right now (Levine 1982)?

Many religions and sages have suggested that a healthy preoccupation with death and dying enhances our life. On his death bed, Plato was asked for a sentence describing his philosophy of life. He answered, " Practice dying " (cited in Sheikh 1983). Many people are comforted and can even have a contact peak experience when they hear others talk about their near-death experiences. These are people who died and who were brought back to life. While no words can substitute for actually hearing these descriptions, they are consistently similar and are very reassuring (Moody 1976; Ring 1980; Gallop 1982; Sabom 1982). By these descriptions death is almost entirely peaceful, and it appears to take us through three stages: physical, psychic, and spiritual. As in other mystical experience, a sense of time and space are reported not to be meaningful in the near-death experience (Meadow et al 1979).

In the physical stage, we usually have an out of the body experience. We actually leave our body through a physical letting go and detachment, and transcend to a position where we are looking down at our physical body. It is as though we are in another dimension, yet for the moment connected with our earthly dimension. There is a sense of timelessness (Sabom 1982; Ring 1980; Kubler-Ross 1975).

In the psychic stage, we see those who we love and value, and we review our life experiences. And in the spiritual stage, we experience no fears or negative feelings, only a total peacefulness, a feeling of unity with the universe. Commonly we see a warm and glowing, but not glaring, white light, often with the appearance of looking down a tunnel (Grof & Grof 1980). The white light and the whole experience has been described as possibly being the unconditional love of the universe. It feels as though we are re-uniting with the core of the universe, often with a sense of mission. It is totally peaceful and joyful (Kubler-Ross 1982).

By an analysis of several hundred people who have reported such an experience it was found that nearly all were not on psychoactive drugs at the time, did not appear to be hallucinating, and oxygen deprivation or endorphin stimulation alone did not explain these changes, the total genesis of which remains unknown (Gabbard & Twemlow 1981; Sabom 1982). An estimated 23 million Americans have had a near-death experience, and of these, at least 8 million, or from 43 to 48% of them, remembered their experience (Gallup 1982). All but less than 1% who remembered it said that it was a very positive experience, and usually felt that it was the most positive experience in their life. This was all regardless of prior religious affiliation or experience (Gallup 1982). In another series, 60% of 102 people who died and were resuscitated reported having at least the early stage (Stage 1 - undescribable peace and contentment). Stage 2 (out of body) was reported by 38%, stage 3 (going further, sometimes with a "presence") by 25% and stage 4 (entering the light) by 10% (Meadow et al 1979).

Active alcoholics die about 12 years earlier than non-alcoholics. Because of their lifestyle and the toxicity of the alcohol, it is likely, though unproven, that alcoholics have more near-death experiences, ranging from serious auto accidents to suicide attempts, than does the general population.

The question remains, why do many people have to experience severe suffering or even a near-death experience to get in touch with their spiritual nature (St. John 1959)? Active alcoholism and co-alcoholism, with all their suffering and frequent near-death experiences, can push the person to one or more " bottoms " that may be the key that opens the channel to higher levels of consciousness. However, for many a comfortable sobriety may be delayed even then, and for some it may never occur.

The transition from active addiction to recovery is similar to a death-rebirth experience. And throughout recovery, as psychological growth occurs, our being tested by our attachments and then giving them up is like a repetition of smaller death-rebirth experiences. During recovery alcoholics/CDs and their family members can recognize these death-rebirth experiences as being normal grief reactions (Bozarth-Campbell 1984). There may be feelings of sadness, hopelessness, "depression," despair, emptiness, frustration, tension, anger, rage, struggle, bargaining and psychosomatic illness. This is the suffering of recovery, and it is a sign that we are getting well. The person may have much to grieve about, including giving up alcohol or other drugs, the lifestyle that accompanies it, the lost relationships, opportunities, bodily functions, and life during the drinking and/or drug using, lost self-esteem, and other losses.

In addition to these, the family member may have to grieve over a lost childhood, or marriage, other lost relationships, and other lost aspects of life that would have been productive or enjoyable. To work through this grief, this hurting and suffering, takes time, usually a period of from several months to a year. Working through grief in a healthy manner is blocked by drinking or using any psychoactive drug, and by "holding it in," not telling anyone about it. To work through it, we can share it with a trusted intimate friend or relative, or in group therapy or with a self-help group sponsor, or with a counselor or psychotherapist.

When we grieve, a part of us is dying and a part is being re-born. What is dying each time is not who we really are, it is not our real Essence, but a bit of our ego/mind, the way we thought it was or had to be. Our ego/mind doesn't let go easily. Frightened by anything that operates or thinks differently than it does, it wants to be right and "in control" of everything it touches. It wants to be in control of that which is in space and time, and thereby becomes attached to them. But space and time are constantly changing, and our attachment to them brings about suffering. The way out of the suffering is to experience our suffering and then to transcend to the freeing and empowering experience of being our Self, which I will further describe in the next part of this book.

Part II BEING

Being our Self

While using alcohol or other drugs may have given us a glimpse of tranquility, serenity, fulfillment, or of our Self, that experience was either only transitory, or worse, it eventually drove us away from our Self, leaving us with a feeling of emptiness, alienation, and loss of meaning in our lives. However, numerous spiritual practices - that are drug free - help us to be that part of us that is Understanding, Compassion and Unity Consciousness, that which is peaceful and serene. One could use terms like " enter " or " become " our Self, except that our Self is already here, within us, right now. In fact, who we are is our Self. The following are some introductory principles to being our Self.

Chapter 7. Living in the Here & Now

Living in the here and now is a powerful way to be. But our mind pushes us to live outside of the now, to live in the past and the future. Our mind is composed largely of memories and anticipations, and it therefore makes us preoccupied with time. There may be no greater obstacle to our serenity than being preoccupied with time (Krishnamurti 1976).

Many of us have observed during an altered state of consciousness that time becomes either slowed or irrelevant. Becoming lost in watching a sunset, an enraptured embrace or in a creative project, we are totally absorbed in the present moment. Wilber (1979) said, " Clearly, in this present moment, . . . there is no time. . . . and a timeless moment is an eternal one - a moment which knows neither past nor future, beyond nor after, yesterday nor tomorrow. To enter deeply into this present moment is thus to plunge into eternity, ..." A major component of having a peak-experience, another name for which is a " high, " is living in the now.

Remembering our past and anticipating our future are not " then and there " experiences. Rather, they are present experiences. We know them only right now. Yet the mind has a built-in block to this knowledge, and by doing so it creates uncomfortable feelings, such as anxiety and guilt. Guilt is a state of being lost in the past, and anxiety is a state of being lost in the future (Perls 1971; Wilber 1979). We are, in fact, bound to time. Yet our bondage to time and all its problems is an illusion. We exist in a no-boundary moment because the past as memory and the future as expectation are in it, not around it (Wilber 1979).

We can handle our human bondage to time by both experiencing* our uncomfortable feelings, which means feeling and ventillating and thereby completing them, and by then transcending them.

Emerson said, " These roses under my window make no reference to former roses or to better ones; they are for what they are; they exist with God today. There is not time for them. There is simply the rose; it is perfect in every moment of its existence . . . . But man postpones or remembers; he does not live in the present, but with reverted eye

---

* This word will be underlined several times more throughout this book to emphasize its importance in spirituality, and will be discussed in more detail under "Forgiving", "Using Our Imagination" and "Hitting Bottom".

laments the past, or heedless of the riches that surround him, stands on tiptoe to foresee the future. He cannot be happy and strong until he too lives with nature in the present, above time." We thus have to live with and in our lower self and in nature, but we are not them. We can rise above time, i.e. transcend it. And that which is above time is the Eternal Now. To transcend the lower self is to take care of it and to live and work from the heart, right now, in this moment. The Christian sage de Caussade (1975) said "... seek for the fountain of living waters; it springs close to you in the present moment ... The present moment is the name of God ..."

Many alcoholics have a time distortion. This comes about when the person begins to develop a personal notion of what we can call "free time," which for him or her means drinking time or drug using time. All other time then becomes obligated time, which means bothersome time. As the disease of alcoholism/CD progresses, the person turns more and more of his or her life to "free time." By drinking or using drugs, he or she also blots out present time, leaving only the past to ruminate over or the future to fantasize about. However, neither the past nor the future can be changed by intoxicated wishes, so that nothing changes positively (Davis et al 1984).

The human condition, with its ego/mind, makes us a slave to time. And alcoholism and other chemical dependence not only potentiate, but greatly exaggerate this enslavement. The solution is both complex and easy - just be, right now. Where and when else could we be? Group treatment, which consists of self help groups and therapy groups, tends to promote learning to live and be in the now. The AA sayings "One day at a time" and "First things first" invite living in the now. Some individual psychotherapy, such as gestalt, also emphasizes it.

Wilber (1979) said, "... to see all memory as present experience is to collapse the boundaries of this present moment, to free it of illusory limits, to deliver it from the opposites of past vs. future. It becomes obvious that there is nothing behind you in time nor before you in time. You thus have nowhere to stand but in the timeless present, and thus nowhere to stand but in eternity." Now is the closest experience of eternity that this world offers. Indeed, the only aspect of time that is eternal is now (Course 1975).

Accepting What Is and Letting Be

Accepting what is and letting be are part of giving up control, surrendering and detaching, all a major part of recovery from dependence and co-dependence. Yet doing so is difficult. The mind clings to being right and to controlling, even in the face of deteriorating function. And active alcoholism and other dependence exaggerates and potentiates such righteousness, just as it distorts time and living in the now. Yet the grandiosity and anger on the surface only hide the hurt, fear, shame and guilt underneath. The solution - becoming honest + working through our pain + suffering - is difficult. But to do so one needs to go through Acceptance through conflict, the level of the heart. Only then can one let go. Only then can one fully surrender + forgive, and then be free.

Bill

The following vignette of using spirituality in recovery illustrates one aspect of accepting what is and letting be.

Bill was a 26 year old business manager. He began attending Alateen for the teenage children of alcoholics, at age 18. Over the next year he discovered that he was alcoholic himself, and began attending AA. He has been active in both since then. His father, an alcoholic, is still drinking. The following tells his story in his own words.

Before Alateen I didn't think about spirituality or God in my terms. I blamed him for all the bad things that happened to me. I had the worst luck of anyone in the world. I never had a real sense of God in the family. Perhaps my mother thought of him as a benefactor.

Once in a while I would feel some kind of a need or hunger. At Christmas Eve for example, I attended church. I went all alone one time to a church that I knew my school friends attended. I was about 18 years old. I remember waiting outside the door for a long time. I felt as thought I didn't really fit in. I felt kind of unworthy. Finally I went in when the service was almost over. There were all my school friends dressed in frocks and holding candles. And it seemed to me that what they were involved in was good and kind of healthy. But I still felt outside of it. I felt that I once could have been involved but by now it was too late. Then I had the first of about eight depressions. Before, my mother and younger brother were involved in religion a little, but I couldn't do it. I felt like a complete jerk about it, and it seemed so "out" socially to think of God. I worried about what my friends would say.

The first few years in Alateen program I felt the same way. But gradually I found something in the group that I could trust somehow.

The first, second and third Steps of AA mean to me a very personal experience that all the things of my life that I used to validate myself were really not necessary. It dawned on me after I got over my first depression that my perfectionism, my desire to be a great actor and to be very smart, all these things were unnecessary, and I simply accepted myself as I was without qualification, just in that moment. And that happened a few times: A real deep depression, immediately followed by this realization. I had a feeling of the presence of God. And I also realized I had to stop all this desperate "trying".

More recently, I've been looking for a spiritual life. I've been to church, but I remain on the fringes. I've started to read spiritual books. Reading about Christ and early Christianity. I'm a little afraid of that too. So now I'm on a quest. AA helps, Al-Anon helps, Alateen helps. Without spirituality, I'd be in pretty bad shape.

Bill's story illustrates a common problem among alcoholics: the need for perfectionism. They expect perfection in others and in themselves if they do not do everything just right and if they are not the <u>best</u> in everything. This is related to the major issue of control. Working the Twelve Steps and beginning to accept what is and letting be are powerful practices to free oneself from the burden of suffering that alcoholism/CD/co-dependence inflict upon people.

To let be and flow with life seems to be a major part of both ancient and modern wisdom. The Tao of Lao Tsu, written around 600 BC, says, " Tao abides in non-action, yet nothing is left undone. It does not show greatness, and therefore is truly great. The world is ruled by letting things take their course. The Tao of heaven does not strive, and yet it overcomes. It does not speak, and yet is answered. It does not ask, yet is supplied with all its needs. It seems at ease, and yet follows a plan" (Lao Tsu 1972).

Around 600 AD, the third Chinese patriarch of Zen wrote " The Great Way is not difficult for those who have no preferences" (cited in Ram Dass 1974-83). A similar modern saying is " Happiness is a function of accepting what is, without adding anything to it or subtracting anything from it. " Slogans from Alcoholics Anonymous addressing acceptance and surrender are several: Let go and let God. Be willing. Easy does it. Live and let live (Alibrandi 1978). The paradox is that to get well the alcoholic and the co-dependent must let go and take charge, i.e. surrender to a higher process, power or creator and become a co-creator.

Frost's poem " Acceptance " reminds us of our link to part of our lower selves - to nature - and its flowing with what is, without trying to change it, yet doing so as if by some higher knowledge:

When the spent sun throws up its rays on cloud
And goes down burning into the gulf below,
No voice in nature is heard to cry aloud
At what has happened. Birds, at least, must know
It is the change to darkness in the sky.

Murmuring something quiet in its breast.
One bird begins to close a faded eye;
Or overtaken too far from its nest,
Hurrying low above the grove, some waif
Swoops just in time to his remembered tree.
At most he thinks or twitters softly, " Safe!
Now let the night be dark for all of me.
Let the night be too dark for me to see
Into the future. Let what will be, be. "

We can become so attached to our relationships that it is painful to let the people in them go where they need to go. We are not free until we let go of others. So long as we need to control other people's choices, actions and destinies, however loving or benign our motives may be, we are held a prisoner of that need. We work through such letting go as level four, Acceptance through Conflict. Then we can transcend to levels five and especially six, Compassion, where we peacefully let others be. Giving others freedom, we free ourselves. And they are free to grow in their own way (Ferguson 1980). We can then learn that it takes less energy to be free and flowing than to be locked up in the stress of resistance. One of the ways we can get free of our suffering is by the process of detaching.

Chapter 8. Detaching

Detaching is useful not only for the family and close others. It is a valuable practice even for the alcoholic/CD during recovery. While this chapter generally focuses on the family member or other close person, most of the principles can be useful for everyone during recovery. Indeed, experts say that inside every alcoholic/CD is a co-alcoholic or co-dependent (Cermak 1985; Wegsheider-Cruse 1985).

Al-Anon (1981) describes detachment as " . . . a recovery tool for the family . . . it helps members to help themselves. In Al-Anon we learn individuals are not responsible for another person's disease or recovery from it. We let go of our obsession with another's behavior and begin to lead happier and more manageable lives, lives with dignity and rights; lives guided by a Power greater than ourselves. In Al-Anon we learn: 1) Not to suffer because of the actions or reactions of other people, etc.; 2) Not to allow ourselves to be used or abused in the interest of another's recovery; 3) Not to do for others what they should do for themselves; 4) Not to manipuulate situations so others will eat, go to bed, get up, pay bills, etc.; 5) Not to cover up for another's mistakes or misdeeds; 6) Not to create a crisis; 7) Not to prevent a crisis if it is in the natural course of events.

"Detachment is neither kind nor unkind. It does not imply evaluation of the person or situation from which we are detaching. It is simply a means for us to recover from the adverse affects on our lives of living with someone afflicted with the disease of alcoholism, or other chemical dependence . Detachment helps families look at their situations realistically and objectively, thereby making intelligent decisions possible" (Al-Anon 1981). A helpful saying of Al-Anon is the " 3 C's ": We didn't Cause it, we can't Control it, and we can't Cure it ("it" referring to their close person's alcohol or other drug problem).

Outside the fellowship of Al-Anon, detachment is sometimes mistakenly interpreted to mean "not caring about", but the word actually means "to separate from". The task in recovery for the co-alcoholic person is to separate from the inappropriate behavior of taking responsibility for the behavior of the alcoholic, including the drinking, and all of its consequences. Detachment includes an insistance to oneself, the alcoholic and to others that the alcoholic retains the responsibility for him or herself. Moreover, it requires a willingness to let go and to allow him or her to have that responsibility. It is making peace for oneself, with oneself. Often co-alcoholics <u>want</u> the person to have the responsibility But they continue to <u>feel</u> guilty, ambivalent, or anxious because they want the person who behaves irresponsibly to behave responsibly. Detachment includes becoming aware of and healthily ventillating one's feelings, and then separating from those feelings, and being at peace. Frequently the alcoholic refuses to accept the responsibility for his life and occasionally is desperately hurt by his irresponsibility. Although family members would not in their heart wish for such hurt, and would care if it happened, they also can let it happen without feeling guilty. This is detachment.

Many of the principles of Buddhism and related paths illustrate similarities with Al-Anon's view of detachment. The Four Noble Truths of Buddhism include:

1) Life involves <u>suffering</u>. Unenlightened human life inherently is like a wheel that turns off center. It is "off the mark" (which is the original Greek meaning of the word "sin".) Our six major occasions of suffering include birth, sickness, decrepitude, the fear of death, being tied to what one abhors, and being separated from what one loves. (Living with or being close to an actively drinking alcoholic usually brings about all but the first. Birth comes in recovery in the form of a re-birth.

2)Attachment, desire, selfish craving or clinging of our ego causes our suffering. In some way, we have become estranged or separated from Reality. We suffer in our isolation and separation. Our ego is "oozing like a secret sore."

3) Detachment is the cure for suffering.

4) Detachment can follow an Eigthfold Path (Smith 1957).

The basis of the Path is Right Association, i.e. with people who have positive attitudes and clarity (in this case those who are in Al-Anon and in couples or spouse's group therapy).
The Eightfold Path includes:

Right 1) Knowledge (including the Truths and the Path),
2) Aspiration (what our hearts really want),
3) Speech (language, honesty, charity, positivity),
4) Behavior (selflessness & charity),
5) Livelihood,
6) Effort (including will),
7) Mindfulness (alertness, self-examination, who we are and where we are going), and
8) Meditation or absorption.

But these actions or practices are not easy to do, whether one is a Buddhist or a recovering co-alcoholic or co-dependent.

Leite (1980) suggests that detachment occurs in stages. One of the first is realizing that there is a way out of our suffering, and to begin taking better care of ourself. Next we can begin to observe our daily life, from the observer self. We neither attack nor apologize. We begin letting go of "control" and we start attending Al-Anon meetings. We can then stop enabling, which means protecting our problem drinker/user from the consequences of his or her drinking or using. We can begin to reframe the way we used to look at the events of our life; we can stop being a victim. We can then begin to learn what does not help. We work only on ourself.

Like "tough love" and letting go, detachment involves levels two, three, four and six of our consciousness. We have to rebuild our ego and then let go of it. And all of this takes time, so that we have to be patient. Detachment is made easier by attending Al-Anon meetings regularly and by working its program of recovery.

Leite (1980) says, " You will know that you have found detachment when you can feel empathy for the alcoholic in your life without feeling tied to the alcoholic's drinking and behavior, when you can accept constructive criticism without the old feeling of failure, and when you can hear impassioned pleas without giving in to them. You will know that you have found detachment when you are accused falsely and do not feel guilty, when you can laugh at the funny things in your life, when you can cry and not care who sees it, when you can show anger in a positive way. You have gained detachment when you can see, truly see, that the people whom you love must live their own lives, make their own mistakes, and live with the consequences of their acts. And that they are not doing it to you. Fill yourself with self-worth, not self-importance. Put all things into perspective. Practice detachment. It is the key that finally frees one from the strongest of all chains, the bondage of self. "

Detaching and Our Higher Power

Teresa of Avila believed that detachment was one of three practices helpful in communicating with one's Higher Power, the other two being love and humility. She said that the happy result of detachment is inner freedom. Al-Anon and AA call this freedom "serenity". While detachment may be useful in meditation and in prayer, there are other aspects, components, or practices of meditation and prayer that can be useful in detaching (Figure 6). We can divide these arbitraily into those practices that can emanate from our lower self and those that can emanate from our Higher Self. First is what we can call non-resistance. By not struggling or fighting against something, we retain a freedom from suffering (Small 1983). This freedom then gives us the power of

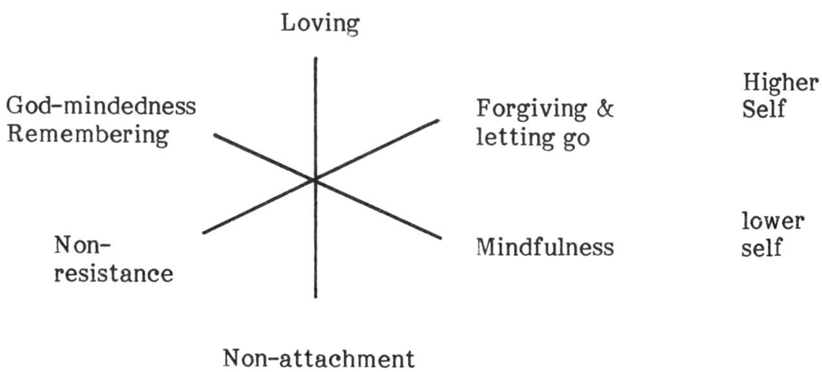

Figure 6. Some Components & Practices of Detachment

(modified from Naranjo 1983)

strength and flexibility to make constructive choices in our daily lives. Non-attachment is not clinging to the way we think things "should" be. It is keeping our expectations as close to zero as we can. The saying "The Great Way is not difficult for those who have no preferences " addresses both of these practices of non-resistance and non-attachment. Mindfulness is as described in the Eightfold Path above: being alert, self-examining, and being aware of who we are and where we are going. A problem with co-dependents is that they are hyper-alert, but for others' behaviors and cues, and not often for themselves (Gravitz & Bowden, 1984). Also, living in the Now is helpful in detaching. From our Higher Self can come God-mindedness, which can be called remembering, i.e. remembering our Source. When we remember, we can begin to forgive and then to let go of our attachments. Then we are free to love, which means that we are free to be Love, which is what we are anyway - already and always.

Jeff

The following is a case vignette of Jeff, a 24 year old man who grew-up in an alcoholic family. He came to join Alateen, at age 18. He is now an Al-Anon member and sponsors an Alateen group. His father is still actively alcoholic. He tells his story and reflects upon the meaning of spirituality, detachment, and his higher power, as follows.

> God was really non-existent in my life before Alateen. I think the most powerful force I knew was my father's alcoholism, although I didn't know it as that. My father's destructive behavior dominated everything. Both my parents were raised as orthodox Jews, but somehow religion was never an important element in our house.
>
> My mother began to go to Al-Anon, and after about a year she began to take my twin brother and me to Alateen.
>
> In the program, I have come to believe that there is a power greater than myself, some kind of unearthly force and upon which I'm dependent and which controls life around me. I don't really have the need to control anymore. I feel that things will work out. He, she, or it directs things and I don't need to intervene. And the way it will turn out will often be a lot better for me than anything I could dream up on my own. "Thy Will be done". The point is I don't have to hold everything together. I guess before the program I felt so powerless and frustrated that I had to try to control the emotions of others, what they felt about me, etc.
>
> My father is still drinking. I fee compassion for him, but I can surrender to the idea that I can do nothing about his disease. I am detached. And I hope he will recover. But I realiize it's not in my hands.
>
> I feel my father loves me, although I didn't feel that before. And even now a big part of me wants to believe that he didn't love us, but I know better. The thing that hurt before most before was the anger and frustration I always felt, and the resentment - particularly the resentment.
>
> I don't think recovery would be possible for me without some sense of the Higher Power. I would have had to do everything myslef. And that would have overwhelmed me.

Detachment involves letting go of our expectations, of our wishful thinking, and of always wanting things to be otherwise than they are. It also involves forgiving others and forgiving ourself, and being patient. Thus our ultimate detachment is from our own ego or personal self. I will further describe detachment throughout this book, and will discuss the family and other close people in Chapters 23 and 24.

Watching the "Dance" or Melodrama

Perhaps the next stage beyond letting go is watching the " dance " or melodrama of our life events. Closely related to detachment, this involves transcending to the acceptance level and into the Self, which has been called the watcher, the witness, the observer, or the experiencer (Watts 1965; Muktananda 1981; Ferrucci 1982). For example, many people have experienced becoming extremely upset and then detaching from their upset and feelings to such an extent that they find themselves actually observing themselves in the upset. Sometimes there is an out of the body experience, so that they are able to see themselves or a representation of themselves having the upset. This ability can be facilitated by practicing guided or eidedic imagery and visualizations (Gendlin 1978; Small 1982; Ferrucci 1982). Closing the eyes, the person visualizes or otherwise imagines the scene or activity about which there is concern (see " Imagining " below). One can then visualize a positive solution to the upset. This can also be done while meditating. Done constructively, this is a healthy practice.

Deikman (1982) and others call this powerful and freeing part of us the observer or observing self. The Western psychological or psychiatric literature refers to the observing self as "the observing ego", but does not explore the special nature of that "ego" and its implications for understanding of the self. It thus continues to miss the dynamics, meaning, and importance of the observer self, and its theories of the self remain somewhat confused.

Figure 6-A

Relationship of the Observing Self and the self (object self)

(compiled from Deikman 1982)

Observing Self

Awareness Consciousness

Aspects of the self

Thinking, Planning, Solving, Worrying

Emotion, Feeling, Affect

Action, Behavior, Functioning

Desire, Wish, Fantasy

But the observing self is central to the work of recovery, as well as, to the work of psychotherapy of all sorts. An illustration of the observing self is shown in Figure 6-A. This scheme shows the interrelationships of the self (or "object self") and the observing self. The self, i.e. the ego/mind, is concerned with thinking, feeling, acting, desiring and other survival-oriented activities. However, the observer self, who we really are, is that part of us that is watching our object self. We might say that it watches us when we watch. It is our Consciousness, it is the core experience of our Self. It thus cannot be watched - at least by anything or any being that we know of on this earth. It transcends our five senses, our ego/mind, and all other lower, though necessary, parts of us. Deikman (1982) said,

> The observing self is not part of the object world formed by our thoughts and sensory perception because, literally, it has no limits; everything else does. Thus, everyday consciousness contains a transcendent element that we seldom notice because that element is the very ground of our experience. The word transcendent is justified because if subjective consciousness — the observing self — cannot itself be observed but remains forever apart from the contents of consciousness, it is likely to be of a different order from everything else. Its fundamentally differenct nature becomes evident when we realize that the observing self is featureless; it cannot be affected by the world any more than a mirror can be affected by the images it reflects.

As the observer self becomes more prominent, the lower or object self tends to recede. Primary identification with our lower self tends to be associated with suffering and illness. However, building a strong and flexible ego or object self is usually required before we can transition into our observer self for any lasting duration. Thus, early in recovery, it is the task of the alcoholic and co-alcoholic to begin to discover - or to rediscover - their ego, mind or object self, and through a constructive process, to build a healthy ego, i.e. one that is flexible and that uses mature defenses (Kaufman and Raphael 83; Branden 1983; Deikman 1982). To do so, one can work the 12 Steps of AA/NA/Al-Anon, and/or an equivalent process. Appropriate group therapy for chemical dependence or co-dependence can be very helpful in this building or growth process. For some, and usually later in the course of the first few years of recovery, individual psychotherapy with a therapist who is skilled in working with CD and co-dependence can also be helpful. The process of growth, in this sense, is similar, whether in self-help, group therapy, or in individual psychotherapy. An outline of this process is shown in Figure 6-B. Note that in item five, identification with the observer self,is an advanced stage in the recovery from many forms of mental illness and suffering.

Figure 6-B
General Goals and Steps in
Ego-Oriented and Transpersonal Psychotherapy

Ego-Oriented (items 1–4)

1) Seeking relief from suffering
2) Recognizing, facing and experiencing feelings
   Learning to tolerate frustration
3) Working through and sorting out fantasy and reality
4) Beginning to work on life issues and change belief systems
   Realizing that I prevent getting what I want and need

Transpersonal (items 5–7)

5) Perceiving new and more possibilities
   Recognizing and experiencing observer self
6) Maximizing freedom of choice (assumed ethical)
   Feeling empathy regarding and compassion for others
7) Becoming able to perceive the oneness of all being
   Becoming a co-creator of my life

Deikman (1982) relates a delightful and freeing case history that further illustrates the liberation of a person's observer self.

> A woman I had been seeing in once-a-week psychotherapy entered my office almost frantic with distress, proclaiming anxiously that she was about "to go to pieces." My usual approach would have been to listen, draw out some explanation of the precipitating circumstances, and bring into awareness the repressed emotions, wishes, or ideas that presumably were the bases for her acute symptoms. This way of proceeding would most likely have been of some help. What actually happened was that I began to smile, feeling amused. The woman's distress was genuine by all the criteria customarily used in such situations. She was not prone to having crises and her statements were not

hysterically exaggerated. Yet I found myself smiling. Her situation seemed funny to me because I perceived her as being in no actual danger, but completely caught up in the contents of her mind, identifying with the commotion she was reporting, forgetting that she was observing it. Speaking metaphorically, it was as if the patient were standing on a hilltop overlooking the ocean and on seeing large waves crashing far out to sea had become fearful that she would drown, forgetting where she actually was.
The woman suddenly became aware of my facial expression, stopped, and indignantly demanded the reason for my "unfeeling" smile in response to her desperation. Her question made me smile even more broadly, and I actually began to laugh. She stared at me in disbelief, and then a look of outrage took possession of her face. However, in the midst of her rising anger, despite herself, she started to smile, too. Damm you!" she exclaimed and began to laugh. We laughed together for a long while. The desperate air of crisis, the emergency, the impending breakdown vanished in that laughter like fog evaporating in the sun. The "going to pieces" never happened.

Note that this action is done by a skilled psychotherapist who knew when and how to make this type of intervention.

Expanding our consciousness, we can soon become aware of our part in the larger drama - the " cosmic drama " (Watts 1975). By watching our own personal dance or melodrama, we can begin to learn that our Self is that part of us which, when we realize we are " really carrying on ", can step back and observe the carrying on, through the power of our imagination. By doing so, we often bring into play the powerful defense of humor, e.g. by laughing at ourself for taking it all so seriously.

Laughing

Laughter is therapeutic (Cousins 1979; Peter & Dana 1982; O'Connell 1976; Moody 1978) and is a way to be the Self. Weil (1980) said, " Have you ever laughed so hard that tears streamed down your face and you found yourself collapsed on the floor, almost unable to breathe? How did you feel immediately afterward? Cleaned out? Invigorated? Healthy? High? ... A condition of open communication between the conscious and unconscious obtains whenever the observing ego gets out of the way. In a fit of laughter there is no ego. ... Mind and body are laughing together; the channels are wide open .... Any situation encouraging social disinhibition favors laughing fits. Perhaps the best trigger of all is the sight of someone else doing it, for laughing, like yawning, is highly contagious. A really good laugher in the right setting can get a lot of other people to join in. Done ritually and regularly, group laughing fits could serve as the basis for a new system of psychotherapy. . . ."

Humor and laughter are regularly seen and heard at self-help group meetings, such as AA, NA, and Al-Anon, and are a sign of maturity and of a strengthening recovery, especially when we laugh at ourself. Laughing is closely related to crying, both processes opening channels to higher consciousness, and both helping us to feel better, possibly by a combination of ventillation of emotions, stimulation of endorphin release in the nervous system, and by unknown mechanisms.

When Norman Cousins was suffering from a painful illness, he noticed that one ten-minute of interlude of laughter produced two hours of painless sleep. His recovery program also included nutrition, thinking positively, letting go, nurturing himself, loving, and using hope and faith (Cousins 1979). Humor and laughing can be an effective healing agent, with no detrimental side effects. They can control both physical and mental pain in four major ways: 1) by distracting attention, 2) by reducing tension, 3) by changing expectations, and 4) by releasing endorphins. Described as a form of "internal jogging," laughter exercises the heart, circulation, lungs, and muscles. When it subsides, the pulse rate drops below normal and the skeletal muscles relax (Peter & Dana 1982).

Humor and laughter are great aids to healing.

Chapter 9. Meditating

While meditation is mentioned in most stress management books, it is not generally discussed as being a spiritual practice, but more as one for relaxing and decreasing tension. However, meditating is one of the most effective practices to be the Self. It quiets the mind and opens the heart and higher levels (Goldstein 1976; Eswaran 1977; Goleman 1972, 1977; Ram Dass 1978; Muktananda 1981; Puryear & Thurston 1982; Washburn 1978; Boals 1978; Walsh 1982). While there are many types of meditation (Table 6), and other practices that are meditative, from daydreaming to doing yoga to exercising to praying, common to them all are a focusing away from and a letting go of the ordinary mental activity of our ego. This allows an opening of the channels to higher levels of consciousness. One effective practice of meditation is by using a disciplined, regular pattern of doing so once or twice daily, every day, for about 20 minutes each time.

A simple form of meditation is to sit quietly with eyes closed, and to repeat in the mind a sound or " mantra ". Silently saying a mantra is a trigger that allows the mind to journey, by automatic reflex, into a quiet and relaxed state. One such mantra is " I am ". If thoughts come into the mind, let them come, and then let them go. The mantra will return, being repeated every few seconds. A mantra can also be written, visualized or touched. In AA there are several slogans, in addition to those mentioned above, that one can say to oneself periodically or even repeatedly, such as " One day at a time " and " No pain, no gain ". While doing so is not generally considered as being meditation, these slogans can each be viewed as a kind of mantra.

Table 6

APPLIED TYPOLOGY OF MEDITATION TECHNIQUES

TEACHER, SYSTEM, OR SCHOOL	TECHNIQUE	TYPE	NAME OF FIFTH STATE
Hindu Bhakti	Japa	Concentration	Union
Sufi	*Zikr*	Concentration	*Baga;* Objective Consciousness
Hesychasm	Jesus Prayer	Concentration	*Quies;* Purity of Heart
Meher Baba	Varied spectrum of meditations	Integrated	Sahaj Samadhi; Sadguru
Sri Aurobindo	"Bringing down the Overmind"	Concentration	Supermind
Patanjali's Ashtanga Yoga	Samadhi	Concentration	Sahaj Samadhi
Ramana Maharshi	Self-inquiry	Concentration	*Jivan-mukti*
Maharishi Mahesh Yogi	Transcendental Meditation	Concentration	God-consciousness; Union
Swami Muktananda	*Shaktipat-diksha*	Concentration	*Turyatita*
Kirpal Singh	*Shabd* Yoga	Concentration	True Master
Tantra Yoga	*Yantra, maithuna,* mantra, visualization, etc.	Concentration	Siddha
Tibetan Vajrayana	Mahamudra: *shiney* and *thagthong*	Integrated: concentration and insight	Bodhisattva
Zen	Zazen: koan, breath, and *shikan-taza*	Integrated: concentration and insight	"No-mind"
Gurdjieff	Self-remembering	Insight	Objective Consciousness
J. Krishnamurti	Self-knowledge	Insight	Choiceless Awareness

from Goleman 1977

The two basic ways of focusing attention in meditation are concentration and insight (Table 6). Concentration includes sustained attention directed toward a single object or point of focus, such as is used in mantra meditation. Insight involves maintaining a special awareness or mindfulness toward objects or events as they arise spontaneously (Goleman 1976).

I have referred to the importance and power of surrender in attaining spiritual growth and serenity during recovery. A major part of our mental, emotional and spiritual growth occurs by our letting go of (surrendering) our defensiveness and our expectations, thereby removing obstacles to our ever-present expanded potential. Quieting our mind through daily meditation can prepare us to begin letting go of and removing these obstacles or barriers to our wholeness (Walsh & Vaughan 1980). Aurobindo said, "The fundamental task which gives the key to many realizations is the silence of the mind . . . all kinds of discoveries are made, in truth, when mental machinery stops, and the first is that if the power to think is a remarkable gift, the power not to think is even more so" (cited in Satprem 1968).

The improvement in our consciousness, in our being, from daily meditation may produce an immediate, though often subtle result. We can feel more relaxed, more energized and crave alcohol or other drugs less - or at times when we meditate none of these may occur. Thus, even though occassionally we may not experience any immediate benefit, the longer term effect of the meditation is slowly accumulating. Often being use to wanting things in a hurry, we can at such a time have our patience tested. The more enduring and lasting effects of meditation, if practiced regularly over many months and years, have been documented both scientifically and experientially. Some of these effects are: an improved ability to handle stress, an improved ability to concentrate, a lessening of general anxiety, a stability of the autonomic nervous system, equanimity and evenness in responding to emotionally loaded and threatening stimuli, and a peaceful alertness (Goleman 1976). If one meditates in the early morning, it may be better to do so on awakening, before one has had any stimulants, such as tobacco or caffeine. Indeed, regular meditation can be a helpful factor in letting go of these addictions.

Aurobindo describes the serenity that we can gradually and subtly obtain from daily meditation over the years, "The experience ends up by acquiring so much agility, if we may say so, that in the full run of the most absorbing activities, in the street,when discussing things, when working, one plunges within (or without?) and nothing exists any more, except a smile - a fraction of a second suffices. Then one begins to know Peace; one has an impregnable Refuge everywhere, in all circumstances. And one perceives more and more tangibly that this Silence is not only within, in oneself; it is everywhere, it is as the deep substance of the universe, as though each thing stood out against this background, came from there, returned there" (cited in Satprem 1968). This feeling and being is our higher consciousness; it is the serenity of our Self.

Meditation is a part of the Twelve Step program of self-help groups such as AA. The Eleventh Step says, "(We) sought through prayer and meditation to improve our conscious contact with God, as we understood Him, praying only for knowledge of his will for us and the power to carry that out." Based on my clinical experience working with many recovering alcoholics, other chemical dependents and their families, I believe that maximum benefit in recovery is obtained by working a self-help program regularly long term, participating in a therapy group for about two years, and practicing daily a method such as meditation or prayer. Some Christians have raised the question of whether they might "lose their Christianity" if they were to meditate. I have reminded them that Christ meditated regularly, and that doing so is quite comfortable and compatible with being a Christian. Some obsessive - compulsive people might be too closed to new experience to try meditation, or if they do, may be over-zealous in their efforts (Goleman 1976).

Meditation, Our Unconscious, and Our Self

We can view our chronic distress and suffering as our unconscious " talking " to us (Figure 5). The three parts of our unconscious - personal, perinatal and transpersonal or collective - communicate with us in other ways. Linking us to our Higher Power, it speaks in both benevolent and less benevolent ways. The less benevolent may come as " bad " dreams and symbols, life events such as "accidents", unpleasant "coincidences," body tension, chronic distress, illness, and other suffering - including " hitting bottom ".

from © Laughing Man Vol 4, 1984

The more benevolent include " good " dreams and symbols, hunches, joy, ecstasy and peak-experiences, pleasant "coincidences," creative discoveries and insights, and inner peace. By meditating we can listen to our inner voice more directly. The silence of meditation allows the truth to become manifest.

Meditation is actually only one of a number of trance states, wherein we connect our ordinary waking consciousness with the wisdom and power of the three levels of our unconscious. We spontaneously go into and out of trance states every day, for example, when reading an interesting book, listening to music that is emotionally moving, daydreaming, exercising, or when we drive a car (Francuch 1981). Trance states, including meditation, are normal and healthy parts of our lives, and can provide us with creative insights that we need to complete our life's journey.

During meditation, we can ask our Self or our Higher Power a question with which we may be struggling at the start of meditation, and if we suspend our belief systems and listen, we may hear the answer in one form or another. The way the Self talks to us, its language, is both subtle and powerful. Sometimes called our " inner voice " or " soul voice," it usually comes to us when we are in a meditative state. It is not derogatory, nagging, cajoling, degrading or abusive (Newton 1981). It does not argue or superimpose its wishes upon us; free will is ours. It does not hold long conversations; it says what it has to say, and then is usually quiet. It may remain silent for long time periods. Yet through it we can gain knowledge and wisdom with the full knowing of facts without the formation of words. When our Self talks through symbol and imagery, there are often multiple meanings for each. When it spontaneously communicates with us, such as in our dreams, it seldom speaks directly in words. It encourages and guides us through its knowledge of both our wants and our needs. It is thus up to our mind to listen to it and then to take any necessary action (Newton 1981).

By contrast, the less benevolent voice is the one that we often consider as being undesirable. It is thus generally less obviously loving, and it usually comes to us in either our ordinary waking state or during our dreams. However, both our less benevolent voice, or part of our personal unconscious, and our Self are telling us the same message, because they both emerge from our collective or transpersonal unconscious, which comes from our Universal Consciousness (Figure 5 in Part 1). That message is " Remember, Forgive, and Love ".

Muktananda (1980) said, " Inside every human being is a source of complete fulfillment and contentment. To know that source we meditate. As a method of self-discovery, meditation has been practiced since the beginning of humanity. Although techniques vary, the purpose has always been the same - to gain a deeper understanding of who we are, of our inner most self. The ability to meditate is natural to everyone. Whenever we concentrate on something, we are, in effect, meditating. However, when we turn our attention inward and concentrate on our own inner Self, a new kind of experience takes place. An inner process begins to unfold which leads to expansion on all the levels of our being ... . The benefits of meditation go far beyond physical and mental well being. Meditation can actually transform our entire lives. When we meditate, we contact an unchanging state of awareness within us which contains wisdom, creativity, joy and contentment. "

Meditation can also provide a model for concentrating, focusing and centering in other areas of one's life (Gendlin 1978). With regular and continued meditation, combined with positive and right thinking, and with being honest with ourself and with others, we can gradually purify our being, and experience inner peace.

Praying

Praying is so similar to meditating that the two can be viewed as being nearly identical. The Eleventh Step of AA says "(We) sought through prayer and meditation to improve our conscious contact with God as we understood Him, praying only for knowledge of His will for us and the power to carry that out." I remember that the first few times I read this Step it had little personal meaning for me. Sometime later, during a dark night of my soul, a friend reminded me of it. I have since come to use it as one of my most frequent prayers. I have discovered its simplicity and its power: "...Praying only for knowledge of His will for us and the power to carry that out." Indeed, I have learned that the members of the most rigorous religious and other spiritual orders or practices seek an almost identical communication with their Higher Power (McKeon 1983).

Some people have a problem with the word "will". This is especially difficult in the Third Step "(We) made a decision to turn our will and our lives over to the care of God as we understood Him." Seeking the knowledge of our Higher Power's will for us is usually not as difficult as turning our will and our lives over. I have found a helpful clarification: We can think of our will as the will of our lower self, of our ego/mind, our will with a "small w." It is the "free will" we have been given (or that our ego has taken). By contrast, the Will of Universal Consciousness is also the Will of the Self. On our earthly journey, the Will of the Self is what our Self, which includes our lower self, needs to complete its return to Itself, to the Higher Power.

A Course in Miracles bypasses much of the struggle to resist the Higher Will by making a few suggestions: "There is no strain in doing God's will as soon as you recognize that it is your own. God's will for you is complete peace and joy; unless you experience this you must be refusing to acknowledge His Will. All real pleasure comes from doing God's Will". The AA slogans "Let go and let God" and "Turn it over" enact Steps Three and Eleven in our daily lives. Related to the concept of surrender, these are similar to spiritual practices in many disciplines, including that of the Tao - "Letting be." I further discuss the concept of will briefly under "Working a Self-Help Program" below.

How do we listen and talk to our Higher Power, to something that is so mysterious, powerful and pervasive that we often have difficulty even conceiving of It? A person can pray at any time, needing no special physical posture, paraphernalia, house of worship, or ceremony. While it can be helpful to close one's eyes and take few slow and deep breaths to get into a higher state of consciousness to facilitate praying, even that is not necessary. What is more important is our "state of heart". Perhaps the only "requirements" for effective prayer are faith, surrender or true humility, and a loving attitude to God and our fellow creatures - states of being which are often difficult to reach (Fosdick 1951; Rahner & Metz 1981; Sherman 1958; Hallesby 1959; Teresa of Avila 1980; Graham 1982). Christ said (Revelation 3: 20) "Behold, I stand at the door and knock: if any one hear my voice and open the door, I will come in to them, and sup with them, and they with me." It is thus not we who move us to pray, but our Higher Power, through our Higher Self, which invites us and moves us.

Even if we do not have the above "requirements" for prayer, we can still pray, in any way we chose that will begin to open ourselves to Universal Consciousness. Whatever comes - whether it be struggle, resistance, or frustration, or joy and peace - we can experience it. If we continue to pray, with patience and trust, the "required" humility, love and faith will come. Prayer and meditation are the breath of the Self, with each respiration transferring the radiant and healing energy from Universal Consciousness into us.

Our prayers are always answered. However, we may not realize the answer immediately, and sometimes not until a long time later. Also, the answer is often not what we want, although it seems to be always what we need. Paradoxically, prayer comes from our belief. Christ said, "When you pray and ask for something, believe that you have received it, and you will be given what you ask for. And when you pray, forgive anything you may have against anyone...." (Mark 11: 24 & 25). When we pray we know that what non-material aspect of our life we are sincerely asking for has already been given. From the instant of the prayer, it is already coming. If we are asleep or passive, we may pass it by. In a balance of our Higher Self and our lower self, in our wholeness, and by taking responsibility, we reach out and claim what we are asking (Holmes 1984). If we do not use it as fully in our wholeness as possible, we will likely not benefit completely from its power.

Just as meditation has been the acme of spiritual practice in the East, so contemplative prayer has been and is the highest development of esoteric religious practice in the West. Bonder (1981) writes "To enter through prayer into naked confrontation with the living presence of God and then to endure the transforming fire of divine love for a lifetime - this is an immense, heroic gesture. Anyone who has prayed for even a moment with a truly open heart can only feel awe and inspiration in the face of such an act." By contrast, Free John describes "neurotic" prayer, which involves self-attention, the binding up of energy and attention into the separate sense of "me", presuming our separaton from our Higher Power, not understanding our true relationship, in which Higher Power is alive as us (Bonder 1981). (Of course, neurotic prayer is probably more helpful toward our life's journey than no prayer at all.)

When we release ourselves, when we totally relax and surrender into the radiant energy of our Higher Power, we begin for the first time to practice with the basic feeling, as well as the intuitive understanding that all things and beings are already only direct manifestations of Universal Consciousness. We are connected. Our fear and suffering are gone. We are One.

Fillmore (1982) writes "The highest form of prayer is affirmation of that which is Being. It is praise of the good. Praise the peace of your own inner self. Rejoice and be glad in the actual posession of that Holy City within, and its gates will swing open to your inner eye, and its peace will pervade your whole consciousness." If we want knowledge and we believe, we can go into our Self, thanking our Higher Power and exalting us and It, and in some way, through a vision or a dream or a flash of spiritual discernment, we will receive the knowledge we are seeking (Fillmore 1982). And all the while, we remember the peace of our humility.

Yogananda (1957) writes that our Higher Power is talking to us, saying, "Call Me, speak unto Me from the depths of your heart, from the core of your being, from the very depths of your soul, persistently, majestically, determinedly, with a firm resolve in your heart that you will go on seeking Me, no matter how many times I do not answer. If you unceasingly whisper in your heart to Me, 'O my silent Beloved, speak to me' ; I will come to you, My devotee". We need but open ourselves in any way to our Higher Power, be it through prayer, meditation or any other practice. And, "...Silently and surely, as you walk on the path of life, you must come to the realization that God is the only object, the only goal that will satisfy you; for in God lies the answer to every desire of the heart" (Yogananda 1957).

Exercising

Just as meditation is not generally discussed in most stress management books as being a spiritual practice, neither is exercise. One can view exercising as a form of meditation, since many of the characteristics of meditation operate when we exercise, such as discipline, concentration, and letting go. Similar to a mantra, the game or task at hand can be the vehicle for entering an alternate state of consciousness.

Exercise is also an effective stress reducer. Depending on its intensity, duration and regularity, exercise works by eliminating or " burning up " many of the accumulated and toxic stress related chemicals, such as the catecholamines, glucose and fats. It also induces a particularly pleasant form of fatigue and relaxation that tends to last for hours and often for days (Girdano & Everly 1979; Sharman 1979). This effect may be in part related to release of endorphins in the nervous system. Other advantages of exercise are that it is widely available, cheap, and self-administered.

Accepting Paradox

From the Yin-Yang of ancient China to the rock and whirlpool of ancient Greece, we have long known, though so often forgotten, that we are suspended between poles, meeting at cross roads, hanging on crucifixes, or meeting on narrow ridges (Hampden-Turner 1982). Rather than either-or, we humans are both-and. We are right and wrong, good and evil, divine and lowly; in our humanity we represent the ultimate paradox. We are a divine animal, a " God who shits " (Becker 1973). While we will never reach perfection in a linear-rational sense, we are already perfect, just the way we are and in exactly what we do (Ram Dass 1974-83).

The processes of active chemical dependence, recovery and of life itself are full of paradoxes. Related to surrender and seeing the " bad " as a gift, learning to become aware of and to accept paradox is a highly spiritual practice. There are numerous paradoxes about alcoholism and recovery. Recognizing and accepting them can make the work that helping professionals do become easier and more pleasant. Many patients and their family members can also benefit from experiencing and knowing these paradoxes, although doing so may take from months to years of recovery and learning about alcoholism and co-alcoholism.

One paradox has to do with self-recognition of having a problem. While the alcoholic or co-alcoholic may have some degree of knowledge that he has a problem related to drinking, he doesn't know that he has a problem. A second paradox is that while the alcoholic or co-alcoholic cannot recover on his own, needing help from others to get better, the only way that he can recover is by his own internal resources.

A third is that while alcoholics cannot drink normally or safely without losing control, they sometimes can. Another is that the disease alcoholism, its treatment and its followup are at the same time simple and complex. A paradoxical statement heard at AA meetings is that " Alcohol was my best friend and my worst enemy, " (similar to the ego from a spiritual perspective - see Table 2). Another is that you can help an alcoholic only when he wants help, while with early or with coercive intervention, treatment is more effective and can save a lot of suffering.

Another paradox is that understanding or insight about one's problems is helpful, and it is worthless (e.g. Utilize, don't analyze - from AA). Then there is the idea that during recovery it is bad to be an alcoholic, while it is also wonderful to be in the growing process of recovery.

Finally, there is the issue about whether alcohol is a good or a bad substance. The paradox is that it is neither and it is both. For some people under some circumstances, alcohol use can bring about positive results, while for others, or under certain circumstances, using alcohol brings about negative results. And there are many more such paradoxes, some of which are mentioned throughout this book.

An ancient Chinese saying suggests that to get inside the temple of truth, one must pass by two pillars or guardians at the entrance. These guardians are confusion and paradox. Recognizing and accepting that alcoholism (or for non-alcoholics, any suffering), its recovery, and its treatment may be confusing and paradoxical for both the clinician and the sufferer. Yet doing so is important because it can make understanding and the helping process go more efficiently and enjoyably. These paradoxes are a part of those that exist throughout anyone's life. Helpful and specific paradoxical interventions can also be made by the therapist in treatment of the person who is stuck in or resisting letting go in their recovery (Shore 1981).

The Self knows no paradox as such. This is because to the Self everything that exists -whether contradictory or not- is not only acceptable, but perfect, just as it is. The AA saying " Everything is just the way it is supposed to be right now " applies here. This statement is to remind the mind, which tends not to accept opposites as being the same or at least compatible, to settle down. In order to make sense of the seemingly endless flow of opposites that it continually experiences, the mind needs a concept like paradox.

Early in recovery, the person is usually still stuck in the lower levels of consciousness, i.e. Survival, Passion and the lower parts of the Ego/mind. It is therefore difficult to comprehend paradox this early. Many of the patients I treat have required at least a year of being drug free and attending self-help and/or group therapy meetings to begin to comprehend the importance of paradox. And when they do, they often enter into the realm of surrender, acceptance, serenity, and the Self.

from © Wall Street Journal 1985

"You mustn't think it's carved in stone just because it's carved in stone."

Chapter 10. Suspending Our Beliefs

Much of what we come to believe about the nature of ourselves, others and the universe is useful to us in our daily lives. Without a foundation of beliefs or personal doctrines, sometimes called belief systems, our existence can become chaotic. Examples of some common beliefs that are helpful to use are, " I am responsible for my own life ", " I usually get what I give ", and " It is helpful to be kind to people. " However, many of our beliefs are not so helpful, and some are even destructive. Examples of some common beliefs that tend to cause us problems are, " I should be happy and feel good all the time ", " I am my personality; my body; my job; etc. ", " I am basically inadequate ", " The world has me as its victim, " and " Everyone else is happy and strong, and I am unhappy and weak. "

Holding on to our belief systems is similar to limiting ourselves to living only in ordinary consciousness. Ferguson (1980) said " A mind not aware of itself - ordinary consciousness - is like a passenger strapped into an airplane seat, wearing blinders, ignorant of the nature of tansportation, the dimension of the craft, its range, the flight plan, and the proximity of other passengers . . . (By contrast) The mind aware of itself is a pilot. True, it is sensitive to flight rules, affected by weather, and dependent on navigation aids, but still vastly freer than the ' passenger ' mind . . . Anything that draws us into a mindful, watchful state has the power to transform, and anyone of normal intelligence can undertake such a process. Mind, in fact, is its own transformative vehicle, inherently prepared to shift into new dimensions if only we let it. Conflict, contradiction, mixed feelings, all the elusive material that usually swirls around the edges of awareness, can be reordered at higher and higher levels. Each new integration makes the next easier. This consciousness of consciousness, this witness level, is sometimes referred to as a ' higher dimension ' . . . . " Like the passenger in the plane, we can remain blind to what is happening around us and within us. Our beliefs can thus bind and limit us, producing failure and low self-esteem.

There is a freedom and a feeling of peace and serenity in suspending one's beliefs. Doing so quiets the mind, similar to meditation, and opens us to higher levels of consciousness. Guided by the ego/mind, the lower self creates what it thinks is reality. Lie Tsu said, " Once upon a time a man whose axe was missing suspected his neighbor's son. The boy walked like a thief, looked like a thief, and spoke life a thief. But the man found his ax while he was digging in the valley, and the next time he saw his neighbor's son, the boy walked, looked and spoke like any other child. " Our realities change as we cycle through our death and rebirth, our involution and our evolution, and our suffering and growth.

Suspending our beliefs allows us to learn more about ourselves, others and the universe through direct experience, which is our best teacher. Joni Mitchell (1976) said, " People will tell you where they've been and where you ought to go. But until you get there yourself, you never really know. " Joy (1979) describes three injunctions to help us suspend our beliefs: 1) make no comparisons, 2) make no judgements, and 3) delete your need to understand. By using each of these we can begin to free ourselves from the bondage of our beliefs, of the way we think things are. Our mind's need to make comparisons and judgements and to understand everything indicates a need to control and to live by the idea rather than flowing with what is and with the reality of a higher consciousness (Joy 1979).

Suspending one's beliefs is difficult for the actively drinking alcoholic, and does not come easy for the alcoholic early in recovery or for the family member at anytime, where control, dependence, and surrender are major issues. Yet doing so has been accomplished by millions of recovering people. AA can remind us by some of its sayings, such as "keep an open mind" and "If you don't believe, make believe" (i.e., that life will get better not drinking or using other drugs). Suspending our beliefs is intimately related to and is a prerequisite to another spiritual practice: using our imagination.

Using Our Imagination and Imagery

Our imagination is one of our most powerful assets. Emerson said, " Imagination is not a talent of some men, it is the health of every man " (cited in Sheikh 1983). When we imagine something, we can transcend into our Self, at our Understanding level. Working in concert with the mind/ego, this is the source of all of our great art, literature, and scientific discoveries (Weil 1973; Harman and Rheingold 1984).

Many people in recovery get into a rut, for example with a lingering depression and/or a feeling of emptiness, at times even after they have worked the Twelve Steps. They cannot imagine their feeling good. The statments sometimes heard in self-help groups "If you don't believe, make believe" and "Fake it till you make it" can apply here. Indeed, we have not fully appreciated the power of pretending. The old Nat King Cole song can remind us, "Pretend you're happy when you're blue. It isn't very hard to do, and you'll find happiness without an end, whenever you pretend." Pretending is part of the dynamic of how affirmations work to heal our negative attitudes and our suffering.

We are limited in life only by the boundaries of our imagination. We can train our imaginitive abilities by many routes. One effective way is by a method called psychosynthesis (Assagioli 1976; Ferrucci 1982). Imagining works through levels three, four and five of our consciousness. While alcohol and other drugs at low doses can stimulate our imagination, there are equally effective or better ways using non-drug techniques. At higher doses of alcohol or drugs our imagination is decreased or blocked.

If we do not use our imagination, we will likely become chronically distressed and can develop an illness. Imagining is healing, both in prevention and in therapy. We use it

"My wife and I are deeply in love, my children are a delight, my career is exciting, I find solace and inspiration in my religion, I'm as healthy as anybody I know. But, still, something is missing."

Drawing by Weber; ©1982 The New Yorker Magazine, Inc.

in a broad range of healing techniques, from becoming aware of unsolved inner conflicts in psychoanalysis to hypnosis and biofeedback to the creative healing of guided imagery (Gendlin 1978; Thompson et al 1955; Williams 1980; Bry 1978; Gawain 1978; Houston 1980; Pachuta 1982; Vaughan 1979; Jaffe & Bresler 1980; LaBoeuf 1982; Samuels & Samuels 1975; Small 1982). It can be used in four general categories: 1) imagining health - e.g. healthy organs or healthy self, 2) imagining by classical or operant conditioning, 3) imagining by psychodynamic techniques, and 4) imagining by transpersonal techniques, such as going on an imaginary journey (Sheikh 1983). However, we use our imagination in most things that we do, including the psychological and spiritual practices described in this book.

Guided imagery is being used in some alcoholism treatment programs. It is a technique of expansion or going beyond and an integration of our whole being that can result in a deeper and fuller dimension of growth. With our eyes closed, we use images - with or without the combination of sound effects, music or pictures - that aid a flow of energy throughout all of our levels of consciousness and our being. While it can be used early in recovery, Dreitlein (1983) suggests that using guided imagery tends to come easier when the recovering person 1) is beginning to accept the disease of alcoholism/CD, 2) is recognizing feelings, 3) is working on interpersonal relationships, and 4) is open to personal growth. Some people can learn to use it almost immediately, while others tend to require a lot of practice for it to become effective.

Experiencing in our imagination can have the same therapeutic and healing effect as in experiencing something outright. When we have an incompleted " upset " - with no access to solving it - we can use the following technique: sit comfortably and quietly, close the eyes, and take a few slow and deep breaths. Now begin to imagine the feeling of the upset, with any concomitent sounds or images. We can then ask ourself the following: Where in our body are we feeling the upset? (Pause, and feel and describe its extent in our body.) What shape is it? (Pause again, and likewise for each of the following.) What color is it? What temperature is it? How does it smell? What does it sound like? If it had a voice, what does it say to us? If we could touch it, how does it feel? What patterns from our past does it bring up? Then take a few more slow and deep breaths, and notice whether our feeling of upset is less. We can repeat these same questions until the upset no longer bothers us (Ferrucci 1982).

Since it has no boundaries, imagery can help us handle worries we may have about our past or our future. For example, in psychotherapy it can help us get into our childhood experiences easier than we can do so verbally. It can bring out our feelings and emotions more easily than many other techniques. Indeed, since imagery is both spontaneous and simultaneous, and not linear, it is in a sense a truer representation of our experiences (Sheikh 1983). It is useful in getting rid of or handling anger, sadness, anxieties about death or other events, and in accepting our shadow. Using music as a facilitating aid to guided or spontaneous imagery can also be helpful in being our Self.

Using Music

Listening to music can serve several useful and therapeutic purposes. It can help us to experience all levels of our consciousness. It can help bring out our repressed emotions and it can directly link us to our unconscious. Music therapists and thinkers have said the following (cited in Bonny & Tansill 1977).

Michel (1951) Musical language has an ability to express a number of ideas at one time, in contrast to verbal language in which only one idea is expressed at one moment.

Noy (1967) (Music is) a symbolic language expressing overt feelings and contents . . .

psychoanalytic theory regards it as a language lending symbolic expression to unconscious contents . . . psychoanalytically minded authors agree that music may be considered as structured according to more or less the same rules as the dream.

Pratt (1952) Music presents to the ear an array of auditory patterns which at a purely formal level are very similar, if not identical with, the bodily patterns which are the basis of real emotion.

Kohut & Levarie (1950) The sounds of music are felt as coming, not only from the outside, but also from his own emotions . . . such an experience induces an "oceanic feeling" which is joined by a feeling of magical omnipotence and a return to a primitive kinesthetic pleasure, as if the listener were flying through the universe on the wings of sound.

Bonny & Tansill (1977) (Music) . . . serves as a catalyst between mental and emotional processes. The morphology of music - instrumental timbre, vocal color, rhythm, dynamics of pitch, intensity, harmony - contributes subtly and powerfully to mood, emotional involvement, and insightful introspection.

When appropriate, evocative music is combined with imagery and psycho-therapy. It can help people become aware of parts of them that were otherwise repressed or unconscious. Many alcoholics/CD's and their family members have difficulty becoming aware of their emotions. And we know that held in emotions will usually eventually cause us to suffer. When used by skilled clinicians, such use of music can be a valuable aid in the recovery process. One recent technique using evocative music is holonomic integration.

Holonomic Integration

This is the name given by Grof & Grof (1979) to a clinical technique that allows a person to experience an inner, mind expanding and emotionally expanding journey without using drugs or any other artificial mechanism. One or several such experiences usually facilitates a person to begin freeing up excess psychological "baggage" that has been burdensome. By using appropriate, evocative music, controlled breathing emphasis on introspection, and a special abreactive technique, the person opens a channel to both the unconscious and to higher levels of consciousness.

Holonomic integration can be helpful in exploring some of our deep life issues, among which may be unresolved sadness and grief, anger, confusion, needing to be in control, frustration, and a feeling of emptiness. It often facilitates an improvement in ongoing individual and group psychotherapy and in discovering one's personal spiritual path.

Chapter 11. Thinking Positively

Of all the spiritual practices available to us, one of the most powerful is thinking positively. By thinking positively I mean viewing our life as a productive part of the "cosmic drama ", a concept and practice similar to what Boorstein (1980) calls " de-emphasizing ". To do so involves many of the above spiritual practices, including surrender, viewing the " bad " that befalls us as a gift, watching our life's dance or melodrama, and accepting paradox. Pulling us back, however, is our always busy mind, with its tendency to view or to categorize each thing and each event in our lives as either good or as bad, and as being separate from everything else, including ourselves. Such dualistic thinking with its concomitant attachments, is paradoxically responsible for both our suffering and for our ability to transcend it all to be our Self.

It can be useful here to ask, if the source of us all - Unity Consciousness - is all positive and all loving, why does the bad or evil exist in our lives? Numerous authors over the centuries have written explanations. The answers end generally with two possibilities. It is all either a cosmic good vs. evil drama, or it is all good, with the evil used in favor of the good, perhaps to celebrate it. What all this has to do with recovery from alcoholism, co-alcoholism, or any suffering will hopefully become clear toward the end of ths chapter.

A Model of the " Cosmic Drama "

The " cosmic drama " may go something like the following. In " the beginning " there was only Universal Consciousness, timeless, spaceless, infinite and eternal (Wilber 1982; Watts 1975). For several possible reasons, it then created the negative, the bad, the evil or the darkness. The first possible reason is that it was lonely or bored, and wanted something with which to relate. Another is that it wanted to realize itself more fully, or to celebrate itself. Still another is that it was dreaming, and that some day - perhaps periodically - it awakens (Watts 1975). There may be other explanations, including that our finite ego needs a reason; infinite Universal Consciousness, being ultimate perfection, needs none (Watts 1965).

To make the cosmic drama, dance, game or sport unfold, that part of consciousness that has wandered into the darkness or has become evil forgets that it is a part of the Universal Consciousness, and acts as though it is separate (Watts 1965, 1973). Hindu tradition calls this play of Brahma by the Sanskrit word the lila (Morrison 1970) or the leela (Johari 1980). In our human consciousness we have inherited all of these characteristics: an aspect that has forgotten that is is part of the One, and so views itself as separate and isolated. It is thus perhaps the intention of the One to awaken into the two, or the many, in order to better know or celebrate its Oneness (Ram Dass 1974-83; Steinberg & Martin 1981, Fremantle & Trungpa 1975). Without darkness or evil, there would be no drama, nothing to overcome, no celebration, and perhaps "nothing to do".

Some of these concepts are illustrated in Figure 7. At the top of figure 7, represented by the triangle, is what we can call our Higher Power, God, or whatever we chose to call Universal Consciousness. Although this state it indescribable, it may be called Unmanifest Unity Consciousness, a state of non-duality, of pure silent Being, and Ultimate Reality. To begin its celebration of itself, it creates a part of itself that blossoms forth to be its Self, and which includes Unity Consciousness, Compassion, Understanding and the upper part of Acceptance. In order to make the cosmic drama or celebration unfold and work, it turns away from its light of Unmanifest Unity Consciousness and thus creates the exact opposite or absence of its Self, as pure darkness and evil. From these two opposites then emerge various parts of our cosmic consciousness, among which have been described as being archtypal, ancestral, phylogenetic, kundalini, racial, and past " incarnations " (DiLeo 1983). This area of our cosmic consciousness is actually mostly unconscious, and Jung began to describe it as our collective unconscious. We can include these parts of us under the transpersonal, as shown in Figure 5 and 7.

The next realm of our consciousness' development is the perinatal, which includes human consciousness from our conception to our birth. These would include our experiences while in the uterus and our struggle during our birth process. The final realm is the personal, where we are born with both an ego and a Self, both being still connected - through their personal unconscious - to the perinantal and the transpersonal realms. A major problem for most of us is that when we are born, and throughout much of our life, no one tells us "the rules". Or they tell us the "wrong" rules. (Or are we told the "right" rules?)

One view is that the darkness/evil disenfranchizes itself from responsibility and then scapegoats each of us through our individual ego. Although ambivalent, our ego accepts the blame for the existence of evil. This blame or guilt is then manifested by our mental and emotional misery that we can carry throughout our lives, or which we can choose to let go (DiLeo 1983). Through its " distorted lens " viewing of these three levels of reality, our ego forgets that it came from God, from its Self and from evil. And to protect itself from destruction, it projects both its own evil and goodness onto others (Course 1975). Although we each want to return to God, we each want to shortcut claiming our evil, our shadow, or our " bottom "without confronting and experiencing it. Psychotherapy, if done with the right therapist, teacher, guide, or guru, i.e. one who is not overly attached to his or her own ego, who lives and works " from the heart ", and who has appropriate skills, can help us over time to confront and experience both the good and the evil within us (Di Leo 1983). A major goal in such a growth process is to learn that we are our own ultimate therapist-teacher-guide-guru.

These areas described within Figure 7 also parallel the seven levels of consciousness. And within each of the three areas of personal, perinatal and transpersonal, the seven levels also are present. Each area is also shown as being connected with the other two through the open spaces in the diagram.

Watts (1975) expands the cosmic drama: " Suppose that God is the one playing all the parts, that God is the child being burned to death with napalm. There is no victim except the victor. All the different roles which are being experienced, all the different feelings which are being felt, are being felt by the one who originally desires, decides, wills to go into that very situation. " Since in our humanity we have aspects that are both divine and animal, could it be that we are a tiny fragment, like a drop from the ocean, of Universal Consciousness acting out our part in this cosmic drama?

Figure 7. A Map of Universal Consciousness and It's Creation of Our Self, Ego and Unconscious

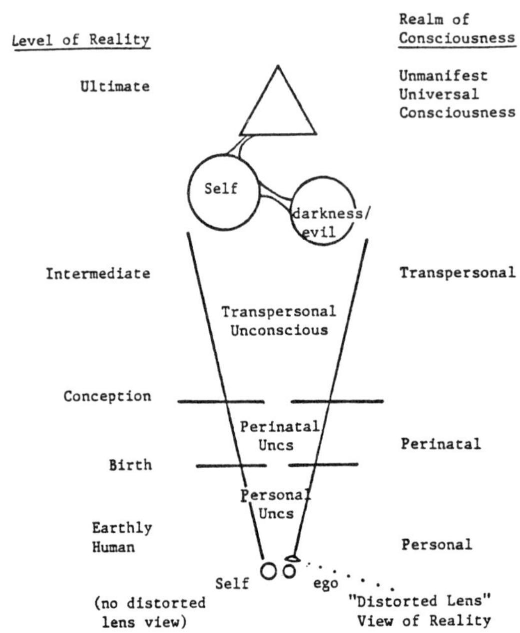

The aspects of evil may be threefold, and are the opposite of the three positive infinites: 1) existance and non-existance, 2) awareness/knowledge (or remembering) /meaning and ignorance/forgetting/meaninglessness, and 3) bliss and negative emotions (Grof 1980-b). The creation of the evil and of the lower self in humans by the Higher Self is called involution (dissolution, death, thanatos), and the movement from the lower back to its source of Consciousness is called evolution (emanation, rebirth, eros, transcendence). According to the perennial philosophy, history can be viewed as a cycle of involution and evolution over the millenia and the centuries. This cycle also recreates itself from moment to moment, endlessly, and instantaneously (Wilber 1982). The boatman said to Siddhartha, " Everything changes, and everything returns " (Hesse 1951).

We can use Plato's cave as another model for our drama. Humankind can be seen as being stuck inside a cave. On the outside is pure, bright light, some of which gets into the cave. Deep inside the cave is pure darkness, mysterious and evil. In between are shadows. We in the cave can use the darkness and the shadows as clues and mechanisms to reach the light (Happold 1970). Hall said " He who knows not that the prince of darkness is but the other face of the King of Light knows not me " (cited in Ram Dass 1974-83). Paradoxically, evil allows and even pushes us to realize our Oneness, through Universal Consciousness' unconditional love and total positivity.

In order to reach the light, the inner peace or eternal bliss that it craves and to emerge with the One from which it came, the separate ego self would have to forget itself and remember the One. But to do so would mean that it would have to die, i.e. it would have to accept the death of its sense of being separate, and of this it is terrified. Since it both wants release <u>and</u> is afraid of it, it arranges a compromise and a substitute. It pretends to be a separate god, cosmocentric, heroic, all-sufficient, and immortal. To accomplish this, it builds what it thinks are indestructible monuments, searches for eternal life through youth, and does numerous other such activities (Wilber 1982). All of these either lull it into a slumber <u>or</u> eventually through their resulting pain, push it toward higher levels of consciousness. If we can experience that it is alright to have this knowledge of good and evil, then our ancient fear disappears forever.

<u>The Curse into the Gift</u>

We can then see the evil, the darkness or the separateness as <u>a means of returning us to our Self, to the One</u>. Evil is positive because it teaches us about the good. This is why the sages say " It is all perfect ", and that suffering is grace. There appear to be only two paths back to the One: 1) confronting and <u>experiencing</u> our suffering and our evil, and then transcending it, and 2) <u>forgiving</u>, which then frees us to love unconditionally. And forgiving and loving unconditionally usually require that we confront and experience our evil, so that the two are inseparable.

These concepts all tie in with viewing of alcoholism as a gift, discussed above. Alcoholism and other chemical dependence, and co-dependence are <u>part</u> of our evil. We confront them in many ways, including by telling our story, by hitting our bottom, (our suffering), by experiencing and handling it, and by accepting their existance. We can do likewise for our other suffering and evil. With this rationale, thinking positively, i.e. that we <u>can</u> turn our curse into our gift - if we only choose - becomes easier and even more exhilarating and exciting.

Our ultimate positive thinking is to remember that we are part of, and thereby are, the One - not sometime later or when we die - but <u>right now</u>. In the St. Thomas gospel, omitted from the Bible (Pagels 1979; Guillaumont 1959), Christ said, " The Kingdom of Heaven is on earth, and men do not see it. " This is in part why mediation, which takes us to the One, our Self, is called remembrance or recollection (Wilber 1982). Thinking positively elevates our consciousness to the acceptance and the understanding levels and into our Self. And the only way that our Self can see is positively, since it is pure positivity. Positive thinking can also be facilitated by writing out in repetition the positive statements that one wishes or knows about oneself, a useful technique called affirmation (Ray 1980; Kirtsberg 1983; Fankhauser 1983). One continues writing the positive statements - and any negative or doubtful ones that come up - until the negative statements become positive. Like all spiritual practice, writing affirmations is merely a technique, and not an endpoint, to reach and to be our Self. There are many other techniques that we can use to stimulate us to think positively (Boorstein 1980; Ferrucci 1982), including the realization that while on this earth we will never attain absolute knowledge or certainity.

Knowledge and Uncertainity

After these somewhat elaborate, beginning attempts at explaining some of the whys of the universe, we must ultimately admit and accept that we are profundly ignorant about it all. Free John (1984) says " Do you know the old saying, Ignorance is bliss? It is one of the 'secret teachings' floating around in our trivia. Nirvana is Ignorance. Realization is release from the illusion of knowledge. All knowledge is an illuson, because it does not actually amount to knowledge. There is no reduction of the Mystery or the Paradox. All things arise and nothing is known - that is Nirvana. This is why I call this Way the Way of Divine Ignorance. When you realize that you do not know, that nobody ever knew, nobody knows now, nobody ever will know, then you are Enlightened! Then you are free.

"... being Ignorant is not exactly like being stupid. Being stupid is a matter of thinking that you know what is happening. I am not stupid - I am Ignorant. People conceive of the Unknown not as the unknowable but as what they do not yet know about, and so whenever they come across something new, they worship it in some fashion or other. Or they acknowledge it and become fetishistically fascinated with it as if it were God. ... But the Unknown, which is the presumed goal of religion, the Divine, is the inherently Unknown. ... It is not that we do not know about God. We cannot know God. God is not the kind of thing that can be known. We can Realize God, enter into God, be Ecstatic in God, Commune with God, be Liberated in God, but we cannot know God. Because knowing about something implies a different kind of relationship than is possible with God ... the Realization of God transcends the subject-object confusion.

"How much would you pay for all the secrets of the universe? Wait, don't answer yet. You also get this six-quart covered combination spaghetti pot and clam steamer. Now how much would you pay?"

"No matter how much we learn, our knowledge will remain finite. Only Ignorance is infinite. While the ego would seek salvation, truth, and survival through knowledge, the Truth that surpasses all understanding is found only in inherent Ignorance . . . we presently 'do not know what anything is.' No matter how much we know about any object, whether it be a tree, or a thought, or a feeling, or 'I', when we consider the thing itself, we do not know what it is. At the level of sheer existence, Mystery prevails. In Divine Ignorance, no 'one' attains union with God. The separate knower is utterly transcended in Mystery alone, and that Radiant Mystery is recognized to be none other than God, Radiant Transcendental Being, the Consciousness of which everything is only a modification."

Bronowski summarized the wisdom of many of the great physicists, mathematicians and other scientists. While we can advance in our knowledge, we will never, no matter how hard or how long we may try, know anything totally or with ultimate certainty. Bradbury said, " We all go on the same Search, looking to solve the old Mystery. We will not . . . ever solve it. We will climb all over it. We will, finally, inhabit the mystery . . . . " (cited in Ferguson 1980).

Free John (1984) concludes, " Our fundamental relationship to God is expressed in the recognition of inherent Ignorance. In the recognition of inherent Ignorance, we are entirely associated with Mystery. Our very Condition is Mystery. It is not expressed or defined by knowledge in any sense. No matter how much we know, we still do not know what anything is . . . By expanding our awareness beyond the lower perceptual and mental model to higher brain and higher psychic states, we think we are finding God. There is no more reason to consider God or presume the Reality that is Divine when seeing internal lights and visions than there is when we are doing anything ordinary in our daily life. God is no more apparent (nor any less apparent) in the one case than the other.

" So, let your Life-impulse be Magnified Infinitely, since you have no possibility to restrict it. Your prejudices are all bullshit. Your knowings are a cramp in the gut Your presumptions are like the hairs on a wart - useless, and only a distraction . . . That is all there is to it. All the rest is nonsense. Do not believe any of it. There is just this incredibly profound, mind-blowing, ego-destroying, humbling Mystery . . . when you stop knowing things, you get Happy."

A Course in Miracles boils down its wisdom to the realization, repeated throughout its three volumes, that there is one reality - Love. And if we want to realize it and be it, and thus have inner peace and serenity, we can find it only through forgiveness. We are here to become whole, to return to the One through forgiveness.

Chapter 12. Forgiving

Often our mind, in its attachment to time and to separation, keeps us feeling guilty about our past and fearful of our future. Such a preoccupation can maintain our anger and resentment at others and at ourselves. And unventilated anger is stress producing, and eventually it is crippling. Intimately related to surrendering, letting go, detaching, and accepting what is, forgiving is a spiritual practice that can move us from lower to higher levels of consciousness. By forgiving, we give ourselves serenity. But whom should we forgive? Jampolsky (1982) has described ten pathways to inner peace: 1) Forgive my parents, totally and consistently; 2) Forgive everyone and forgive myself; 3) Forgive nature, the weather and other conditions; 4) Let go of all concepts of God; 5) Let go my rational mind, and trust in Love and in God; 6) Chose to experience peace rather than conflict; 7) Chose to experience Love rather than fear; 8) Chose to be a Love finder rather than a fault finder; 9) Chose to be a Love giver rather than a Love seeker; and 10) Teach only Love, for that is what I am.

But such forgiving and chosing do not come easy. There appear to be at least two steps, at least early in the process, before one can forgive. These are working through and experiencing the uncomfortable feelings, such as anger, hurt, guilt, and fear, that we have about the person or problem in question. We can do so either 1) directly - by communicating or by " fair fighting," (see below) or 2) indirectly - through imagery, dreams, in psychotherapy, and in other ways. Then we can begin to detach from the bondage of both the uncomfortable feelings and our needing to be right regarding conflicts with a person or situation. Generally, only then can we forgive. However, forgiving totally and consistently does not happen all at once, and this is why the process so often takes a long time. To allow the time that we need, we can chose to be patient. All of these can be facilitated for the alcoholic by working the Steps of AA, especially Steps four through ten, and by participating in a therapy group long term. Perhaps the most constructive of group treatment ultimately is in either a couples therapy group or in family therapy or a family group. This is because it is usually the people closest to us with whom we have the most conflict. And the closest of all to us is ourself, who we have the most difficulty forgiving.

Jampolsky (1983) said, "To forgive does not mean we must remarry our ex-spouse; let prisoners out of jails; return to our old job, or anthing else overt. The ego believes that if it forgives the one who has harmed it, it must translate this forgiveness into some behavior. But true forgiveness requies no bodily action, even though some gesture may perhaps accompany it. Forgiveness is an inner correction that lightens the heart. It is for our peace of mind first. Being at peace, we will now have peace to give to others, and this is the most permanent and valuable gift we can possibly give.

"The root meaning of the verb to forgive is to let go. Forgiveness is a relinquishing of an unhelpful train of thought, a giving back to the ego that which is now recognized as undesirable. Forgiveness is a gentle refusal to defend ourselves against love any longer. It sees that all things are forgiving. It is a willingness to perceive everyone, including ourselves, as either expressing love or feeling a need for love. Any form of attack is a call for help, and the answer to every call for help is gentleness. . . . practicing forgiveness does not imply we must tell people we forgive them or act holier-than-thou around them. . . . true forgiveness is not the adopting of a morally superior position. Nor does it acknowledge someone else's cruelty and pronounce it acceptable, for to do this would be dishonest. Forgiveness sees that no real grounds for innocence must be recognized. Certainly the person's behavior cannot be rationalized away. He did behave the way he behaved. Possibly another motivation can be attributed to his behavior, such as fear instead of selfishness, and although this can be a good first step, it is not sufficient in itself to allow us to see the splendor of God's light within him. Forgiveness is a gentle turning away from what we see with our body's eyes and a searching for the truth that lies beyond the individual's ego.

"True forgiveness is based on reality. It overlooks the evidence gathered in from the point of view of a single body and turns instead to universal truth. The truth of our reality is that each of us is innocent and loved completely by God. It's not that we haven't made countless mistakes and will probably continue to do so for some time. But true forgiveness distinguishes between the deep urges of the heart and the more superficial desires of the ego. All mistakes come from the ego and are part of a learning process that everyone must go through. Forgiveness is a gentle vision that sees the maturity, the goodness of heart, and wholeness of character that will come in time to each person. And it recognizes the inappropriateness of condemnation to this growth process.

Jampolsky concludes, "Most people understand that deep urges for goodness exist in everyone's heart no matter how overlayered they may be with guilt, defensiveness, dishonesty and inhumanity. Forgiveness looks past the more superficial motivations of the inidividual, no matter how extreme these may be, to the place in his heart where he yearns for exactly what we yearn for. Everyone wants peace and safety. Everyone wants to make a difference. And everyone wants to release his potential for love. It is deep into this desire that forgiveness gazes, and seeing there a reflection of itself, it releases the other from judgement." And in releasing the other, we release ourself from our attachment or resentment, and our own suffering.

This entire process of forgiving is a great experience in being all levels of consciousness. Experiencing involves our consciousness levels one through four, detaching involves levels four through six, and forgiving involves levels five and six. And the final step in the process, for those who dare to risk it, is to thank the person whom we have forgiven for their involvement and for their teaching us this experience of transcendence and of experiencing inner peace. We can also thank the person through affirmations (Fankhauser 1983). One affirmation might be "I release ____________ to his/her highest good." Another is "Thank you, ___________, for this valuable teaching." Working through all of the above need not necessarily involve telling the person who we thought instigated our problems any or even all that transpires regarding their involvement with us. We can work it out, if appropriate, in our individual or group therapy, in a self-help program, with a trusted friend, in imagery, and/or in our dreams. The ultimate communication that we have for these people with whom we are so involved - and for ourself - is " I love you ". When we can do that, we are free of suffering, and we can feel inner peace. All forgiving is a gift to ourself (Course 1975).

Forgiveness begins first with awakening, which is similar to remembering our connection to our Higher Power. The flow to serenity, to inner peace, follows a path that we each can choose, as follows:

Practice	Condition
Loving	
↑	
Forgiving	Inner Peace
↑	↑
Remembering	Awakening (or Re-Awakening)
↑	↑
Forgetting Our Source	Suffering

This is a universal path to inner peace, health and wholeness. It is the same one as that of the Twelve Steps, the levels of consciousness, and many spiritual quests. Each of the spiritual practices for being our Self described in this book and in others can facilitate us on our journey. And when we "arrive", we realize that we were there all along. We were serenity. We were Love. We were and are always and already that for which we had been searching.

Once we realize that we are unconditional love, that we are serenity, forgiving becomes easier and easier. We learn that we can forgive our ego its mechanical nature and its forgetting, and we can forgive others, the world, the universe and even our Higher Power. And each time we forgive, we experience inner peace. This is why forgiveness is a gift to ourself.

Jampolsky (1981) said, " Inner peace can be reached only when we practice forgiveness. Forgiveness is the vehicle for changing our perceptions and letting go of our fears, condemning judgements and grievances. . . . Love is the only reality there is. . . . Forgiveness allows us to see only the Love in others and ourselves . . . (it then) becomes a process of letting go and overlooking whatever we thought outher people may have done to us, or whatever we may think we have done to them. . . . Forgiveness corrects the misperception that we are separate from each other, and allows us to experience a sense of unity and at-one-ment with each other. . . . I cannot forgive myself unless I forgive others. . . . Only through forgiveness can my release from guilt and fear be complete. "

I will return to the importance of forgiveness and unconditional love in Part IV.

Chapter 13. Communicating

Communicating is a spiritual practive that helps us better know both our lower and higher selves, and others. In perhaps its most effective form, especially between intimates, it consists of three stages: 1) the communicater gives a clear, concise message to a person, 2) the person reflects back to the communicater what s/he heard, and 3) the communicater feels heard accurately, and says so, or not.

Ventil ating and communicating in a healthy manner includes having an awareness of our feelings, living in the here and now, risking with openness and honesty, and being assertive. While doing so is difficult, even if we can't get in touch with our feelings and risk, we can say something like " I'm finding it hard to get in touch with my feelings about this. I wonder if you can help me with it? " Communicating in these ways can allow us to feel that we have made a contribution, to feel more alive, and to complete our expression. And completion allows us to move to higher realms of our consciousness.

Communicating verbally comprises only about one fourth of all of our communicating. While the majority is non-verbal, we can make our verbal form as clear as possible. Communicating requires listening, which is a manifestation of love. Peck (1978) said, " . . . true listening . . . requires tremendous effort . . .it requires total concentration. You cannot truly listen to anyone and do anything else at the same time ."

Being Assertive

Communication also includes being assertive. However, many alcoholics and their family members have difficulty being assertive. Often related to their low self-esteem and even self-hatred, they find it diffucult to ask for what they want and need. Frequently, only when they are drinking or using other drugs do they erupt with an outburst of agressive attacks or responses. By contrast, some people even when sober communicate aggressively and with hostility (Wallace 1978).

Assertiveness is a positive and productive expression of oneself (Girdano & Everly 1979). Assertiveness training is helpful for everyone, and is especially so for recovering alcoholics and their family. It is an effective way to substitute positive, self-assertive behavior and perceptions in the place of passive, angry, withdrawing or generally inhibited behaviors and perceptions, which themselves tend to produce or aggravate stress.

"You sprang that question on me quite unexpectedly, Karen. Could you give me a few minutes to get in touch with my feelings?"

Many inpatient alcoholism/CD treatment programs are beginning to teach assertiveness. Group therapy is another place to learn assertiveness, both within the group and preparing for needs outside the group, such as breaking off a destructive relationship, confronting an unfair or unrealistic supervisor or authority figure, or saying no when one does not want to do something. Actions may include leveling about one's feelings, wants and needs, setting limits by saying what one will and will not permit, and making demands or giving warnings (Wallace 1978; Materi 1977). In most communities there are inexpensive courses on assertiveness available, and I often recommend that my patients take them.

<u>Sally</u>

Being assertive is related to having a healthy and authentic self-esteem. Often just knowing that we are a child of God, a part of Universal Consciousness, is helpful for building our self-esteem. Sally was a 23 year old office clerk who's father was active alcoholic and mother a dysfunctional co-alcoholic. She began attending Alateen meetings when she was 16, and has been active in Al-Anon since age 20. She tells her story as follows.

> I was brought up Catholic and I've never had any trouble with the idea of God as my higher power. But it was never a "presence" and I never really thought much about it. Oh I prayed for good grades and things, but for the most part, God was passive when it came to important things like my father's drinking and my mother's confusion. I just went along and didn't question. I never thought of him as someone to help me out of jams. I had a feeling that he was there, but being frightened all the time I just assumed that he didn't care much about me. I was biding my time until I graduated from high school and then I was going to split.
>
> Gradually, I came to trust my Alateen group. And the way they talked about the higher power, and the way they called on him for help. Now whenever I have something difficult to do, I have a feeling of some kind of support. For example, I don't like my job and I want to quit. But there are a lot of reasons why it's not a good idea yet. Even if I did just up and quit, I know God wouldn't let me starve. Something would turn up. I'd have the strength to find something because he would give it to me.
>
> So many things are in my life since I've been in the Alateen program. I finished college instead of stopping at high school. I feel that God really cares about what happens to me. I know sometimes things are difficult, but I also know that he will help me to rise above the difficulties.
>
> I don't just "go Along" anymore. I make decisions about my life and some things work out and some things don't, but it's all OK.
>
> As far as spirituality in recovery, I don't know whether I would have gotten better without it . . . but I think it would be hard. I think my self esteem comes from my feelings about the higher power. He created me. And I'm one of God's children. I must be good if God loves me and watches over me.

<u>Risking</u>

Communicating often involves risking. And risking is being vulnerable. When we are vulnerable with a close person, we are communicating in perhaps its most intimate form. Such open and vulnerable communication allows us to learn about ourselves, and thus to heal ourselves and to transcend the suffering of our ego/mind. Recovering people communicate intimately when they tell their story at a self-help group meeting or at a group therapy meeting in their "shared honesty of mutual vulnerability openly acknowledged" (Kurtz 1983b). The essence of such risking and sharing is expressed in a work by an unknown author.

To laugh is to risk appearing the fool.
To weep is to risk appearing sentimental.
To reach out for another is to risk involvement.
To expose feelings is to risk exposing your true self.
To place your ideas, your dreams before the crowd is
to risk their loss.
To love is to risk not being loved in return.
To live is to risk dying.
To hope is to risk despair.
To try is to risk failure.
But the risk must be taken, because the greatest
hazard in life is to risk nothing.
The person who risks nothing, does nothing, has
nothing and is nothing.
He may avoid suffering and sorrow, but he simply cannot
learn, feel, change, grow, love, and live.
Chained by his certitudes, he is a slave, he has
forfeited freedom.
Only a Person Who Risks - is Free

Risking is a powerful spiritual practice. While it is healing, it can at times have unpleasant side effects, for example when another rejects the risk we have taken, or when a person betrays our confidence. Thus, risking nearly always involves trust, which is another important spiritual practice. It also involves letting go, suspending our beliefs, and other spiritual practices.

Work that may provide further breakthrough in communicating suggests that all communication can be categorized into one of four areas: assertion, declaration, request and promise (Orman 1984; Flores 1984). By listening carefully for these, we can clarify nearly all of the communication we hear from others, and respond to them more accurately. Vaughan (1983) believes that every statement that we make is both a perception and a projection. Ultimately, communicating is both a search for love and an expression of love. Every communication that does not extend love is a search for it (Course 1975).

For close relationships, a form of assertiveness called " fair fighting " can be helpful (Dayringer 1976). An outline of this technique is listed in Table 7. My colleagues and I have used it in our couples therapy groups and have found it to be very helpful for couples during their recovery from alcoholism/CD.

Touching and Bodywork

Another form of communicating is through touch. Touching gives us the reassurance that we are not totally separate and totally alone, even if for only that instant. It is also an anchoring device for communications, and can at times be a link to our unconscious (Bandler & Grinder 1982). And it is an effective centering device when we are frustrated or when our nerves are frazzled. " Four hugs a day " has been recommended, even for those who feel they are most in control.

Many people have difficulty touching, and are often out of " touch " with their own bodies. They are blocked in this crucial part of their lower self. Their body and energy flow may also be off center. Bodywork, ranging from exercise to massage to yoga (which are also kinds of meditation), can be an effective remedy (Ryan & Travis 1981). Stimulated and centered through our lower levels of consciousness, we are thus able to let go into higher levels and be more fully ourselves.

Table 7

Summary of Fair Fighting Techniques

1. Ask permission to talk about a single complaint.
2. If busy, make appointment. Assure no or minimal interruptions.
3. Hug to affirm positivity.
4. One complaint per session.
5. Relate the here-and-now only; avoid past and future.
6. No anger museum complaints.*
7. Use " I message ". Feelings work better than logic or reason. Expressing feeling hurt is usually more effective than anger.
8. For unequal discussions, each have 3 minutes to talk, until both done.
9. Negotiate for change in behavior.
10. Affirm agreement of specific change.
11. Hug to affirm positivity, thank partner.

*can make list, exchange, agree to bury, bury. Also decide time limit for complaint validity, e.g. 3 to 7 days.

modified from Richard Dayringer, So Il Univ School of Medicine, Springfield

Creative Dreaming

Our dreams are a major language of our Self. They come to us most every night, whether we remember them or not. A spontaneous product of our unconscious, they function to maintain our psychic balance and to further our growth to wholeness. Dreams show us a reality within us. A problem is that they communicate with us through symbol and metaphor, and so to comprehend them and to use them we may have to learn to understand their universal human language.

A key to helping understand our dreams is that each figure or actor in a dream at the same time likely represents we, the dreamer, as well as several others in our life. Also, with practice, we the dreamer are likely to be the most accurate interpreter of our dreams. Our dreams are a rich and profound source of our journey to wholeness. To participate more consciously in and to make use of our dreams, we can use various techniques of creative dreaming, from dream analysis to consciously creating some of what happens in our dreams (Garfield 1974; Sanford 1982; Williams 1980). We can enter our higher consciousness through our dreams.

Being the Dream or the Dreamer

Using the word "dream" in another way, as a metaphor for our life, we can view our melodrama or "victim act" as a "dream" of which we think we are a part. We can take our life and our suffering seriously, and think that they are all there is. But we have another choice. We can be the "dreamer", which means that we can be more our witness, watcher or observer self. By being the dreamer, we are empowered so that we can more easily detach from our ordinary waking victim - and suffering - oriented consciousness (Silverman 1980; Course 1975).

Being Patient

For many of us to realize and to be our Self, it takes time. Being patient is related to living in the now, surrendering, accepting what is, thinking positively, and other spiritual practices. Jung suggested that the first half of our lives was concerned with our developing our mind, and the second half with our developing and becoming higher levels of consciousness. Many people resist, struggle and fight early in life, and only later become more accepting, patient and more spiritual. We each receive test after test to strengthen our patience. AA's slogan for being patient, perhaps its most powerful, is " One day at a time. "

Saint Gregory said, "All holy desires grow by delays." He advised that we not prejudge our difficulties; they may be painful disappointments when they happen, but they may also be the carriers of unwanted delays that have a valuable and constructive purpose (Progoff 1980). Being patient frees us from the suffering of being attached to the future.

Chapter 14. Ventil ating and Telling Our Story

Identifying and healthily ventil ating our feelings is a major psychological and spiritual practice. These feelings come from the level of Passion and the level of the Heart, which is Acceptance through conflict. There are also higher level feelings of joy serenity, and compassion to share. As part of the mind's continual blocking of its transcendence, it tends to discourage a healthy ventil ation of feelings. Again, opposites come into play: if we don't ventil ate we will get sick, and if we do, the mind discourages it. The process of experiencing a feeling or an upset can help the upset to disappear. There are specific imagery techniques for completing our experiencing that are available to use when we are alone (Ryan & Travis 1981; Ferrucci 1982), and we can also ventil ate to a trusted loved one, our therapy group, self-help group, therapist, or friend. Doing so allows us to complete the feeling, which can then elevate us to higher levels of consciousness.

Telling our story and listening to others' is a foundation of the AA program of recovery. All stories, whether read in mythology, other classical literature or told at a meeting, are similar, and can even be viewed as having the same collective theme (Table 8). Each mythical story has three movements: separation, initiation and return (Campbell 1949). The story may represent the movement of the Spirit through the challenges of transcendence. The classical story or myth is similar or even identical to our stories in self-help groups (Figure 8).

The Hero/Heroine's Journey

First there is a call to adventure. Most do not respond, as there are too many distractions. For those who do respond, pride, from the ego level, often pulls them into the adventure. As the hero or heroine enters the phase of separation and initiation, a period of extreme stress, " sacred blunders ", betrayals or symptoms occur. Separation represents the break with the ego's world and a journey into a sacred place, from which the traveler can eventualy reach a completion and learn transcendence. It often follows ritual or a rite of enactment to remind the hero of the transforming power of the adventure that is his personal story. We frequently encounter the shadow side of our personality, which is often accompanied by experiencing confusion and paradox. A series of trials must be faced along the way, including the fear of losing control or losing our self. To meet the challenge, the hero has to surrender to the trial, i.e. drop previous belief systems and behaviors. After the surrender, the hero transcends the duality, and there is a sacred union of hero and God as one. Thus, the hero/heroine learns from the initiation-adventure, with all of its struggling, discomfort and frustration, and returns a more whole person. At this time he shares the knowledge with fellow humans (Campbell 1949). The curse becomes a gift, in a " fall upward ".

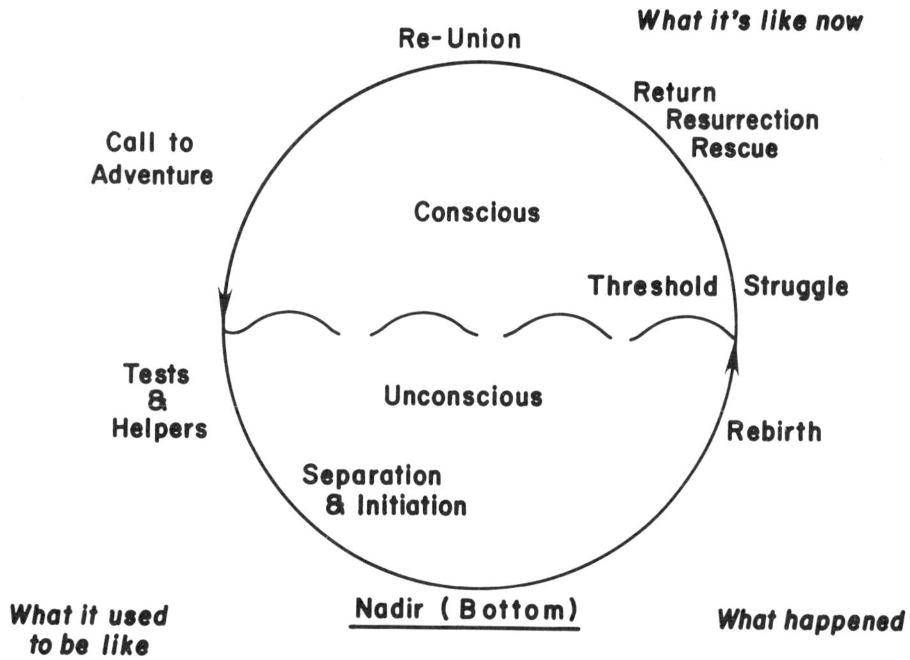

Figure 8. THE MYTHICAL HERO-HEROINE'S JOURNEY

Throughout the story there is paradox. One is that the evil gods or "tricksters" may also provide some kind of help for the hero to meet the challenge. Even so, the hero often gets angry at the gods - either for tempting him with a lie or telling him the truth. A second paradox is that one has to let go and surrender in order to return and to transcend. And a third is of the curse becoming a gift. The journey is the story, i.e. getting lost and trying to find one's way home (Schreder 1982). The self gets lost and finds itself as a new and more whole Self. It is the cycle of death and rebirth, of involution and evolution (Table 8).

Table 8. Phases of Our Life Journey and Its Stories According to Six Models or Views

Model Or View	Phases of Our Life Journey and Its Stories 1	2	3
Classical mythology	Separation	Initiation	Return
Disease	Pathogenesis	Active illness	Recovery
Telling our story	What we were like	What happened	What we're like now
Levels of Consciousness	Lower self	Acceptance thru conflict	Higher Self
Spiritual	Forgetting & Separating	Suffering	Remembering & Forgiving
Thanatological	Death	Rebirth	

Story in Our Life

Our lives are one big story, in which we are continuously creating little stories, or melodramas. Knowing this and sharing our stories makes life less frightening, and more complete, which then pushes us toward transcendence. We can also use these stories as metaphor, which can allow us to grow and to live a richer life (Metzner 1980; Romanyshyn 1981; Valle & von Eckartsberg 1981). There may also be a hidden metaphor in some, so that what we learn comes to us later. From the brevity of a Zen koan to the most elaborate and complicated predicament into which we and our friends may fall, we can learn from our stories.

We repeat the same adventure and tell the same story over and over - whether it be in literature, movies, or with friends or with ourselves, because, perhaps through its variations, it gives us the chance to know ourselves better, and to grow to wholeness and fulfillment. And the repetition is also the continuous cycle of the One becoming the many (or the two, or the separate), and returning to the One, in an exquisite dance or play (Ram Dass 1974-83). It thus bridges the separateness of our lives, both externally and internally, to completion, wholeness and health. Story connects us to others and to ourselves. Alcimion said "Men die because they cannot join the beginning to the end," i.e. they cannot complete their story (Hillman 1979).

When shared, psychotherapy - whether in a group meeting or individually - is nothing more and nothing less than story telling. To the content of our lives it gives context, e.g. that a curse is a gift, and even vice versa. Story gives spiritual meaning to the whole. We then can discover that the story, also called a myth - which means an eternal truth, and not an untruth - is the language of the Self, communicating with itself. And all the time it is watching, participating, and enjoying seeing the dance unfold. Hillman (1979) said, " From my perspective as depth psychologist, I see that those who have a connection with story are in better shape and have a better prognosis than those to whom story must be introduced. . . . to have ' story awareness ' is per se psychologically therapeutic. It is good for soul. . . . One integrates life as story because one has stories in the back of the mind (unconscious) as containers for organizing events into meaningful experiences. . . . Story-awareness provides a better way than clinical-awareness for coming to terms with one's own case history. Case history too is a fictional form written up by thousands of hands in thousands of clinics and consulting rooms. . . .(It) follows the genre of social realism; it believes in facts and events, and takes with excessive literalism all the tales it tells.

" I think children need less convincing of the importance of story than do adults. . . . childhood tends to mean wonder, imagination, creative spontaneity, while adulthood, the loss of these perspectives. . . . I wish to remove story from its too close association with both education and literature - something taught and something studied. My interest in story is as something lived in and lived through, a way in which the soul finds itself in life " (Hillman 1979).

The language of the psyche is story, told or enacted through basic units of experience. Some names given to these basic units of experience are 1) sensation (sensory-perceptual), 2) emotion (feeling), 3) impulse, desire, or motivation, 4) thought, reason, symbol and ideas, 5) motor and speech, 6) autonomic nervous sytems and hormonal, 7) intuition, 8) will, and perhaps the most powerful unit of this language of our psyche, 9) imagination (Assagioli 1976; DiLeo 1983-84). The human will is generally described as being in the center of these units, as a major part of our personal self. However, our will is vaster than that, and I discuss the concept of "will" further under Working a Self-Help Group Program below.

Kurtz (1983b) describes how stories in AA are effective: remapping our belief systems into a new way of life that involves a new way of thinking, and the process of identification with the stories of others. Many of my patients tell me that they hear the same story over and over at self-help group meetings. Some may use this observation as an excuse to stop attending meetings. They usually need either a gentle or a more forceful push back, so that they can gain what still others tell me - that even though the stories are similar or even the same, they benefit from hearing them all, each one providing a teaching, although some may be boring or make them angry. To grow, we need to live in and allow a tension. It may be just the challenge of the boredom or anger that pushes us to learn about ourselves and others, and thus to transcend and transform. We often experience a shift in awareness and in committment from learning that their our ego now can serve our true identity - our Self.

We can also catalyse, expand and deepen our story by keeping a diary or a journal. This can range from a few words written daily or periodically in a diary about our life experiences and observations, to a more intensive journal. The latter may include a looseleaf notebook that is divided into sections, with dividers. Journal entries are made in the different sections of the journal. As the person grows, so does the journal (Progoff 1975, 1980; Kritsberg 1983). Keeping a journal is a powerful method of facilitating and becoming more aware, more conscious of one's physical, mental and spiritual growth.

Completing Our Story

Telling our story - with genuineness and honesty - helps us with a powerful psychological and spiritual task: that of completing our story. When we tell it, we, the storyteller, get more in touch with our story and with ourself.

Completing our story generally takes an awareness of and a commitment to doing so. A breakdown of "our story" as shown in figure 8 is further detailed in Figure 8-A. Some key points in this representation of our story are in the downswing, where we can create the possibility of being aware that we do not have to be the victim of unawareness. Rather, we have a choice, with practice, of being aware, and thus the powerful practice of making a commitment to facing and dealing head-on with our suffering and our grieving. We do so by experiencing and ventil ating, participating and, after several "rounds" with our particular story that we are currently working on, by completing it. Having learned a new experience, lesson, or teaching, we then integrate our story into our life. By so completing our story, we generally have to experience some pain. Some people in recovery have jokingly referred to working through their suffering in this fashion as an "A F -G E " ("another fucking growth experience"). By so using humor as a mature ego defense mechanism, one can detach from the trap of becoming overly involved or stuck in his or her story.

Co-Creating Our Story

Each time that we complete our story, i.e. that "episode" of our life story, we are then free to create a new, bigger and more truthful or honest story. As we progress and grow in life, we then complete and create bigger and bigger stories, i.e. a story that is closer and closer to the "Truth," to Higher Power (Fig 8-B).

However, we usually eventually learn that we are not creating our story alone. Indeed, we are co-creating it, with our Higher Power, which we may here also call "Life" or "Process". We thus discover that when our story is in harmony with the story of the Universe, we are in harmony, we are free, and we experience serenity.

To co-create a new story, we have to let go of our old story, once we have completed it. Telling our story through working the 12 Steps and working in group therapy can be helpful in both completing and letting go of our old, painful story.

Figure 8-A

In our recovery our individual stories change as we discover and experience new wholes within us. Our stories in both self-help and therapy groups are a marvelous blend of tragedy, humor and humility. They show us the strength, competence and beauty of human character that can flow from the disabling and dehumanizing malady of alcoholism. As mentioned above, in their "shared honesty of mutual vulnerability openly acknowledged," they are healing (Kurtz 1983b). Thus, our story telling and listening in groups or in individual psychotherapy or counseling, or with a friend, is a powerful spiritual practice. We seem to benefit from being reminded where we have been - separate, fearful, and lonely - and where we are now - recovering, together, joyful, and One. And by so telling our story we help ourselves attain humility.

Figure 8-B CO-CREATING OUR STORY

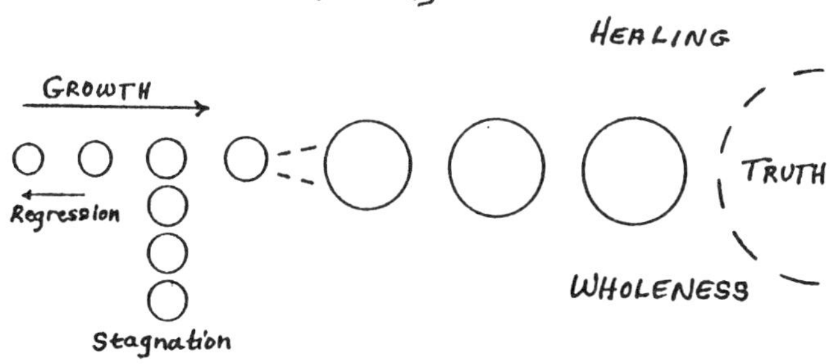

Being Humble

Gaining humility is a major milestone in recovery. It usually signifies a life transformation, in that the person flows more with life, functions better, and tends to be at a much lower risk of drinking and using drugs again. In the case of the recovering person, the term " humble " is thus positive and is a great strength, and is not generally viewed as a weakness. Taken from its origin humus, meaning " earthly ", the general dictionary definition of " humble " is twofold: " Not proud or arrogant; modest " and " meek; submissive; low in rank or conditions " (Random House 1980; Oxford 1971). It is in part the former definition that the alcoholic or any obsessive, compulsive, controlling or manipulating person can acquire to help solidify their road to recovery, and about which numerous therapists and recovering people speak so positively. It concerns, in addition, a substantial decrease in grandiosity, and the acquisition of being open, listening, and non-defensive, while at the same time being honest with oneself and others, and having an improved self esteem. It is part of the strength obtained through surrender.

However, becoming humble for a recovering alcoholic may be more difficult, and at the same time paradoxically easier, than is doing so for a non-alcoholic. For the non-alcoholic there is one cycle, from becoming ego-attached or " somebody special ", to then becoming ego-detached or " nobody special. " Ram Dass & Levine (1976) said " We are in training to be nobody special. And it is in that nobody-specialness that we can be anybody. The fatigue, the neurosis, the anxiety, the fear, all comes from identifying with the somebody-ness. But you have to start somewhere. It does seem that you have to be somebody before you can become nobody. If you started out being nobody at the beginning of this incarnation, you probably wouldn't have made it this far . . . it's that force of somebody-ness that develops the social and physical survival mechanisms. It's only now, having evolved to this point, that we learn to put that somebody-ness, that whole survival kit, which is called the ego, into perspective . . . .

" At first you really ' think ' you've lost something. It's a while before you can appreciate the peace that comes from the simplicity of no-mind, of just emptiness, of not having to be somebody all the time. . . . You spent the first half of your life becoming somebody. Now you can work on becoming nobody, which is really somebody. For when you become nobody there is no tension, no pretense, no one trying to be anyone or anything, and the natural state of the mind shines through unobstructed - the natural state of the mind is pure love, . . . pure awareness. Can you imagine when you become that place you've only touched through your meditations? . . . You've cleared away all of the mind trips that kept you being who you thought you were. . . . You experience the exquisiteness of being in love with everybody and not having to do anything about it. Because you've developed compassion. The compassion is to let people be as they need to be without coming on to them. The only time you come on to people is when their actions are limiting the opportunities for other human beings to be free " (Ram Dass & Levine 1976).

The reason that it may be more difficult for the early recovering alcoholic or co-alcoholic to be humble, to become nobody special, is that from their active disease and in early recovery they usually do not have a healthy ego and self-esteem to give up (and nor do many non-alcoholic people). With their strong fear, guilt, shame, ambivalence, and low self-esteem, they may find it difficult to surrender their ego because there is little to surrender. The ego is too rigid, too inflexible to let go. Alcoholism creates a false sense of self-esteem, manifested in part by an over-concern with being in control and by a surface grandiosity. The heavy drinking or drug use of alcoholism/CD cause at least five other dynamics that contribute to the lower self-esteem of active CD. Memory blackouts can cause the person to be fearful of " going crazy ". Their loss of control over drinking or drug using usually causes " recurring trouble " in the areas of self, relationships - especially family, legal, education, health and finally job, usually progressing in that order. The toxicity of the alcohol or drugs causes brain damage and frequently depression. Dealing with the many enabling co-alcoholic people around them promotes an extreme of either frozen or volatile feelings. Finally, the person becomes isolated, alienated, and feels spiritually empty (Whitfield 1983).

Thus, a major goal of early recovery is to begin to break down the unhealthy ego and to rebuild a healthy one. This is usually best accomplished successfully through modern treatment, a major component of which is group treatment (self-help group and group therapy), with its story telling and sharing, modeling, identifying, working the Steps, confronting and strong supporting. For this to occur, usually at least two years of abstinence from alcohol and other drugs and participation in group treatment is required for a healthier ego to emerge (for some this may be an even slower process, lasting many years or even a lifetime). For alcoholic/CD people who are also adult children of alcoholics, further work in group treatment may be needed to help rebuild a healthier ego. Only then can the person begin to see the way and the advantages to letting go of the ego and letting go of being somebody special. Assertiveness training can also be helpful in beginning to build a healthy ego. Since it takes great strength to surrender one's ego, one must generally have a fairly strong, i.e. flexible, ego to let go completely. The process of gaining humility is usually composed of a string of cycles of strengthening and then letting go of parts of one's ego.

In a society where everybody has to be somebody special, what a joy it can be to walk along and be nobody special (Ram Dass & Levine 1976). It is freeing, peaceful and serene. We learn to listen. And where we are when we are nobody special is in our heart and in our Self. The fellowships of AA, Al-Anon, NA, and others also suggest being nobody special by their principle of anonymity. Their 12th Tradition says, "Anonymity is the spiritual foundation of our Traditions, ever reminding us to place principles before personalities."

Since we are each a part of Universal Consciousness, it would seem that we would know that and spend all our days in a state of serenity. But by its nature, our mind builds a wall of defenses around us, around our Self (Figure 9). This is one way of viewing our " forgetting " and our ego's " distorted lens ", mentioned above under Thinking Positively. To help us remember our unity with the One and open us to its life-giving and positive energy, we can eliminate as many of our unhealthy ego defenses as possible.

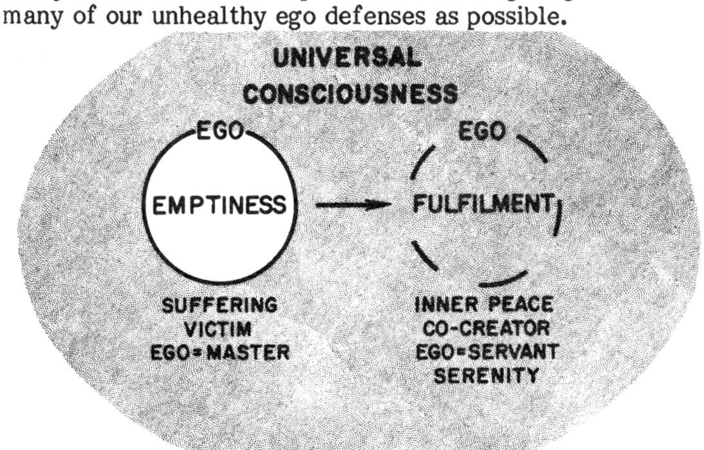

Figure 9. Letting go Unhealthy Ego Defenses Opens us to Universal Consciousness and Serenity

These unhealthy defenses may be: intellectualization, repression, dissociation, displacement, and reaction formation (considered neurotic) and projection, passive-aggressive behavior, acting out, hypochondriasis (Vaillant 1977), grandiosity, and denial (considered immature and at times psychotic). By using mostly these ego defenses, we suffer by being a victim. Our ego is our master. We feel that the world, i.e. things and events outside of us, is causing us to suffer.

Eliminating our unhealthy defenses may be in part what the founders of AA, borrowing from James and from Jung, meant by the term " ego deflation at depth " as a requirement for recovery (Kurtz 1979). Reducing these unhealthy defenses then leaves many openings in the wall between the previously isolated ego and Self, and thus the chance for being an un-isolated Self, whole and serene (Figure 9). Thus, the mature ego defenses remain: humor, altruism, anticipation, sublimation and suppression (Vaillant 1977). These are mature not only because they are efficient, but because they also open us to higher realms of consciousness, especially so for humor, altruism and sublimation (see right side of Figure 9). Appendix C illustrates how the Twelve Steps of AA are concerned with helping the recovering person attain the use of mature ego defenses.

With our forgetting, and with using all of the unhealthy defenses of our ego, we suffer needlessly. Our ego becomes our master. We become a victim. Being attached to our own ego, we become self-righteous, and we suffer even more. Our ego's wall of unhealthy defenses blocks out the healing energy, love, and serenity of universal consciousness. By surrendering and working a self-help group program and being in a therapy group, we can begin to let go of our unhealthy ego defenses. When we do that, and re-build a set of healthy ones, we can, little by little, begin to experience more and more inner peace. Only a person with a strong ego, i.e. a flexible one, can let go into the freedom of forgiveness. When that happens, we are no longer a victim of "the world", i.e. our own ego. We are now a co-creator with our Higher Power. Our ego is now our servant. We not only have serenity. We discover that we <u>are</u> serenity.

Part of becoming "somebody special" is coming to admit and finally to accept being an alcoholic. This struggle occurs at the Acceptance level. One learns that s/he is not only an alcoholic, which implies that s/he cannot drink or use drugs safely, but is also a <u>recovering</u> alcoholic, which implies a state of growth and the potential of attaining <u>serenity</u>. Thus the person becomes a healthier and strong lower self, both to survive <u>and</u> eventually to let go and become his or her Self, "nobody special." At this point being an alcoholic may be irrelevant, because s/he is now <u>sober</u>.

A paradox is that we constantly and simultaneously alternate between being somebody and nobody special in our cycle of involution and evolution, of death and rebirth.

A reason why it may be easier for an alcoholic to become humble is because the illness is so painful and it pushes so hard that the person is forced to either grow or to die. With all of this pressure and suffering and with the increasingly wide availability of appropriate treatment and of coercive methods for holding a denying and resisting alcoholic/CD in treatment, it thus may be easier for an alcoholic or co-alcoholic to recover and to transform his or her life, than if one had, for example, solely a personality disorder or a neurosis, in which s/he would be less likely to be so pushed or coerced into treatment. Being humble is also facilitated by another powerful spiritual practice, accepting our shadow.

Chapter 15. Accepting Our Shadow

Each of the Twelve Steps involves accepting our shadow in some way. The name of <u>shadow</u> has been given to that part of our personality that we do not want and which we <u>dislike</u> (Jung 1965; Hampden-Turner 1982). In the discussion thus far, I have described some ways of being the Self that involve a combination of experiencing our lives now, quieting our mind, and transcending to wholeness. Of the several parts of us from which we close ourselves, and thereby avoid fully experiencing our lives, our shadow is one of the most difficult for us to accept, whether we are alcoholic/CD, co-alcoholic, or not. What follows is an explanation of the shadow that approaches the hierarchy of consciousness from a different viewpoint: its relationship to our creation of boundaries.

To create the " cosmic play " of our forgetting and of our re-discovering, of our involution and our evolution, we " begin " as Consciousness that is unlimited in time and space, with no boundaries and with no opposites, as shown at the bottom of Figure 10 (Wilber 1979). As part of our forgetting, we create at least three boundaries that result in isolating ourselves from our wholeness. We draw the first boundary between our body-mind, which also can be called our total organism, and our environment. At the next level we draw a boundary between our ego/mind (ego) and our body. And we create the final boundary between the parts of our ego or personality that we like and want, which we can call our persona, and the parts that we minimize, disclaim, dislike or do not want, our shadow.

Figure 10. Therapies and the Levels of the Spectrum (from Wilber 1979)

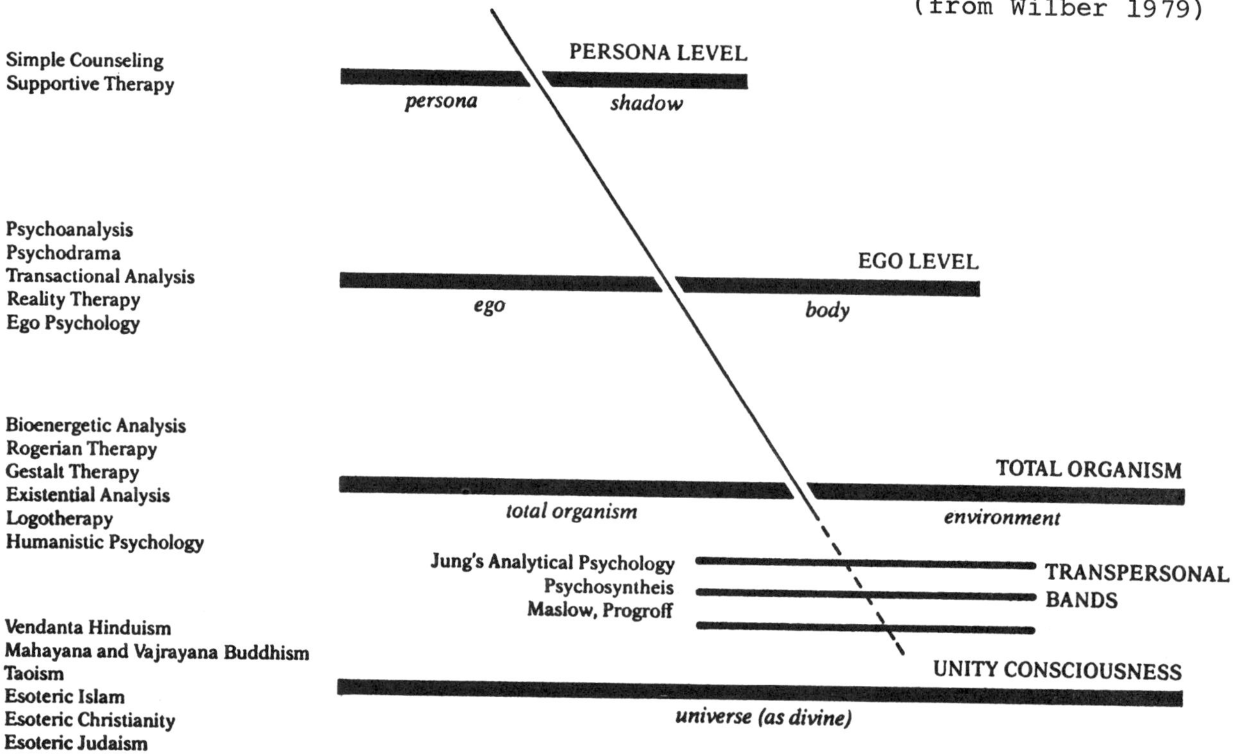

With each successive level of the spectrum of consciousness we view more and more aspects of ourselves as those which appear to be external to our mind or ego. We are thus left with a narrow part of us that is isolated from our wholeness (Wilber 1979). Similar to our attachments, the more boundaries we create and the stronger we make them, the more we suffer.

A boundary line can be viewed as a battle line, which sets up two potentially warring camps. Wilber (1979) said, " The persona is a more or less inaccurate and impoverished self image. It is created when the individual attempts to deny to himself the existence of certain of his own tendencies, such as anger, assertiveness, erotic impulses, joy, hostility, courage, aggression, drive, interest, and so on. But as much as he may try to deny these tendencies, they don't thereby vanish. Since these tendencies are the individual's, all he can do is pretend that they belong to someone else. Anybody else, as a matter of fact, just not him. So he does not succeed in really denying the tendencies, but only in denying ownership of them. He thus comes to actually believe that these tendencies are not-self, alien, outside. He has narrowed his boundaries so as to exclude the unwanted tendencies. These alienated tendencies are therefore projected as the shadow, and the individual is identified only with what's left: a narrowed,

"To begin with, I would like to express my sincere thanks and deep appreciation for the opportunity to meet with you. While there are still profound differences between us, I think the very fact of my presence here today is a major breakthrough."

impoverished, and inaccurate self-image, the persona. A new boundary is constructed, and another battle of opposites is on: the persona vs. its own shadow. . . . The essence of shadow projection is simple to comprehend but difficult to enact, because it throttles some of our dearest illusions."

Our shadow is thus an impulse, trait or tendency that we resist, dislike and reject to such an extent that we project it onto one or more others or onto the universe. AA describes it thus: " It is a spiritual axiom that every time we are disturbed, no matter what the cause, there is something wrong with us " (12 Steps & 12 Traditions 1953). Kubler-Ross (1982) has described the worst aspects of our shadow as " . . . a little Hitler inside each of us. However, it is a gift to us to allow us to get in touch with some unfinished business. " Regarding our tendency to project our shadow onto others, she said, " Whenever I react negatively to someone, whenever I feel hateful toward someone, I look for a part of myself that is mirrored in them. "

A common trait of active alcoholics, and of many non-alcoholics as well, is to believe that the world is causing their problems, when in actuality they themselves are causing them. By abstaining from alcohol and other drugs and by relating honestly to themselves and to others, they slowly discover the truth, and gradually begin to take responsibility for the problems that they and their drinking have created. They are accepting their shadows. They accept not only by simple acknowledgement, but in the healthiest of recoveries they begin to laugh at their prior behaviors and to express gratitude for the gift of their recovery and their shadow. And by doing so their life becomes more serene, because their ego is now more complete and can transcend to the next higher level of consciousness.

Table 9. The Common Meaning of Various Shadow Symptoms (a dictionary for translating symptoms back to their original shadow forms) (from Wilber, 1979)

Symptom translated to	Its Original Shadow Form
Pressure	Drive
Rejection ("Nobody likes me")	" I wouldn't give them the time of day! "
Guilt (" You make me feel guilty.")	" I resent your demands "
Anxiety	Excitement
Self-consciousness (" Everybody's looking at me ")	" I'm more interested in people than I know"
Impotence/Frigidity	" I wouldn't give him/her the satisfaction "
Fear (" They want to hurt me ")	Hostility (" I'm angry and attacking without knowing it ")
Sad	Mad
Withdrawal	" I'll push you all away! "
I can't	" I won't, dammit! "
Obligation ("I have to ")	Desire (" I want to ")
Hatred (" I despise you for X")	Autobiographical gossip ("I dislike X in myself ")
Envy (" You're so great ")	" I'm a bit better than I know "

A projected shadow impulse, trait or tendency that is not experienced and handled in a healthy manner generally becomes a symptom, such as anxiety, boredom or fear (Wilber 1979). Table 9 lists the common meaning of 13 shadow symptoms. As uncomfortable as they may be, we have to experience them, rather than resist or avoid them, because by doing so we can then translate them into their original shadow form and thereby accept them. And then they tend to disappear. Wilber (1979) said " We must touch our symptoms with awareness and as much open acceptance as we can command. And this means to allow oneself to feel depressed, anxious, rejected, bored, hurt, or embarrassed. It means that where formerly we resisted these feelings in all sorts of ways, we now simply allow these feelings to display themselves. Indeed, we actively encourage them. We invite the symptom right into our home, and we let it move and breathe freely, while we simply try to remain aware of it in its own form. That, very simply, is the first step in therapy, and in many cases it is all that is required, for the moment we truly accept a symptom we also accept a large part of the shadow concealed in that symptom. The problem then tends to disappear. " Recovering alcoholics invite their shadows into their homes by telling their stories, by working the Twelve Steps, by helping others in need, by possibly eventually disclosing their anonymity, and by numerous other ways.

We can thus begin to view our shadow symptom as a positive part of our own unique personality. It is there to warn us that we have an aspect of us with which to be concerned. Rather than suffer from it, we can now use it as a point of self-knowledge and growth. Jesus died (humanness, lower self), only to rise as Christ (Godness, Higher Self). In accepting our full humanness, we become more divine, more our Self. In our weakness we find our strength.

Earlier, I mentioned the problem of evil, which is part of our collective shadow, as being part of the "cosmic drama". Evil may be natural, e.g. earthquakes, floods, and diseases (Sanford 1981; Siegel 1981; Kushner 1981), or it may be human evil (Peck 1983). Peck defines human evil as any human force that seeks to kill life or liveliness, i.e. that seeks to kill the human spirit. Active alcoholism/CD and co-dependence usually eventually dampen or "kill" the human spirit. However, this spiritual damage is nearly always reversible through treatment and recovery. Since most workers in the field of alcoholism/CD believe that these problems are illnesses, they appear to be a natural form of evil. However, they are often a disguised form of natural evil that appears on the surface as human evil. Whichever way we view alcoholism/CD and co-dependence, until the victims face the terror of it all, including their own shadow, they cannot let go of it and be free. A description of the pathogenesis and the natural history of this illness with an evil component is described throughout this book and in others (Johnson 1981; Vaillant 1983; Whitfield 1984b). In most references, alcoholism/CD and co-dependence are not referred to as being evil, but as being an illness. A Course in Miracles views everything other than love as being an illusion. Thus, even evil is an illusion. I will discuss this concept further in Part IV.

The recovering alcoholic or family member can learn to know, accept and befriend his or her shadow by at least four possible ways. These are by: 1) working a self-help program, 2) participating in group therapy long term, 3) using visualization exercises and 4) using psychotherapy. Visualization exercises can be powerful inducers of getting in touch with our shadow, as well as other aspects of our beings (Samuels & Samuels 1975; Bry 1978; Small 1982). Psychotherapy also may be helpful, as long as one remembers the " rule of one thirds ": about 1/3 of psychotherapists will help us get better, with 1/3 we will get worse, and with 1/3 we will make no change (cited in Wolfe 1975). The various types of therapies that can help the person to reach the corresponding level of consciousness are listed in Figure 10 (although it is not indicated on this list, working a self-help program, such as AA or Al-Anon, long term can help a person reach all of the levels).

Chapter 16. Being Responsible

Being responsible means taking responsibility for our life, our feelings and our well being. Doing so is crucial in reaching a lasting and comfortable sobriety. But there is a part within each of us that wants not to be responsible, whether it be for our thoughts, behaviors, emotions, or any other aspect of our lives. It is the part of us that wants to be the suffering victim, but without playing any other role or making any other contribution to our condition. While we all so inflict such suffering on ourselves, people with alcoholism, other chemical dependence, and their family members have as part of their illness an especially strong inclination to being victims. For example, I may often say things like, "The world is doing it to me. I'm just trying to get along". I project onto others and onto the world my own fear - the fear that I am victimizing myself.

"I'm sorry. My responsibility doesn't go beyond this bubble."

It is not so easy to break free from the role of being a victim. In a way, we are attached to - we are addicted to - being a victim, being at the effect of others and the world. Breaking free from any addiction or attachment usually comes in stages, in fits and starts, "two steps forward, one stap backward", little by little. The text of A Course in Miracles says, "If you realize that all the attack [and suffering] you perceive is in your own mind and nowhere else, you will at last have placed its source, and where it begins it must end."

The first step in getting free is to become aware that we are trapped. We begin to become more aware of our feelings, and then to experience them. We can do so more easily by working in a therapy group, whether it be in an inpatient or an outpatient program. We can share with trusted family, friends, or a self-help group sponsor. Working the Twelve Steps is also helpful, especially Steps One and Four through Ten.

I hear some people say, "No, I don't want any help, thank you. I can do it on my own". I often remind them that each time they come for group therapy or for self-help group or to take Antabuse, etc., that they are doing that on their own. No one is pointing a gun at them. It is entirely their choice to use a treatment method to get well and to stay well.

Other people are forced to come to treatment, or else they might lose their job or go to jail, for example. However, even they have a choice. They can choose to get the most possible out of their treatment, since they have to be there anyway. Making such positive choices is an example of taking responsibility for one's own life.

The part of us that wants to be a victim is in our lower self, most specifically level two, passion, and the lower half of the Ego/mind level. Once we work through our suffering, which is best done in the Acceptance - through - conflict level, we are then free to look back at it all from our Higher Self, our observer self, and see that it was just our soap opera, our melodrama. From such a vantage point, we have transcended our karma and our suffering. At this stage on our journey, at this level of our awareness, we can now see that we caused our suffering. No one else did. And since we caused it, we can chose not to continue causing it. We can chose to stop causing our own suffering. A Course in Miracles summarizes this powerful realization as follows:

> I am responsible for what I see
> I choose the feelings I experience and I decide upon the goal I would achieve
> And everything that seems to happen to me I ask for, and receive as I have asked.

We can take responsibility by remembering our Source and by remembering our melodrama. We can then forgive others and forgive ourself, which then frees us to see and to be the highest level of reality, which is Love. Through forgiveness, we see that everything other than Love is an illusion, and we experience inner peace.

Chapter 17. Working a Self-Help Group Program

Twelve Step Recovery Programs

Working a self-help group program uses nearly all of the above-described spiritual practices. By doing so, one is able not only to stay sober one day at a time, but to grow well beyond the realms of ordinary existence (i.e. levels one through three). While there are numerous discussions of AA that are much more complete than this one (AA 1976; Twelve Steps 1953; Kurtz 1979, 1982; Bean 1975; Bean et al in press), and while I have previously related many important spiritual aspects of AA, NA, and Al-Anon above, I will mention a few additional ones.

Alcoholics Anonymous may be the most important phenomenon of the 20th century. The Twelve Steps of AA - the heart of it s program - are the result of the wisdom of many recovering alcoholics who were struggling to stay sober and to improve their lives, and who did so. Comprising about 200 words, the steps are principles and "rules" of psychological and spiritual life. These Twelve Steps can be condensed into six words. The alcoholic doesn't need to drink if he or she will: Trust God, Clean house, and Help others (McKeon 1983). The Steps are listed in Appendix C. It is probably no

Courtesy AA Grapevine

mistake that these Steps, now used by many other self-help groups, ranging from Al-Anon to Overeaters Anonymous to Emotions Anonymous, follow the hierarchy of the seven levels of consciousness (Table 3 in Part 1). Thus, working the AA program, i.e. spending time going over and actually practicing the message of each step in one's daily life, is learning to live, and actually eventually living, on all seven of these levels.

Chapter 5, How It Works, of AA's " Big Book ", begins, " Rarely have we seen a person fail who has thoroughly followed our path. " A problem that perpetuates the suffering of many recovering people in AA is that they never work the Steps, or they work only a few. While many get sober and stay sober in AA, NA, and Al-Anon without working the Steps, it is probably difficult to get its spirituality and to experience serenity without working them (AA 1976). The richness of AA's spirituality is contained in the contrast of emotions that working these Steps can engender, from the lower self's struggle for survival, its passion, and the mind's drive to control it all, through the acceptance through conflict of the heart, into the Higher Self, with its understanding, compassion and serenity.

While the power and effectiveness of working the Twelve Steps cannot be fully explained or understood intellectually, it may be useful to examine and to relate how each Step is associated with some of the major practices and concepts described in this book: the seven levels of consciousness, the spiritual practices for being our Self, and the mature ego defenses (as described by Vaillant 1977). These associations, as I and others in the field of alcoholism/CD have come to recognize, are shown in Appendix C. Many of these levels and practices are associated with every Step, and most of them are associated with several of the Steps. Appendix D shows some highlights of the Twelve Steps as I have paraphrased them in a transpersonal view that may further indicate their power and their effectiveness. (This, of course, is not an attempt to re-write the Steps, which has been tried, but never equaled, to my knowledge.) Finally, Appendix E shows some common and effective tools for recovery regarding staying sober, working the AA program and making self-change, according to the time sequence in recovery, that are not listed in the Twelve Steps (Alibrandi 1978). Many of these tools are simplified reminders of many of the spiritual practices described in this book and elsewhere. Such simplifying is usually very helpful in early, and often in later recovery.

Drawing on Descarte, Heisenberg, Marx, and Sartre, Kurtz (1979) suggests the four paradoxes of twentieth century modern America which also affected the Fellowship of Alcoholics Anonmyous,". . . (1) the very triumph of rationalization and control reveal that ultimate rationalization and control are impossible; (2) the reduction of the sought after meaningful and real gives way to the unreal and the meaningless hollowness; (3) the demand for more meets the inevitable either-or and limited becomes equated with inability; (4) the realization that ever-increasing individual liberty does not mean ever greater social equality."

Appendix E. Tools for Recovery Regarding Staying Sober, Working the Program, and Making Self-Change (modified from Alibrandi, 1979)

	Staying Sober	Working the Program	Making Self-Change
Stage 1 One Day to One Week	Stay away from the first drink. Avoid getting too hungry. Go to AA meetings Come with me to a meeting. Use the 24-hour plan. Eat or drink something-usually sweet. Make use of telephone therapy. Take life a day, even a minute, at a time. Avoid all chemical mood-changers. Listen. Get plenty of rest. Read the AA message. Be willing. Be wary of drinking occasions. Stay sober for yourself. Look for similarities rather than differences. Remember your last drunk.	Admit you are powerless over alcohol.	Believe that you are not alone.
Stage 2 One Week to 2 Months	Laugh. Keep it simple. Have faith. Remember that alcoholism is incurable, progressive, fatal. Avoid major decisions in early sobriety. Easy does it. Be wary of drinking occasions. Remember that alcoholism is cunning and baffling. Try not to place conditions on your sobriety. Do first things first. When all else fails follow directions. Let go and let God. Share your happiness.	Find a sponsor. Try to turn your life and will over to a Higher Power. Share your pain. Use the Serenity Prayer. Come to believe in a power greater than yourself. Get active. Respect the Anonymity of others. Make regular use of prayer.	Salute the daily progress you make. Keep an open mind. Fend off loneliness. Replace old habits with new, sober habits. Steer clear of emotional entanglements. Try not to test your willpower. Get out of the " if " trap.
Stage 3 2 to 6 months	Live and let live. Look at your whole drinking record. Let go and let God. Share your happiness. Count your blessings.	Try the Twelve Steps. Be available for service.	Eliminate self-pity. Change old routines. Look out for over-elation. Let go of old ideas. Accept life as it comes. Avoid nostalgic sadness.

Human Will and God's Will

A central stumbling block and opportunity during recovery is surrendering to God's will for us. Thurston (1984) and others describe various stages of human will and its growth and development. This growth and development parallels our seven levels of consciousness. I have summarized these stages of our will in Table 9-A.

The will of the active alcoholic/CD or co-dependent is at stage zero - it is non-existent. Between this stage and stage 4 (God's will) are three important stages or steps. These include the re-building, or at times building from scratch, 1) a new "masculine" or assertive will, 2) a new adult, flexible or "feminine" will, and 3) then discovering an empowering or creative will. In early recovery it can be difficult to jump from no will to God's will very quickly. This is why Steps Two and Three can be so difficult to work through (Two = Came to believe that a Power greater than ourselves could restore us to sanity; Three = Made a decision to turn our will and our lives over to the care of God as we understood Him). Thus, in recovery we have to keep coming back to these two and each of the other Steps, over and over, as Step Twelve describes.

Before we can surrender our will totally to the Will of the Universe, we have to construct or re-construct a strong, yet flexible and creative will of our own to surrender. This is equivalent to building a healthy, i.e. assertive yet flexible ego (e.g. as depicted in Figure 9). When we are ultimately able to surrender our will to God's will, we discover a powerful insight: God's will is also our will. It was ours all along! "There is no strain in doing God's will as soon as you recognize that it is also your own" (Course 1975).

Discovering that God's will is our will is a powerful and freeing insight and experience, thus liberating our soul to higher realms of creativity. Thurston (1984) defines our soul as having three parts: spirit, mind and will. Spirit is already and always free. Our mind or ego, while very useful, is not as free, as described throughout this book. And our will is in a developing state in recovery. Thus, by the energy of our spirit, the survival and achievement orientation of our ego/mind, and the motivational aspect of our will, we grow toward wholeness, each in our own unique way. What a creative and wonderful gift Higher Power has bestowed upon us and upon Itself!

MISS PEACH

© Field Enterprises Inc. 1978

Since God created us, a central part of Its will for us is that we become and be who we are as individuals, i.e. "for me to be me" as a unique, complete and whole being. This wholeness includes our being in community with other men, women and children. A key to stress management thus lies our celebrating who we are as a total human being. However, it can be risky to be fully ourself. Perhaps some major meanings of the Twelve Steps are described in AA's "Just for Today" and "Twelve Promises" (see Appendix G). These describe who we already are and how we can live in our wholeness (AA 1976). Indeed, not limited to alcoholics, the physical, mental and spiritual recovery program of AA/Al-Anon is a "way out" of needless suffering for all of humankind.

	Staying Sober	Working the Program	Making Self-Change
Stage 4 6 months to One Year	Be grateful. Share your happiness. Count your blessings. Cherish your recovery.	Take a searching and fearless moral inventory. Share your inventory with someone else. Carry the mesage of AA. When you are shaky work with another alcoholic. Seek God's will for you and the power to carry it out.	Accept work to eliminate self-deception. Watch out for anger and resentments. Let go of old ideas. Accept life as it comes. Get out of the " if " trip. Develop the habit of gratitude. Try to heal yourself by helping others. Share your experience, strength, hope. Find the courage to change yourself. Avoid using the truth to injure others. Avoid gossip.
Stage 5 Over 1 Year	Maintain a spiritual condition.	Continue to take a personal inventory. Promptly admit when you are wrong. Meditate. Make a list of those you have harmed. Make amends to them when possible. Practice these principles in all your affairs. Practice rigorous honesty. Admit and correct your errors today. Seek God's will for you and the power to carry it out.	Watch out for complacency. Avoid self-righteousness. Find your own way. Try not to dwell on the faults of others. See adversity as opportunity. Don't fear needed change. Try to do a good mental house-cleaning. Try to become a part of the world you have rejected. Develop self-restraint. Suspend judgment of yourself and others. Find the serenity to accept others. Beware of phony pride. Avoid using the truth to injure others. Be good to yourself. Cherish your recovery.

THE BORN LOSER ART SANSOM

Since its founding in 1935, AA has helped to make the word "spiritual" more acceptable, no small feat in this modern world. It presents alcoholism as a threefold illness. As described by Kurtz (1979): "The pinch of alienation AA suggests comes less from man's separation from the product of his labor than from modernity's claim and attempt to separate three aspects of human life and experience that are in reality essentially conjoined - the physical, the mental, and the spiritual. The AA insight insists first that body, mind, and spirit are so intimately related within each individual that what affects one influences the others."

Failure to recognize our three essential parts contributes to our suffering in a major way, in that it leaves us feeling empty, incomplete, and, at times, sick. Participation in AA heals that suffering.

However, many people reject the spirituality of AA, often because they have been hurt by their experiences with organized or other religion. But the Spirit is not a prisoner of religion. Every day thousands of people enter self-help group meetings feeling the pain of sadness, fear, guilt, shame, and anger, and leave the meeting feeling good, feeling renewed and whole. The spirituality attained through sharing their own stories and through listening, through honesty and trust, and through surrender and more, opens the heart, and thus the channel to the Self and serenity.

Appendix D

The Twelve Steps of AA
Paraphrased in a Transpersonal View

1) Honestly admitting hopelessness, and ego deflation at depth. Insight. Beginning of physical recovery. Oriented to survival. Initial step to being humble.

2) Possibility of surrendering to a higher consciousness. Viewing our life optimistically. Beginning of ego strengthening through another.

3) Deciding to surrender to a higher consciousness. Starting to transcend isolation. Beginning of active spiritual recovery.

4) Self-examination in anticipation of transcendence (positive change). Introspection. Self objectivity as the basis for honesty.

5) Honest self-revelation to another. Continuing to transcend our isolation.

6) Chosing transcendence by being a co-creator with a higher consciousness.

7) Asking our higher consciousness to help us accept and transcend our shadow and our ego. Being humble.

8) Preparing to transcend our isolation through relationships by asking possible forgiveness.

9) Carrying out #8 above. Restitution.

10) Continued self-examination, experiencing, surrender, and ego transcendence. Continued reorganization.

11) Continued transcendence through meditation or prayer. Communicating with a higher consciousness. Faith as an answer to fear.

12) Awakening, leading to altruism and continued spiritual practice.

Appendix G

JUST FOR TODAY

1. **Just for today** I will try to live through this day only, and not tackle my whole life problem at once. I can do things for 12 hours that would appall me if I had to keep them up for a lifetime.

2. **Just for Today** I will be happy. This assumes that what Abraham Lincoln said is true that "most folks are about as happy as they make up their minds to be." Happiness is from within, it is not a matter of externals.

3. **Just for Today** I will try to adjust myself to what is, and not try to adjust everything to my own desires. I will take my family, my business and my licks as they come and fit myself to them.

4. **Just for Today** I will take care of my body. I will exercise it, care for it, nourish it, not abuse or neglect it, so that it will be a perfect machine for my bidding.

5. **Just for Today** I will try to strengthen my mind. I will learn something useful. I will not be a mental loafer. I will read something that requires effort, thought and concentration.

6. **Just for Today** I will exercise my soul in three ways. I will do somebody a good turn and not get found out. I will do at least two things I don't want to do, as William James suggests, just for exercise.

7. **Just for Today** I will be agreeable. I will look as well as I can, dress as becomingly as possible, talk low, act courteously, be liberal with praise, criticize not at all, nor find fault with anything and not try to regulate or improve anyone.

8. **Just for Today** I will have a program. I will write down what I expect to do every hour. I may not follow it exactly, but I will have it. It will eliminate two pests: hurry and indecision.

9. **Just for Today** I will have a quiet half hour all by myself and relax. In this half hour sometimes I will thank God, so as to get a better perspective of my life.

10. **Just for Today** I will be unafraid, specially I will not be afraid to be happy,to enjoy what is beautiful, to love, and to believe that those I love, love me.

THE TWELVE PROMISES OF AA

1. **We will attain** and maintain sobriety.
2. **We are going to know** a new freedom and a new happiness.
3. **We will not regret** the past nor wish to shut the door on it.
4. **We will comprehend** the word "serenity" and we will know peace.
5. **No matter** how far down the scale we have gone, we will see how our experiences can benefit others.
6. **That feeling** of uselessness and self-pity will disappear.
7. **We will lose** interest in selfish things and gain interest in our fellows.
8. **Self-seeking** will slip away.
9. **Our whole attitude** and outlook on life will change.
10. **Fear of people** and economic insecurity will leave us.
11. **We will intuitively know** how to handle situations which used to baffle us.
12. **We will suddenly realize** that God is doing for us what we could not do for ourselves.

Table 9-A. Stages of Human Will (compiled from Thurston 1984, Ouspensky 1949 & Assagioli 1969)

	Stage	Will	Further Description	Sense of Identity	Stance	Possibility /Choice; Co-Creation	Tasks
Turning it over	4	Transpersonal Real Universal or God's Will	Transcendence. Total Self-reflection. Surrender of stages 0 thru 3. Total creativity. Transcendence of paradox. Unconditional Love.	Unity	None Pure Being & Creativity	Total	Total Surrender as a co-creator. Conscious contact. Continued awareness.
Choice	3	Empowering "Good"	Perceptual shift: Ego/mind is limited, eg it s awareness is only of the past; it only wants to be right, be in control, win and survive. More solid recognition of paradox. Dramatic awakening.	Observer Self	"Lucid Living"	Much More	Detaching. Compassionate. Taking responsibility. Beginning to co-create. Continued development of awareness. Knowing have a choice & making a choice.
Awareness	2	"Skillful" "Adult"	More self-reflection; blends and synthesizes. Progressive awakening. Archetypically feminine. Yin. Kind, cooperative, flexible. Early recognition of paradox.	Ego/ mind	Beginning Flexibility	More	Early introspection. Continued development of awareness. Expression of hurt and vulnerability. Surrender. Recognition of paradox.
	1	"Adolescent"	Earliest awakening, beginnings of self-reflection. Archtypically masculine. Yang. Active, somewhat harsh. Negating, rebellious.	Ego/ mind and Body	Struggle. "Willpower" "Macho"	Some, Little	Becoming aware. Beginning to question. Developing self worth. Expression of anger and aggressiveness for survival.
	0	None	Metaphorically asleep. "The world" (others) and Ego/mind control our life. Often chronic distress & illness.	Others plus Ego/mind and Body	Victim	None	Unaware suffering Being stuck Denying

from Whitfield CL: Alcoholism & Spirituality, Baltimore, 1985

In 1975 another self-help group called Women for Sobriety was formed on the East Coast. The founder was a recovering alcoholic who was also seeking to achieve serenity. Having read much literature from such diverse sources as Plato, St. Paul, Emmet Fox, the Unity movement, and others, she began to learn a way out of her suffering. Especially meaningful to her was Emerson's "As a man thinketh, so shall he be," as she wrote the Thirteen Statements of Acceptance (Kirkpatrick 1984):

1) I have a drinking problem that once had me.
2) Negative emotions destroy only myself.
3) Happiness is a habit I will develop.
4) Problems bother me only to the degree I permit them to.
5) I am what I think.
6) Life can be ordinary or it can be great.
7) Love can change the course of my world.
8) The fundamental object of life is emotional and spiritual growth.
9) The past is gone forever.
10) All love returns two-fold.
11) Enthusiasm is my daily exercise.
12) I am a competent person and have much to give to others.
13) I am responsible for myself and others.

(To encourage wider acceptability, I have substituted in No. 12 "person" for "woman" and in No. 13 "others" for "my sisters".)

The progress of these statements follows that of our levels of consciousness and of the Twelve Steps. I see these as being in the spirit of and complementary to the Twelve Steps, and in no way in competition with them. Numbering about 100 words, these statements convey a message of hope, positivity, and emotional and spiritual growth. WFS meets in many cities across the USA (Kirkpatrick 1983), and is expanding to include men in Men for Sobriety meetings. It could become People for Sobriety.

Chapter 18. The Healing Factors of Group Therapy

Group therapy works well in concert with and is complimentary to recovery in self-help groups. The two are compatible. Therapy groups also refer many people to self-help groups who otherwise would not attend them. At the same time, group therapy differs from self-help groups in several ways, some of which are that one usually pays a fee for it, with the same group of about eight to twelve people meeting weekly with the guidance of one or two group leaders or facilitators. There is more confrontation and feedback than in self-help groups, and there is much caring and support for each group member's getting well and staying well. Since alcoholism/CD and co-dependence are illnesses or isolation and alienation, which only aggravate our suffering, being in a group specifically addresses the person's isolation and alienation.

Being in such a group forces the person to confront a fundamental spiritual necessity: relating to self, others and eventually the universe. It takes the person out of his or her own narrow existence, stuck in the lower self, and gently and sometimes somewhat more forcefully encourages communicating, risking, feeling, trusting, being assertive, and caring for fellow members. Over a period of about two years of active working in a well-conducted chemical dependence therapy group, the person undergoes a series of transformations that begin to fill the suffering and feelings of emptiness with a sense of hope and positivity about their ability to stay well and to grow.

While there are several healing factors in group therapy (Table 10), I and other believe that the basic healing ingredient is love, or as Rogers has described, "unconditional positive regard for the individual". I discuss some of the ways that this higher level of love is healing in Part IV: Loving.

Table 10. Healing Factors in Alcoholism/CD Group Therapy and Self-Help Group Participation

Year One	Year Two	Long Term
Learning to ask for help	Asking for help	Continuing to ask for help
Beginning to communicate	Communicating	Continued communicating
Learning about CD : P-M-S	Learning about spirituality	Growing spiritually
Identifying responsibility	Taking responsibility	Being responsible
Learning to trust: S-C-S	Trusting	Trusting
Getting feedback	Asking for feedback	Continuing to ask for feedback
Learning to risk	Risking	Risking
Becoming aware of feelings	Sharing Feelings	Continuing to share feelings
Learning to be assertive	Being assertive	Continuing to be assertive
Ventil ating low self-esteem	Building self-esteem	Continuing to build
Letting go unhealthy ego defenses	Learning healthy ego defenses	Transcending ego

Key: P-M-S = Physical - Mental - Spiritual, and S-C-S = Share - Check - Share

Helping Others

The Twelfth Step says, "Having had a spiritual awakening as the result of these steps, we tried to carry this message to alcoholics, and to practice these principles in all our affairs". While it is gratifying, reassuring and affirming to help a fellow sufferer, ultimately, we cannot save another, we cannot make them happy, and we cannot find themselves for them. This is what can be so exasperating about doing Twelfth Step work. However, when we do help a fellow sufferer, our own pain and suffering goes away. We are focusing. We are giving ourself to another. When we so help them, we are saying that we accept them. When we accept, we forgive. When we forgive another who has been and not is where we have been, we forgive ourself. And the power of forgiveness is that it brings about inner peace and serentiy.

The key in helping is not to be attached to the outcome. It feels good if the person recovers with our help. But if they don't, we don't have to feel guilty or other discomfort ourselves.

Jampolsky (1983) said, "It was a powerful lesson to realize that when I focused on helping, I had no fear. There were other times . . . when I was evaluating what I was getting or not getting, that I was immobilized with fear. The lesson was clear. When a person is concerned only with giving, there is no anxiety. Much later in my life, I was to discover that very often there is also no pain or sense of limitation."

When we help another we are in the sanctuary of the Self. We know when we are moving into lower levels of our consciousness when we begin to feel anxiety or discomfort. But even if we feel anxious or uncomfortable, that is alright. Doing so reminds us of our lower self, and that we are human just as the person to whom we are offering our help.

In helping others we are inevitably lead back to the First Step, "We admitted we were powerless over alcohol - that our lives had become unmanageable". And now we learn not only that once again are we powerless over alcohol, but that we are powerless over another human being. We are powerless! We learn once again that all we can do is forgive and love. We extend our love for our fellow suffer by sharing our story with him or her - the power of example and identification, by answering any questions, and by just being there. Helping others, and other spiritual practices, ultimately bring us to a grand paradox: the paradox of being our Self.

Chapter 19. The Paradox of Being our Self

The paradox of being our Self is that while most of us need to use spiritual practices such as the above to reach or to be our Self, each move that we make toward it pushes us further away from it. There is no path to unity consciousness; there is no way to arrive at that which already and always is. Wilber (1979) said, " Unity consciousness is not so much a particular wave as it is the water itself. . . . as long as you are wave-jumping in search of wetness, you obviously will never discover that wetness exists in its purity on whatever wave you're riding now. Unity consciousness . . . is every wave of present experience just as it is. " The grand paradox of unity consciousness is that while we can't really do anything to get it, if we don't do something, we'll likely remain just as we are. Special conditons such as spiritual practices are useful, but they are not necessary for the actualization of unity consciousness. These conditions and practices do not lead to unity - they are themselves an expression of unity consciousness, of our Self. Our spiritual practice springs from, not toward our Self (Wilber 1979).

From the teachings of the holy men and women such as Christ, Mohamed, Buddha, Teresa of Avila, Gandhi, and others, and from the writings in holy books such as the Bible and the Gnostic Gospels, the Koran, the Talmud, the Bhagavad Gita, the Tibetan Book of the Dead, A Course in Miracles and others, the message is the same: that we have it now. Everything that we do is spiritual and celebrates our Self, the One. However, through our forgetting, we resist being our Self. (Our forgetting may be a manifestation of our fear of letting go of our ego.) And we seem to continue to forget and to resist our present experience. Wilber (1979) said, " If there is some aspect of life that you dislike, there is some aspect of unity consciousness that you are resisting. . . . The understanding of this secret resistance is the ultimate key to enlightenment. " We resist at all levels of consciousness (Figure 10). We resist our body-mind level of consciousness by thinking, intellectualizing, and by not living in the now. And we resist our oneness by holding on to our separateness. Overcoming each of these resistances is crucial in the spiritual, and thus the total, recovery of the alcoholic and of his or her family member.

We both seek and resist Unity Consciousness through the cycle of evolution and involution. Thus, rather than being linear, the levels of consciousness can be described as being distributed on a circle, on which we are constantly moving. The circle is the ancient Chinese and Zen symbol for perfection, and the Yin-Yang symbol is enclosed within a circle. Perhaps most people move around this circle on only levels one through three. Some others move higher, and a few move on the entire circle, and are thus whole, from which the term " wholistic " comes. That most of us resist our Self is a crucial insight. So how can we get out of this paradox of both seeking and resisting? And if spiritual practices are helpful in getting out of the paradox, how are they helpful?

It may be that each spiritual practice and each life condition both frustrates us and shows us a type of resistance. Understanding such a concept gives us a glimpse of our Self, because that which sees resistance is itself free of resistance (Wilber 1979). We can then be free to look upon all experience as a whole, as it is now, and to see and experience that both the seeking and resisting are a part of the celebration of the Self by itself.

But another frustration comes from the next insight: that everything we do, including our seeking of serenity through spiritual practice, is a resistance, as long as we identify ourself in time, space and separateness (Ram Dass 1974-83). We can even become attached to needing to be detached. All seems lost, and we may feel our dark night of the soul (St. John 1959; DiLeo 1981). Absolutely everything seems wrong, because we see that every move we make is a resistance, a movement away from unity consciousness. At our "bottoms" we thus become healthily vulnerable, open to giving up the search, and just experiencing, just being. And it is here that the entire movement and process of our resistance winds down, and we see that we are unity consciousness, we are our Self (Wilber 1979). We are One. There are no boundaries, and we are not separate.

Wilber (1979) said, " It thus becomes apparent why the search for unity consciousness was so exasperating. Everything we tried to do was wrong because everything was already and eternally right. Even what appeared as a primal resistance to Brahman i.e. Unity Consciousness was actually a movement of Brahman, because there is nothing but Brahman. There never was, nor will there ever be, any time other than Now. What appeared as that primal moving away from Now was really an original movement of Now. . . . The ocean waves surge freely againt the shore, wetting the pebbles and shells. "

The search, the alcoholism, the other chemical dependence or co-dependence, the struggle, the suffering, the joy, the frustrations and the growth of recovery - all are a part of us and are a movement of Unity Consciousness, of our Higher Power and of Us. Whether we are suffering or letting go of it, we can do no wrong in the eyes of God.

Part III TRANSFORMING

Chapter 20. Transformation During Recovery

Through various ways, and today most often through treatment and through self-help groups, many alcoholics/CD's and their family members are transforming their lives to become more whole and fulfilling. Transformation is a changing of form, a forming over, a restructuring (Leonard 1972). Ultimately, it is a shift from living our life to get somewhere to living our life as an expression of our being (Erhard 1984). When we transform, we transform our awareness or consciousness. We switch from one domain of reality and being to another. Through such change, we transcend to higher, more empowering, more peaceful and more creative levels of being. At the same time that we experience more empowerment and more possibility, we also begin to take more responsibility for our lives.

Stages of Transformation

Ferguson (1980) describes four stages of transformation. The first is an entry point. It is usually recognized as such only in retrospect. Entry can be triggered by anything that shakes up one's old understanding of reality, of "the way that we thought things were". This trigger may range across a spectrum, from a line read in a book to intense suffering to the unconditional love of or from a fellow human. For some it may be a spontaneous spiritual, mystical, psychic, or peak-experience, and for others it may be the intense change generated by using a psychedelic drug. Whatever guise it may take, the trigger brings about the start of growth for us - the experience of awakening. The Twelfth Step of AA says, " Having had a spiritual awakening as the result of these steps, we tried to carry this message to alcoholics, and to practice these principles in all our affairs " (Alcoholics Anonymous 1976).

Awakening occurs when we get the first glimpses that " things " or "reality " are not the way we thought they were (Ram Dass & Levine 1977). It is an ongoing process of further awakening toward our wholeness throughout our lives (Watts 1973). Awakening is seeing what is true - the joys and the sorrows, the bliss and the suffering, the highs and the lows. Once we have fully experienced awakening, it is difficult to go back to "sleep", although we often " doze " (Ram Dass 1974-83). Some describe the person who is awakening as being on a " spiritual path ", even though the non-awakening person is also on a spiritual path or journey, although doesn't know it.

However, many people give up at this entry point, and go no further. Those willing or forced to take a risk move on to the next stage. Alcoholics and co-dependents who here enter into treatment - probably 15% of all people in these two groups - whether forced or not (though they most generally have to be forced) - enter into possible recovery and possible eventual transcendence into peace of mind and serenity. For most, the time duration of this entry point, which is usually a crisis, is short - usually only about ten days - so that the effective clinician needs to act forcefully, skillfully, and fairly quickly to get the person into treatment during these early days of increased vulnerability. At this point many will say to themselves or to others that they are confused enough or are suffering enough to want to look further inward, as well as outward.

The second stage of transformation is exploration. Having once seen the possibilities, exploration involves struggling, letting go, suspending beliefs and considering and creating new ones. However, we usually go after our transformative experiences in the only way we know how: as consumers, competitors, and still operating from the values of our old paradigm (Ferguson 1980). We may question ourselves and others, and shop from one method or helper to another. And we often become impatient and discouraged. Over and over, we find that change does not usually come easy for us and for others.

We also discover - whether alcoholic, family member, clinician, or non-alcoholic - that in our exploration, everything, everyone, everywhere is a teacher. And we can chose to be conscious of it all in our learning. We cannot leave the trap until we know we are in it. We find that no one but ourselves are the warders and jailers (Ferguson 1980). We learn that God, guru and Self are the same being, teaching itself, learning from itself, and celebrating itself. A guru may be a teacher, physician, psychotherapist, other clinician or helping professional, guide, relative, friend, and even an enemy. Perhaps our greatest teacher is ourself, if we can listen.

From this view, several years of sobriety in AA or one intense relapse, for example, may teach us the same lesson. Often unconsciously, each person choses his or her own scenario, pace, and time for transcendence. At this stage of transformation the person often remains open for new ways of seeing things. For the alcoholic or the family member, this stage of exploration generally occurs over the few weeks and sometimes months after the entry point, crisis or hitting bottom. It is the beginning of treatment and of the recovery phase. For the person beginning to take AA seriously, he or she will often admit powerlessness and unmanageability, as reflected in the First Step (see Appendix C). Interspersed throughout this stage of exploration may be alternating periods of relapse and remission. The person may want to continue drinking or using drugs, but in a more controlled manner. Or the co-alcoholic may want to continue trying to control the alcoholic's drinking behavior and not take responsibility for their role and their suffering, even though they are at the same time exploring ways to heal themself. And all of this ambivalent behavior can test the spirituality and the skills of the clinician from whom they are seeking help. This is why it is helpful for the person to be in a weekly therapy group and regularly attending a self-help group. These groups are experts at constructively helping the person through these crucial stages of exploration and integration.

The third stage is integration, in which we gain further strength through surrender and growth (Gravitz & Bowden 1985). Surrender and many of the above ways of being the Self have opened the gates of the heart and into the transcendence of being the Self. Having seen that many of our old habits, ambitions, and strategies are not appropriate for our new beliefs, we learn that there are other effective ways of being, and we begin to incorporate them into our lives.

At this stage the alcoholic/CD person may comfortably say, " I am an alcoholic or chemical dependent. " Or the family member or other close person may say, " I am a co-alcoholic, co-dependent, or at least co-responsible for my own fate. " Or the person may work another or all of the steps of AA and accept otherwise unwanted aspects of himself, as described in "Accepting Our Shadow" in Part II. By such work or practice, he or she is well into the Acceptance level of consciousness, into the heart, and the channel to the Self. To be fully realized or accepted, this period of integration often takes from several months to up to three years if worked through in a self-help group and/or group therapy, and may take longer, depending on the individual's circumstances and journey.

The final stage of transformation can be called being, in which we are and live what we have integrated into ourself(Ferguson 1980-a). When Gandhi was asked one day what message he had for the people of India, he said, " My life is my message " (Ram Dass 1974-83). Not only does the new way of being work in our own life, but if we have transformed, it may also begin to work for others. Not only can our individual mind and Self heal and transform, but our minds and Selves can join to heal and transform society (Ferguson 1980). This is a major part of what the whole recovery movement is about. Also, working AA's Twelfth Step, the recovering alcoholic or co-alcoholic now lives his or her life to help both self and others.

At this point we can look back at our journey of transformation and see that it is the same as the hero or heroine's mythical journey described above, through separation, initiation and return (Campbell 1949), and is similar to our s and other's stories that we tell and hear. And from the more transformations that we each go through, the more we begin to create and incorporate positive change and serenity into our lives. Knowing when to and when not to risk change is to have wisdom, from the Understanding level of consciousness. This wisdom is reflected in the familiar Serenity Prayer.

> God grant me the serenity to accept the things I cannot change . . .
> The courage to change the things that I can . . .
> And the wisdom to know the difference.

An analysis of some of the power in using this prayer is shown in Appendix E.

Among alcoholics, chemical dependents and co-alcoholics, transformation seems too often to be unpredictable. How much pain and suffering do people need to go through? How low a bottom do they need to hit before they use it as an entry point and begin to awaken? From my own clinical experience and that of others, that answer commonly depends upon others around the person, for example, a loved one, a boss, or a helping professional, as well as the person him or herself. We are all involved with those we touch in this play of transformation. Doing so tests our patience and our flexibility. The key is to be active and involved, and remain unattached to the therapeutic outcome.

Time Duration of Transformation

In time duration, for most people their transformation is nearly always gradual, usually occuring in fits and starts, in a stair-step or cyclical fashion and over a period of from months to years (Figure 11). Probably in only an estimated 1% or less of alcoholics does a dramatic recovery occur. Such a recovery was that of previously atheist Bill Wilson, co-founder of Alcoholics Anonymous, told in his own words: (cited in Kurtz 1979)

" My depression deepened unbearably and finally it seemed to me as though I were at the bottom of the pit. I still gagged badly on the notion of a Power greater than myself, but finally, just for the moment, the last vestige of my proud obstinacy was crushed. All at once I found myself crying out, ' If there is a God, let Him show Himself! I am ready to do anything, anything! '

" Suddenly the room lit up with a great white light. I was caught up into an ecstasy which there are not words to describe. It seemed to me, in the mind's eye, that I was on a mountain and that a wind not of air but of spirit was blowing. And then it burst upon me that I was a free man. Slowly the ecstasy subsided. I lay on the bed, but now for a time I was in another world, a new world of consciousness. All about me and through me there was a wonderful feeling of Presence. . . . A great peace stole over me and I thought, ' No matter how wrong things seem to be, they are all right. Things are all right with God and His world.' "

The Serenity Prayer

God	Saying this word I am admitting the existence of a Consciousness or a Higher Power that is greater than I.
grant	Saying this second word, I am admitting that this Consciousness or Higher Power is able to bestow and give to me and to others.
me	I am asking something for myself. Holy books say that if I ask sincerely, it shall be given. It is not wrong to ask for improving myself. For with the improvement of my character, both I and people around me will be happier, and my relationships will have a better chance to improve.
serenity	I am asking for calmness, composure and inner peace in my life which will enable me to tanscend my ego, to think straight, and to govern myself properly.
to accept	I am resigning myself to conditions as they are right now. I am living in the now, the present moment.
the things	I acknowledge my tragedy, death, suffering, illness & pain, as a part of my life, neither good nor bad. I accept my humanness and fallibility. I am accepting my lot in life as it is. Until I have the courage to change any part of my life I don't like, I must accept it, without doing so grudgingly.
I cannot change	I can't prevent these events or conditions from happening to me or to others.
courage	A quality which enables me to deal with the problems and realities of life without reliance on alcohol or drugs. A determination to stand my ground and "slug it out" with all issues, pleasant or otherwise, that might return me to drinking or using. A strength of my spirit to face and handle the negative. Fearlessness in the practice of faith, humility and honesty.
to change	In facing these negatives directly and honestly, I am asking for myself and my life conditions to be different for me. I am taking an active part in this changing.
the things I can,	I am asking for help to make the right decisions. Everything is not the way I would like it to be in my life. I must continue to face reality and constantly work toward my continued growth and progress.
and wisdom	I am asking for the ability to rise above my ego and form sound judments about myself and my life. I then use my ability to ask for guidance from myself, others and a Higher Power.
to know the difference	I want to be able to understand clearly truths of fact. I want to see things differently in my life so that I will be more aware of myself and of others. I need to sense a definite value in loving over being selfish.

Figure 11. Possible Time Sequence in Recovery of Spiritual Parameters among Alcoholics and Other Chemical Dependent People

Active Alcoholism →	Recovery Begins →	Physical →	Mental →	Spiritual
Emptiness	Organic Brain Syndrome		Learning to " Experience "	
Confusion				
Fear	Depression			
Ego inflation with low self-esteem	Low self-esteem (" weak ego ")	→	" Somebody special " (strengthening ego) →	" Nobody special " (transcending ego)
Shame		Working a self-help group program		Forgiving
Continuing frequent crises		Ventilating & Telling our story	Living in the Now	Loving unconditionally Being humble
Guilt		Awakening	Accepting what is	Accepting our shadow
		Developing natural highs	Improved communicating	Accepting paradox
Ineffective relationships			Mature defenses, eg laughing	Creative dreaming
				Thinking positively
Victimization			Meditating or praying	Being patient
Delusion			Transformation	Watching the melodrama
Other illness		I cannot drink Alcoholic Victim Curse	→	I can not drink Sober Co-creator Gift
	"Hit Bottom" →	Surrender/Ego death (varying amounts cyclically)	→	Cyclical, for lifetime
			Suspending our beliefs	Belief in a higher consciousness or power
Suffering	3 to 4+	4+	2 to 3+	1-2+
Time Duration		1 to 12 months	To 5 years	Lifetime

It was like a divine fate that brought another gift to Bill W the next day, delivered by his friend Ebby who had been treated by Jung, and who was the first alcoholic Bill had seen to recover successfully (and who became Bill's sponsor). It was a copy of one of the most spiritual books ever written by a psychologist: William James' The Varieties of Religious Experience (Kurtz 1979; James 1982). Bill W wrote:

" . . . Spiritual experiences, James thought, could have objective reality; almost like gifts from the blue, they could transform people. Some were sudden brilliant illuminations; others came on very gradually. Some flowed out of religious channels; others did not. But nearly all had the great common denominators of pain, suffering, calamity. Complete hopelessness and deflation at depth were almost always required to make the recipient ready. The significance of all this burst upon me. Deflation at depth - yes, that was it. Exactly that had happened to me " (cited in Kurtz 1979).

A spiritual transformation or conversion was thus both the first and third of the four founding moments in the history of AA: 1) the necessity for a spiritual conversion (described indirectly to Wilson from Jung and from James), 2) the wisdom of the Oxford Group practice (from which part of the Twelve Steps emerged), 3) Wilson's own dramatic spiritual experience, described above, and 4) the meeting between Wilson and Dr. Bob Smith, a surgeon, in May of 1935 in Akron, Ohio (Kurtz 1979). These four parallel the four core ideas of AA, with number three changing to ego deflation from the perception of hopelessness, later replaced by the term " hitting bottom ".

Both these four founding moments and four core ideas are nearly identical to, if they are not at least similar to the four stages of transformation described earlier: 1) entry, 2) exploration, 3) integration, and 4) being. They are also similar to and follow the Twelve Steps of AA, the seven levels of consciousness discussed above, the hero's journey, and the other hierarchies of human functioning described earlier and in Table 3 (in Part I). We thus can see that from the above and from the previous discussions, that much of ancient and modern wisdom is the same.

Transpersonal psychotherapists believe the ego's relationship with the Self to have a central psychodynamic significance, constituting one of our deepest representational systems. This may explain in part the first of both the four founding moments and the four core ideas of AA: the need for a spiritual transformation. DiLeo (1984) said "The aim of this relationship is a fusion of subject and object in a transcendence of the subject - object dichotomy. This fusion involves, subjectively, one of the strongest autonomic arousals known. It involves an experience of intense light, deep feelings of love, bliss, acceptance, redemption, reconciliation, and many other positive affects. It is often alluded to as the experience of 'coming home again' or that of 'Paradise Regained'. It is the ultimate aim of the psyche, the one Freud mistook as the incestual wish for the parent. Difficult stages on the way to this fusion can involve a re-experiencing of the initial trauma of separation (of consciousness) and the anticipation of ego - death of dissolution that usually precedes the ego transcendence into the Self." This emphasizes, among other things, our drive and our need to function on all levels of our consciousness.

The " Big Book " Alcoholics Anonymous cautions that such sudden and dramatic spiritual awakenings as Bill W experienced are unusual, most transformations being what James called the " educational variety " because they develop slowly over a period of time (AA 1976). In Figure 11 I have outlined a possible time sequence of the physical - mental - spiritual progression in recovery from alcoholism/CD and from co-alcoholism. The physical healing or recovery generally takes from as short as one month, which is rare, to one year, which is the most common. The mental and emotional recovery takes from two to five years, and sometimes longer. Active participation in a self-help group and working the Twelve Steps, and/or working long term in an appropriate therapy group can help speed that mental and emotional recovery. Doing so can also help with spiritual recovery, which seems, paradoxically, to take both an instant and a lifetime. As a supplement, and almost never as a replacement, individual psychotherapy with an appropriate therapist can also be helpful. While in Figure 11 I have provided my estimation of when the various spiritual practices and changes may occur during recovery, these may vary among individuals, and research is needed to describe their occurrence more accurately.

I have noticed in my own transformations that ideas and books that I once had heard or read and could not clearly understand, on re-reading or -hearing them later they suddenly became clear. I believe this may be another marker of knowing that one has made a transformation in some way.

Chapter 21. Hitting Bottom

Hitting bottom is an unavoidable part of life. It is important in transformation and in helping heal us to wholeness. It has been described in many terms by writers in diverse areas as: a desolation experience (Laski 1961), a personal crisis (Mogar 1965), an existential crisis (Begental 1965), a dark night of the soul (St. John 1959), ego-deflation at depth (James 1982; Jung 1969) and a nadir-experience (DiLeo 1982). Vaughan (1984) suggests rather than being a dark night of the *soul*, that it may be a dark night of the *ego*.

Hitting bottom is seen in all areas of our lives, ranging across a spectrum from suicidal depression to active alcoholism to anxiety about either real or imagined dangers. It also includes our every day suffering, anxieties, and conflicts, as well as all sorts of common struggles involving feelings of anger, rage, frustration, sadness, opposition and oppression (DiLeo 1982). Although it is painful and unwanted, hitting bottom is 1) not pathological, i.e. it is normal, 2) a critical choice point in life necessitating a "leap of faith, " 3) an essential condition for growth and psychological change, and is 4) often a catalyst for an emerging new awareness or inner conviction (Mogar 1965, DiLeo 1982). Such a personal crisis is a part of any creative effort, whether it be scientific, artistic, therapeutic, interpersonal (Forer 1963), intrapersonal or transpersonal.

As part of transformation, hitting bottom is the first step, the entry point to our growth. It is a *reverse* transformation, in the sense that it is a regression or an involution (Meher Baba 1963; Watts 1965; Wilber 1981). The person slides or drops to functioning at a lower level of consciousness. The lowest bottom is at the lowest part of level one, Survival, a place which many alcoholics and some of their family members visit often. A problem, whether it be a " high " bottom or a " low " or " rock " bottom, is that when we are in the middle of the pain, we usually do not know where we are, or may ignore all of it. It is as though we are in a refractory period, where we cannot see the light of our recovery, similar to the heart muscle's inability to contract for a fraction of a second after each heart beat. And even if we are aware of what is happening, we don't want to be there. We want it to be over with quickly, and usually don't see the usefulness of our suffering, the potential for transformation, and for turning our curse into our gift. And even if partially aware, we often don't realize the intensity of the bottom and all the dangers associated with it.

Paradoxically, hitting bottom is both the opposite of having a peak-experience and it is an opportunity for having a peak-experience. This nadir-experience has been

described as the ultimate state of separation and alienation, identification with evil, a dark passage, hell, the devil, death, agony, final destruction, and ego death (DiLeo 1982). By contrast, a peak or transcendental experience has been called by all the above descriptions of being in the Self, plus the original state of Divine Union, Creation, Perfect Bliss, Paradise, and ego trascendence. The person goes through the process of transformation, from being stuck in the lower self to transcending to the Self. Bogged down in anxiety, conflict, sadness, and suffering, the person rises to a resolution of the feelings and conflicts (DiLeo 1982).

But how does one transform? How does one become serenity? There seem to be so many obstacles. A solution, mentioned frequently throughout this discussion, is to *experience* our pain. And to experience a bottom one must *go through it*. One generally cannot go around it and transform. To experience it fully, one must be totally conscious and aware, feeling every bit of fear, anger, sadness, empathy, and joy. The key seems to be to experience suffering *when it happens*, and not to seek it out or produce it when it is not there. For our unfinished work of experiencing, we can use imagery, creative dreaming, and talking it out with the person involved or with trusted others, as in Steps five, eight and nine of Twelve Step recovery programs. If these methods are not helpful, then group therapy or experientially oriented psychotherapy can help, with gestalt therapy often being among the most helpful types. *If the feelings and suffering are not experienced, we will usually eventually develop a stress-related illness or another problem.* (This does not mean that we should seek out or create unnecessary suffering for ourselves.)

To reach serenity, inner peace or cosmic consciousness, we all want to bypass our suffering. And on our journey we discover that the only way back to the Light, to the One, is *through* our darkness, through our suffering, *through* our "bottoms". In AA the saying "No pain, no gain" is often used. When we have *completed* these we experience inner peace and serenity.

This key principle or concept of transpersonal or spiritual psychology is further developed in Figure 12, which is another "map" of the cosmic drama. Starting at the top is Unmanifest Unity Consciousness, which many have called our Source, the Void or the Undescribable. It begins its journey or celebration by becoming the Light, which we could describe as perfect bliss. Turning away from itself it travels through the darkness or the evil, which can be called unberable suffering, and thus sets the stage for the unfolding of the universe. It then begins to differentiate itself into the multiple areas of the transpersonal realm or unconscious, as described in the discussion on figures 5 and 7 above. Continuing on its cosmic journey, through what DiLeo (1983) calls the Round, it further differentiates into the essence of the human fetus in the perinatal realm or unconscious, and then into the personal realm or unconscious.

Each of us finally emerges as a human infant, which has to deal with life on its multiple levels as a child and then as an adult. But in our journey, we forget our Source, and buy into a cosmic good vs evil game. However, what we each strive for is a feeling of completion, of inner peace. And we want to bypass the evil or the suffering and go straight to the One. That is precisely what can be so compelling to use alcohol and other drugs: they can provide us, for a few minutes or hours, with a glimpse or a suggestion of the One. Some of us, whether it be due to a biochemical abnormality or another factor (see Figure 1), cannot be satisfied with a glimpse, and go for more and more. That is perhaps related to why William James suggested that alcoholics might be "frustrated mystics". But whether we are alcoholic, co-alcoholic or not, we cannot return to our Source, to full knowledge or good, without going through the evil, the darkness, which is our suffering and our "hitting bottom".

Figure 12. The Structure of Psyche
(from DiLeo 1984)

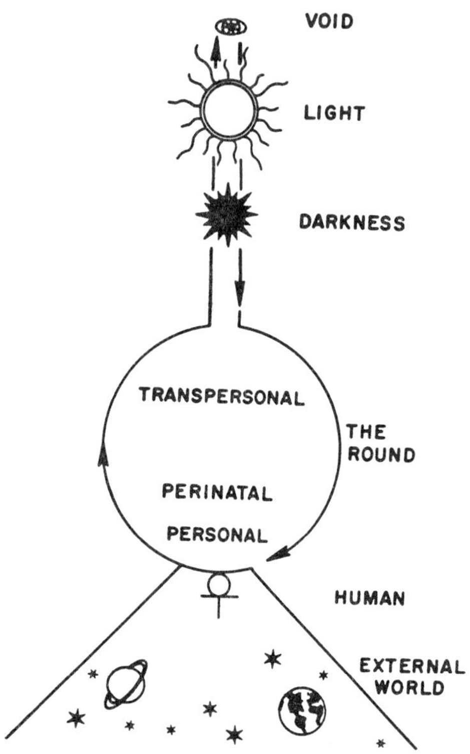

Two major blocks to our experiencing or completing an experience are drinking or using drugs heavily and using unhealthy ego defenses (discussed above in Part II, Being Humble). Both of these tend to decrease the intensity and duration of the experience, thus leaving it incomplete. Having an incomplete experience means that we will have to deal with it again later in an attempt to complete it. To help release these blocks to completing an experience we may have to shift our awareness to another domain, from our ordinary waking state to a more intense feeling state or state of awareness. By so doing, we can begin to extend our understanding and our acceptance of alcoholism and co-dependence and numerous other life issues beyond the physical and intellectual levels, in which many people get stuck, attached, or addicted, and into the emotional and feeling level. This principle is in part why both inpatient and outpatient treatment programs emphasize the importance of identifying and experiencing our feelings. (Again, this does not mean that we should seek out or create unnecessary suffering for ourselves.)

What we resist, persists. What we do not experience completely will likely return for us to experience again, until we complete it. Only when we have fully experienced can we let go and be free of it. Our final level or domain of understanding and acceptance can then unfold: the spiritual level, the level of being.

Going through and experiencing a bottom involves another paradox: to do so we cannot do it alone, i.e. we need others, and the only way we can do it, ultimately, is alone. Involving others means ventillating and telling our story, as well as listening. To involve others is another test: finding someone we can trust, and then trusting them. Trusting is a spiritual practice that we develop, usually by trial and error. And the " higher " we are spiritually, i.e. on the levels of consciousness, the easier it is to trust. (Caution: "higher" does not mean better.) Trusting involves judgement, wisdom and letting go. However, most active and many early recovering alcoholics and their families are stuck in the lower levels of being. The clinician's first task is to help them get alcohol and drug free. Or for the family, to " detoxify " from their addiction to being victimized by and trying to control their alcoholic/CD. Then we can help them to experience the pain and confusion and then to work through it. At this point an important principle of transpersonal and spiritual psychology applies: a person can usually work through, transcend and transform only to a level at which his or her clinician is functioning. The clinician who is attached to his ego, or even lower, may have a difficult time letting the person rise above his own ego level.

This concept of experiencing may also have some validity for the alcoholic who is treated with non-drug and social setting detoxification, wherein drugs are generally not used to ameliorate the experience of the withdrawal syndrome. Here, the patient is allowed to experience the alcohol withdrawal in a drug-free state and in a safe and nurturing environment, aided by the caring and reassurance of others, and thus "completes" the experience. He or she is thus able to remember the alcohol withdrawal more clearly and may then use it more constructively in recovery (Whitfield 1979, 1980a, 1980b). In this sense - and in more - non-drug and social setting detoxification can be a spiritual experience that impacts positively on long term recovery.

With each successful transformation, we will be able to begin to trust ourself more, and eventually may be able to learn not only from our trusted friends, but from those who are not - and even from our enemies. Learning from our enemies does not mean that we have to trust them by ventillating and telling them our story. However, it does mean that we can use them as a mirror. Similar to that described in the AA spiritual axiom (12 Steps & 12 Traditions 1953), other people mirror or reflect back what they see in us. Therefore, the " bad " we see in others is often that which originates from ourselves and then is reflected back to us from them. That " bad " is usually our shadow, as described above. In everyone we tend to see the reflection of what we chose to have him or her be to us. In nearly every encounter we meet ourself, and that encounter is holy, because we are (Course 1975).

As we become higher levels of consciousness and become more aware at each bottom, the experience of each one will tend to become more intense than before, when we may have hidden, denied, repressed or ignored the pain we began to feel. The duration of the bottom experience may last from a few seconds to days or weeks, and sometimes longer. The time of each tends gradually to get shorter and our total suffering tends to decrease in proportion to our awareness and openness, and our willingness to feel the pain and to share.

In recovery from alcoholism/CD and co-alcoholism there is a difference between the terms transformation and reformation. The abstinent alcoholic who has not transcended to the Self or at least to the Acceptance/heart level can be called " reformed ", whereas the person who has entered onto a spiritual path, to be the Self, can be called " transformed " (Small 1982). The clinician who works with people just up to the reformed level, i.e. up to the Mind level of consciousness, has an opportunity to go beyond it and to help them to transform their lives. To help accomplish such a task, the clinician usually has to work from his or her own heart.

Our internal world - our spectrum of human consciousness - appears to be arranged both by a Higher Power <u>and</u> by us, in synchronicity with the external world, to provide an endless series of adventures. Hitting bottom adds the spice for our adventures (DiLeo 1982).

<u>Unwanted Side Effects of Transformation</u>

While there are many positive effects that result from transforming our lives, there are also some unwanted side effects. One of the most common is a feeling of or a <u>fear of losing one's mind</u> or of becoming psychotic. When we make a positive change, we grow from one aspect of our being to a new and more complete one. To do so, we have to give up, surrender and therefore lose a part of us. To process the loss, we go through the painful experience of grieving, which is a normal and healthy way of transforming (Friedman 1984). The grieving process is not just sadness, but a combination of anger, denial, bargaining and depression (Kubler-Ross 1975). This is all often disorienting, and has been called " the melancholy of becoming ". Our fear has some reality: we <u>are</u> losing our mind, although it is but a <u>part</u> of our mind, of the way we thought things were. However, it is not our ability to function long term in our thinking, deciding, and growing that we lose.It is generally a less efficient and constructive way of being that we lose. We gain a more efficient and constructive way of being. When we are transforming, we <u>feel</u> it in all of these ways. This is in part why being aware of, talking about, and dealing with our feelings are such an important part of growth and of recovery.

As our consciousness becomes more aware of itself and as our awareness becomes more acute, each <u>feeling</u> that we have seems to be clearer, stronger and <u>more intense</u> (Welwood 1979). This can be unsettling. However, the intense negative feelings tend to decrease in duration, and the positive feelings tend to increase in duration and intensity.

There may also be a feeling that the whole area of spirituality itself may be an <u>illusion</u>. This may be true, since everything that our ego experiences can be viewed as being an illusion, a dream, due to its " distorted lens " view of the varying levels or areas of reality (Fig. 7, in Part II). However, since our only other choice is the less comfortable and more rigid lower self or ego-attached view of our existence, we may wish to choose the more peaceful and growth oriented view of our life - which includes full functional use of the lower self. And even this choice may be viewed as being an illusion. Our choice may thus be between two illusions: a more conflicted one or a more peaceful one (Jampolsky 1981; Course 1975). Since we have discovered that we are no longer victims, the choice is ours to make.

Fearful of being rejected or of being laughed at, we may avoid telling others of the content and process of our transformations. We may thus end up feeling isolated. Helpful antidotes are having faith and trusting that we are on the right path, which is growth to wholeness, our full potential, through becoming and being our Self, plus talking about it with trusted others who are also on spiritual paths. Combined with the use of the spiritual practices discussed above, all of these will help us through the process of our transformations.

Another unwanted side effect is physical illness. Sanella (1977) found that it may be common for people who are on a spiritual path to suffer symptoms and illness located in the axis of the body, i.e. from the feet to the head, generally excluding the arms and chest. He postulated that these problems may be manifestations of blocks in our basic spiritual energy, called, among other names, kundalini energy (discussed below). There also may be change-related, stress-related illness. As mentioned so often above, we can use these problems as signals and as teachings in our lives. What are they telling us? We can then consider turning our curse into our gift.

Unhealthy attachment is another unwanted side effect. We can become addicted to spiritual practices in unhelpful and in unproductive ways. An example is of a recovering alcoholic who turned it all over to his Higher Power, but neglected to realize that he had the responsibility to take care of the business of his lower self, which in his case was getting an attorney to help him with his two pending driving-while-intoxicated charges (he had two previous DWI convictions, for a total of four DWI's). When he was sentenced to two months in jail, he couldn't understand why his Higher Power had not intervened. The teaching that he received was that we each have to be our own co-creator. The sages have told us that all methods are traps. Spiritual practices are only tools to use to help us actualize ourselves, to discover and to be what we already are.

Another unhealthy attachment is to an ego-centered form of spirituality. Trungpa (1973) said, " Walking the spiritual path properly is a very subtle process; it is not something to jump into naively. There are numerous side tracks which lead to a distorted, ego-centered version of spirituality; we can deceive ourselves into thinking we are developing spiritually when instead we are stengthening our egocentricity through spiritual techniques. This fundamental distortion may be referred to as spiritual materialism".

There is also the related problem of fanaticism. In such a case, we may have only switched our addictions. For example, before, we may have been addicted to thinking we were a victim of the world, and now we are addicted to brand-X religion, recovery method or spiritual practice. We may become so narrow and so clinging to it, that brand-X is all we can think or talk about. The fanatic usually doesn't know that he is a fanatic, and often projects the shadow of his own narrowness onto others. One can even become attached to being detached. It is thus a delicate balance of using the method to be what we want to become and not be attached to the method or to the being. Finally, there may be some people who want to study just the theories of transformation and of spirituality, and not practice it and be it. However, spirituality is experience. In our Higher Self, a quarter inch of experience is worth more than a mile of theory.

Chapter 22. Alcohol, Other Drugs and Spirituality

The relationship of alcohol, other drugs and spirituality is controversial. Some people who read this chapter may become offended and won't want to read the rest of it. A common reaction may be one of anger, shock or even misunderstanding. Some may be angry to hear what I and others say about alcohol, drugs and spirituality. Some may be shocked at finding these concepts about the non-medical use of drugs in a book on spirituality. Some may even erroneously think that I and others are advocating the use of drugs, or even their irresponsible use. By contrast, other readers may feel a sense of relief to have their own personal experience validated. I welcome the reader not to use any of this chapter, and certainly not to use alcohol or any other psychoactive drug.

Psychoactive drugs alter our consciousness. They have been used by humankind for thousands of years. Drugs provide us with a feeling of novelty (Weil 1973). They work by either stimulating, disinhibiting, or otherwise changing our ordinary waking consciousness. In most people ordinary consciousness is ruled by the lower self, and mostly by the mind. At low doses the alcohol or other drug effect can be viewed as a transitory opening of channels, which are usually blocked, to the user's experiencing higher levels of consciousness. They act on the entire spectrum of consciousness, including at the lower part of level one by inducing biochemical changes in the brain, allowing us to reach where we want to go, usually to higher realms. And sometimes - usually depending on our mind set and environmental setting - we go to lower realms, for various reasons. Sedative drugs and psychedelic drugs tend to activate our spirit, which to a small degree has some anology to the "right brain ". Stimulant drugs tend to activate the ego/mind, which likewise has some analogy to the "left brain". (I have qualified above in part 1 that this analogy is reductionistic.) Foods may act similarly, although they usually have a more subtle impact. Some foods when eaten are easier to digest and/or feel more harmonious to the organism. Many vegetarians believe that vegetarian foods are more "spiritually stimulating" and that sweets and red meats are more "ego stimulating". Even so, while helpful, diet alone is not enough to realize unity consciousness (Free John 1984a).

Sometimes under the influence of sedative drugs our consciousness is altered in ways that allow our minds to soar to the spirit, to oneness and a sense of wholeness. While those moments are uncommon, when they happen they are powerful. For many people, sedative and other depressant drugs alter their consciousness in ways that cause their mind to fixate on the negative, the destructive and the isolated parts of their being. While they are not reliable portals to the spirit, people have had enhancing spiritual experiences under the influence of drugs and alcohol. Drugs quickly unlock neural locks in our brains. What lies behind those locks may be the Higher Self or it may be the lower self. It is not always knowable beforehand which it will be in any drug-using experience. Programming the experience to be positive has been worked on by Native Americans in the peyote ritual and by researchers (Grof 1980a; DiLeo 1984).

Used normally (which alcoholics and other chemical dependents cannot do successfully with much consistency) and intermittently, drugs can give us a glimpse of our higher consciousness, our Self. By so doing, they can stimulate us to reach our Self in other ways, without drugs. Probably the most spiritually powerful of drugs are the generally misunderstood psychedelics, such as LSD (Grof 1980-a; Smith 1976). While they may promote any of a variety of emotions and experiences, these unusual drugs tend to promote feelings of positivity, letting go, and oneness, if the right mind set and environmental setting are present in the user (Hoffman 1983). If the substance is not pure and the set and setting are not positive, using these drugs in any situation is ill advised. For a variety of reasons, many of these drugs remain illegal.

Bill Wilson, one of the co-founders of AA, throughout his own recovering and sober life searched for ways that alcoholics who had rejected AA could be helped to reach their own recovery and to experience a lasting and comfortable sobriety. In the 1950's, AA's trustees carefully shielded from public scrutiny the fact that not only had Bill W taken the psychedelic drug LSD during his successful recovery from alcoholism, but that he was, in a loving and totally positive gesture, encouraging experimentation with the drug by those otherwise hopeless and AA - rejecting alcoholics (Kurtz 1979). Although he knew that using LSD had not " cured " him and that it would not " cure " anyone else, he may have known that its profound experience, similar to that of a near-death experience, might be a trigger that could induce a life transformation. Clinical research by Grof and others supports Bill W's notion (Grof 1980-a, 1973, 1975). Psychedelic therapy helped alcoholics and other chemical dependent people to reach a form of unity consciousness, a state they had perhaps been seeking through their drinking and drug use (Leech 1973; Westermeyer & Walzer 1975). Indeed, among all patients, alcoholics and other chemical dependents had the highest incidence of mystical experiences with psychedelics (Grof 1980). This is perhaps related to James' belief that alcoholics are " frustrated mystics ".

The chemical structure of LSD consists of the synthesis of two compounds found in nature: an ergot molecule and two alcohol molecules (Goodman & Gilman 1980). It is most likely the presence of the alcohol molecule - and not some other substance - at a precise location on the ergot molecule that makes LSD the most potent and most "spiritual" of all the known psychoactive drugs. It is also interesting that throughout at least the past few centuries alcohol has been called " spirits ", and that even today some liquor stores are called " spirit shops ". Kurtz (1983a) said that alcoholics seemed to have confused spirit with "spirits" .

Regarding alcohol's existence in the universe, experiments in radiophysics have shown that throughout the space of the universe there exist at least 56 compounds that are also known to us and to be a part of us on earth, and that one of them is alcohol (Blitz 1982). Even throughout outer space, we cannot avoid our most popular psychoactive drug. Like all things, each containing negatives and positives, Yang and Yin, evil and good, alcohol pervades the universe as we know it.

We know that drugs provide us only a glimpse - coming attractions - but they are not the main feature. And drugs also provide disadvantages, ranging from hangovers to chemical dependence to death. Alcoholics and other chemical dependent people in recovery learn that they cannot consistently use any drug safely.

When I have given extended workshops on spirituality, stress and recovery, it is common for someone to ask a question like, " Why are you wasting our time talking about drugs and spirituality, since we all know they don't work? Since they cause only trouble for us? " One man who asked this question had told the audience that he was a recovering alcoholic, and our subsequent dialogue went as follows:

How long have you been sober?

About eight years.

Would you say that you have reached a spiritual awakening during those eight years?

Yes. I was an atheist before I recovered. My life is much better now.

Do you think that if you hadn't become alcoholic you would have had such a spiritual awakening?

No, I probably would not have. I guess that my alcoholism pushed me into it.

It seems to me, then, that it is possible that you used a drug, alcohol, to reach higher levels of consciousness, to have a spiritual awakening. And subsequently, through recovery and AA you have learned to do it without drugs. Does that sound possible?

Yes, maybe.

The paradox of using drugs is that doing so can open us to our Self and can alienate us from our Self. One alcoholic woman who had searched for inner truth from the time of her adolesence, describes her discovery of "... blessed alcohol, which subtly dulled my pain and unshackled my soaring spirit." She became alcoholic and went through eight years of psychiatric treatment while she continued drinking. She then joined the fellowship of AA, stopped drinking, and found that "... with this act I was at last freed to truly look at myself, and with the help of all the other alcoholics who had lived through the same hell, to be myself. ... I learned that there is something infinitely more powerful than my small human mind. And I knew that I must find it, know it, and be it" (cited in White 1979).

Another disadvantageous part of this paradox is that depressant drugs dampen and thereby block our ability to experience our otherwise normal ups and downs. I have already spoken of the importance of experiencing our feelings in the maintenance of our wholeness. Yet many people use depressant and/or anti-depressant drugs to avoid feeling their emotions, and they are commonly encouraged to use them by many health professionals. Alcoholics, CD's and their family members are commonly prescribed and use these drugs, which thereby blocks their experiencing of their wholeness. And paradoxically, the suffering they may encounter from using the drugs can offer them a way out, through recovery and possible transcendence.

These are a small number of teachers of spirituality who have themselves been or become alcoholic/CD. While little is known about the effect of their illness upon their teaching, some of their followers experience being confused about the behavior of their teachers, and many, like non-recovered co-alcoholics everywhere, do not understand that the teacher has a treatable illness. Such situations may raise interesting questions about the relationships among alcoholism/CD, co-alcoholism, and spirituality. The suffering and questioning of all concerned is grist for the spiritual mill.

There are many other people who are on a "spiritual path" who use alcohol or other drugs in a less problematic or in a normal way. There are also many people who are not recovering alcoholic/CD who chose not to drink or use drugs as part of their own life or way of and toward experiencing serenity. Given these contrasting choices, we can sometimes fall into a trap of judging one or the other as being right or wrong. In the eyes of the Self and of Universal Consciousness, there is no right or wrong. This is a delicate balance while we are on earth, since through our lower self we have to deal with the consequences of what we do and what we create.

Drugs work, either through opening channels or by causing suffering, or both, to induce some of us to find our Self. But there are more powerful ways. Probably the most powerful way is through forgiveness and love (Ram Dass 1974-83; Peck 1978; Jampolsky 1984; Course 1975).

Part IV: LOVING

Chapter 23. Love and Unconditional Love

I and others have described the low self-esteem among alcoholics/CD's and their family members. This tends to be especially prevalent during active illness and for the first one to three years of recovery in a constructive treatment program. A major component of this low self-esteem is feeling a deep sense of unworthiness and unloveableness. Related to several important factors, including their inability to control alcohol or drugs and not feeling loved by parents and other intimates, they believe they are simply not worthy of receiving love. Rather than believe one is unloveable, one can shift to believing that one does not need love, which translates into " I don't want to be loved " and then finally " I will reject love, no matter who gives it to me " (Gravitz & Bowden 1984). The person ends up with "frozen feelings," or an inability to experience feelings and emotions, including especially love. This problem around love is crucial in the difficulty that alcoholics/CD's, children of alcoholics and other family members have in forming and maintaining intimate relationships, and in their growth in recovery.

The fellowships of Alcoholics Anonymous, Al-Anon and other self-help group programs begin to address this problem through unconditional love. In their acceptance of everyone and every act, no matter how degrading or humiliating, they welcome, support and love everyone who comes in their doors. The most effective group therapy does likewise, although in a more structured and at times confrontive fashion. Love is the most healing of our resources, and it takes several years of being so loved to get well and stay well. And then we can begin to love others in return.

Some Descriptions & Dynamics

One of our most powerful and difficult acts is to give and to receive love. Yet when we are our Self, we are love. There are numerous definitions of love and books about love. The Oxford English Dictionary (1971) defines it as warm affection, disposition arising from attraction, or instincts or sympathy for the welfare of the object. There is usually delight in its presence and desire for approval. Love is also a strong predilection to liking or fondness for or devotion to something. It is clearly all that, and more.

Table 11. Defining Some Clinical Therapeutic Properties of the Self (Levels 4 through 7): Love, Truth, Healing & Power along the Levels of Human Consciousness. (Levels 1 through 3 represent those for the lower self)

	Hierarchy of Consciousness	Love	Truth	Healing	Power
7)	Unity Consciousness	Peaceful Being	Peaceful Being	Peaceful Being	Peaceful Being
6)	Compassion	Unconditional empathy & acceptance	Love & acceptance	Love, & acceptance	Love & acceptance
5)	Understanding	Commitment to growth	Creativity	Right decision	Wisdom
4)	Acceptance/ Heart	Forgiveness	Forgiveness	Forgiveness	Forgiveness
		Caring through conflict	Total awareness	Caring	Accepting
3)	Mind/Ego	Worship	Experience	Prevention, education	Assertion
		Possession	Beliefs	Psychologic	Persuasion
2)	Passion	" Chemistry "	Sensations	Nurturance	Manipulation
1)	Survival	Neediness	Science	Physical	Physical strength

A helpful way to define love is to do so for each of the seven levels of consciousness (see Table 11). By such a view, we see that in the lower self love is neediness, " chemistry ", possession, strong admiration and even worship - in short, traditional romantic love. Most active alcoholics and many of their family members - and many non-alcoholics - become stuck at these levels. Perhaps some of the only times they are able to experience and be the higher levels are some times when they are intoxicated, whether by alcohol, another drug or, for the family, by needing to control another person's use of alcohol or drugs. A major achievement in recovery -and in life - is to work through, to transcend and to become the higher levels of love : caring through conflict, forgiveness, trust, commitment to growth in one's self and in a loved one, unconditional empathy and acceptance, and pure peaceful Being (Table 11). To do so does not come easy. By experiencing, forgiving, letting go, and using the spiritual practices described above, we can gradually open to the Love within each of us. We can also begin to see that at higher levels love is the same as truth, power, and healing (Table 11).

Peck (1978) describes love as " . . . the will to extend oneself for the purpose of nurturing one's own or another's spiritual growth. " Love is thus both selfish and unselfish, growth inducing, and attention giving. The attention includes focused listening, participating, sharing and confiding. Love is also risking, including the risking of commitment, confrontation, and independence. Love is separateness, being able to be alone or with another other than the loved one, and love is giving and receiving. Finally, love is disciplined, the ability to endure suffering enough to work it out through conflict in a relationship (i.e. acceptance through conflict). These are all characteristics of higher level love. Peck believes that love is not : falling in love, dependency, self-sacrifice or a feeling (Peck 1978); these correspond to love as defined at the lower three levels of consciousness. Falling in love is the anticipation of fusing with the loved one.

Like a drug, falling in love can give us a glimpse of the bliss of re-uniting with Universal Consciousness. But in our lower self alone we cannot attempt to fuse with another without creating inordinate difficulties for ourself.

Powell (1978) said that " Love takes time, demands a history of giving and receiving, laughing and crying, living and dying. It never promises instant gratification, only ultimate fulfillment. . . . clinging dependency and jealous possessiveness are counterfeits of true love. . . . Unconditional love is liberating. It frees the loved one to be authentic and real. . . . Weathering the storms of the love process is the only way to find the rainbows of life.. . . (We can chose) love as a life principle. . . . the surest way to find God is not to make him a private possession, a problem solver, or an instant consolidation in time of need, but rather by opening to love. " Love is paradoxical: we give to be given to, and, unconditionally, we give without expectation.

Biblical references to love include four varieties (Dorr et al 1983; Quell & Stauffer 1951). The first is 'ahebh, which is the most general love; it includes a romantic affection, parent to child, love between friends, and love between God and the faithful. Rahum implies sympathy, nurturing, protecting, accepting and guiding. Filia refers to a brother- or sister-like caring or liking. Agape implies a godly love and a chosen, though sometimes tough love. A fifth form is eros, which includes mature, intense, delightfully sensual, affectionate and passionate love. Starratt (1979) said, "Eros, in all of its forms, is central to the religious life because it is literally true that erotic love penetrates beyond the enchanted veil of isolation and makes us acquainted with the One who is hidden from the unloving". Since Freud, psychology and psychiatry have generally focused little on the broader and deeper dimensions of love, other than its biological-erotic elements. The humanistic and transpersonal movements have strengthened the importance of the highler levels of love in helping and in wellness.

Love is perhaps our most healing and enlivening energy and resource. While it is the foundation of many alcoholism and family fellowship programs, organizations and treatment programs, there is a lack of love in others, where many administrators, clinicians, and staff are stuck in their lower selves. By contrast, among businesses a powerful movement called organizational enlivenment is growing. It is based upon an "unconditional positive regard " (another term for love) (Rogers, cited in Pitts 1984) for every individual in the organization, with a focus on people's strengths rather than weaknesses and on creativity and support rather than passivity, manipulation and mediocrity. Consultants and chief executive officers are beginning to realize that love is the primary energy force within their own organization. With the continued strengthening of the spirituality of all of us, this emptiness, this lack of love, is gradually being filled with the healing, fulfilling, and growth-inducing power of love (Pitts 1984).

Love and Fear

Alcoholics/CD's and co-dependents are quite familiar with the experience of fear. Indeed, with their obsession with control, fear often runs and even dominates their lives. And fear is another word for stress.

Yet Jampolsky says in his book by the same title that love is letting go of fear (Jampolsky 1981, Course 1975). Rather than hate, the opposite of love may be fear.

Through the " distorted lens " or forgetting of our ego, we interpret reality as our being separate from the One. When we are separated from our own being - which is part of the One, and thus is the One - we see it as an attack on both our own being and on the One. In our psyche we thus feel guilty for isolating ourself from our source. And we then feel fear that we will be punished. We suffer. Not wanting the pain of the punishment and fear, we dissociate it from ourself and then project it onto others. What we project is what we see, i.e. projection makes perception, and what we see is what we believe is true, in a vicious cycle. What we see also proves to us our state of mind, so that if we see that which is negative, then we see ourselves as being negative. Active chemical dependent people and co-dependents commonly see their existence in this way. Such projection produces more separation and alienation, and the viscious cycle continues (Steinberg & Martin 1981; Silverman 1980; Course 1975). The way out of the cycle is to listen, moment by moment, to Universal Consciousness, to our Self. In Twelve Step programs this is called " Turning it over ", i.e. turning it over to our Higher Power. Such listening can be achieved through meditation, prayer, silence, imagery, creative dreaming, forgiveness, and other practices described above. When we listen, we ask our Self for an answer, to reinterpret what we see through our ego's distorted lens.

Our fear is a normal manifestation of our stress response as described in chapter 2. The stress response is a simple and ordinary reflex that has only the most minute significance as a practical necessity in our lives, and yet we are overwhelmed by it. We make fear so chronic a mood - in our chronic distress state - that we repeatedly interpret our existence through the medium of fear.

From Hindu scripture the Upanishads say, "Whenever there is another, fear arises". Describing how to transcend fear, Free John (1983) writes ". . . And how does the sense of otherness develop? Through the self-contraction, whereby one feels separated from what one observes, therefore limited by it, and thus limited to what one can seem to be at this moment. Feel mortal and you feel incapable of flow, or change, or freedom. There is no ultimate metaphysical means for getting rid of fear, no ultimate knowledge. The alternative to fear is not some great answer that will ultimately prevent our being chronically and mortally afraid, which we all are, and which people are in general. Such knowledge is not even possible. The alternative is to recognize fear as an ordinary mechanism of the body beyond which we can, and should, in any moment feel and breathe. We should be resting in our natural state, feeling and breathing whole bodily into the Life-Principle in which we are existing, not full of fear, doubt, contraction, becoming a black hole, another universe unto ourselves into which everything is sucked. . . ."

As human beings, we become addicted to psychological fear. But fear is not our natural state. Only when we enter into what can be called "right relationship" to all our possible states, including fear, can we realize our natural state, which is Love. We can do that through the power of forgiveness. Free John continues (1983), "Fear is the root of un-Enlightened existence. It is the essence of egoity and of all conventional models of 'reality'. . . . societies tend to be structured along lives that both accomodate the fear-psychology and reinforce its essential structures. Societies are, in general, collective representations of the common egoity. The common social laws . . . are created by and for people who are afraid. . . . social change in the direction of freedom always requires great struggle. . . . Our fear is represented by socially controlled consciousness in relation to two primary human (and presumably private) processes: sex and death. Enlightened life, sex and death are conscious, intentional and self-transcending participatory actions." If we can surrender into Life through rememberance of our Oneness and through forgiving and loving, we can begin to overcome fear. And then life, sex and death become free meditation (and ultimately, Realization or Samadhi).

Fear is not intended to be our natural or chronic state. We may suffer it chronically only because we do not take responsibility for ourselves. Free John (1983) said "We do not simply rest in That which is controlling us. We will not surrender to That which has brought us into being and which is sustaining us at the present time and which will still be the case after we are dead . . . . We act as if there is something wrong about such surrender, as if we must always be on guard to defend ourselves".

We may have difficulty realizing that love is an act of surrender. Free John concludes (1983) "Once you realize that you need only enter into true feeling Remembrance of the Divine at any moment, you will never be afraid again. " In our self-transformation, we can internally re-frame our experience of fear by turning it into Love, since fear is but the opposite of Love. "Once having contacted the fear, just radiate the feeling. Feel it so intensely that you shine with it. Once you locate it, the feeling ceases to be fear. It becomes free, blissful Energy. What you identify as fear is the Life-Energy of the being contracting upon itself and causing an explosive and unpleasant pressure. Do not force the Life-Principle to contract upon itself through self-contraction, fear and negativity. Allow it to be Radiant. Its will is to be Radiant, to be naturally present without contraction. No fear exists in that Radiance, nor do you engage the mechanism of fear when you are Radiant" (Free John 1983). We are "always already" enlightened. We do not need to wait to be liberated from fear at some future climactic event of salvation. We can transcend our self-contraction of fear in every single moment. And we can do so by surrendering into every single moment and by forgiving.

Getting free of fear is a major step in working the Twelve Steps of recovery and realizing a comfortable sobriety. Above, I summarized the Twelve Steps as "Trust God, clean house, and help others". Throughout this book I have also described the path of awakening, experiencing, and transcending. We can now see that the way out of a life of fear is by realizing this path.

<u>Twelve Steps</u>	<u>Getting Free by Experiencing</u>	
	<u>Transcending</u>	
Help others	(Serenity, inner peace)	Love
↑	↑	↑
Clean house	<u>Experiencing</u>	Forgive
↑	Letting go	↑
	Completion	
	Communication	
	Awareness of Feelings	
	Honesty (open mind)	
	↑	
Trust God	<u>Awakening</u>	Remember

It is not at all complicated. It is the same path. It is a simple one. If we remember our Source, and Forgive, we are left with pure Unconditional Love. Our fear thereby becomes irrelevant, and it disappears.

A Course in Miracles (1975) further describes fear and love, "The presence of fear is a sure sign that you are trusting in your own strength. All healing is essentially the release from fear. What is not love is always fear, and nothing else. There is no time, no place, no state where God is absent. There is nothing to be feared."

The lower levels of love as well as those of truth, healing and power can be close to fear and often create fear. The higher we transcend in levels of love, the more we can see that the corresponding definitions of love are similar to those for the higher levels of truth, healing, and power (Table 11). And they appear to be identical at the* levels of Compassion and Unity Consciousness where they are unconditional love. Jampolsky (1981) said, " To Give Is to Receive is the law of Love. Under this law, when we give our Love away to others we gain, and what we give we simultaneously receive. The law of Love is based on abundance; we are completely filled with Love all the time, and our supply is always full and running over. When we give our Love unconditionally to others with no expectations of return, the Love within us extends, expands and joins. So by giving our Love away, we increase the Love within us and everyone gains. "

Love is indeed letting go of our fear of separation, and it is thereby healing. It means accepting the darkness, the evil, the shadow, within ourselves and others. When we feel like attacking someone, we are perceiving that we are not One and that the other person does not love us, and this generates fear, which can make us ill. But those who we perceive as attacking us are usually fearful in their own lives (Jampolsky 1982). When we experience our Self, which is Love, we can more easily see the other person as feeling fearful, separated and attacking. And when we experience our Self, we know that we are whole, and we can thereby immediately forgive them and react peacefully to their attacking, and it will usually help calm the other person - as well as help prevent an upset in us (Steinberg & Martin 1981; Silverman 1980; Course 1975). Even though they may be attacking or grandiose on their outside, when we view others as fearful or frightened, we can give them our love, without judging them.

Love and Intervention

As another expression of love in helping people with active alcoholism/CD, the phenomenon called intervention has developed and grown. An intervention is an organized session of confrontation and support to motivate a person with an active alcohol or other drug problem into treatment. Family, close friends, colleagues and other potentially influential and caring people meet in a group. They talk, rehearse, and then lovingly confront the person. Requesting that the person enter treatment, they describe the limits and consequences that will result if the person does not enter and complete treatment. I and others believe that the healing energy in such an intervention is Love. Who would devote so much time and go to such trouble for someone about whom thay did not care? It also is a form of tough love, although Love nonetheless.

An analogy might be made of such an intervention with the rare phenomenon of exorcism. The possessed person is taken over by an evil force, and we could view the active alcoholic likewise. Both illnesses are destructive and cause much suffering for the victims and for those close to them. In an exorcism there is a team of people who devote hours of time and loving energy to the process. Peck (1983) describes it thus: "In a sense the team 'gangs up' on the patient. Unlike traditional therapy, in which it is one against one, in exorcism the patient is outnumbered . . . . through prayer and ritual, the team invokes the power of God in the healing process . . . . it is legitimate to use any loving resource . . . . The key word is 'loving'. . . . exorcism stands in relation to ordinary psychotherapy as radical surgery does to lancing a boil. It makes use of analysis, of careful discernment, of interpretation, of encouragement and of loving confrontation. It is psychotherapy by massive assault. Its purpose is to uncover and isolate the

* higher level of Acceptance through conflict, where they are forgiveness, and at the

demonic within the patient so that it can be expelled. The evil's principle weapon is fear which is a spirit of unreality. The team would speak with the patient's healthy core personality or the demon(s) but would refuse to speak with some unclear mixture of the two. . . . the essence of the role is the gentleness and caring and patience and discernment and willingness to suffer. . . ." Unloving people are generally not effective in helping to bring about an exorcism. The similarities between exorcism and an intervention are close. And the basic healing ingredient and energy in both is Love.

The Energy of Love

Whenever we are feeling attacked, stressed, angry or hurt, we can close our eyes, meditate for a few seconds, and then ask our Higher Power to release the energy we are using into unconditional love (Moss 1981).

Our inner energy that is a major part of love has been called by many names: Kundalini, Shakti (India), Ch'i (China), Ki (Japan), Holy Spirit (Christianity), Prana (Ayurvedic), Chiti, Love (universal), Eros and Libido (Hall & Nordby 1973; Thompson et al 1955; Muktanda 1981; Siu 1974). While it is powerful and healing, it is more subtle than our breath. This " inner energy " is the energy of our Self, and is different from our "outer energy", or that of our lower self, which we view as running the biochemical processes of the cells of our body. It is a higher order of energy than our metabolic energy. It appears that once we " receive " this inner energy, i.e. remove the blocks to it and experience it, we will always have it. To receive it we usually have to be in a receptive state of mind, wanting to receive it, practicing spiritually, and having faith that it will come. The ways we can receive it vary in type and duration (Muktananda 1981). It can be slow, coming in fits and starts, or dramatic, or both, and can come from being associated with a teacher, a guru or a caring therapist, or it can come spontaneously.

While many aspects and dimensions of it have been described, this energy is the energy of Universal Consciousness and of pure and unconditional love. Unconditional love is the mortar or cement that holds together the otherwise seemingly fragmented parts of our existence (Steinberg & Martin 1981). It is the energy that encompasses and supports the process of our life and of our growth (Moss 1981). Filling the void or emptiness that we often feel, this energy is transformational energy, as described above in the recovery of Bill W and countless others.

I believe that the energy of Love is what inspired and allowed me to write this book. I describe it in further detail throughout these pages.

Discovering Serenity - Our Natural State

As we clear away the cobwebs and smears on the lens through which we view "reality", we begin to discover that inner peace or serenity is our natural state. Our "human condition," that which we are given or "thrown", is only a way or a vehicle for us to discover and to celebrate our Higher Self and its connection to Higher Power. And in that sense, we begin to experience it as a gift. However, what lies deep within each of us, at our very core, is pure Serenity - our natural state.

In table 11-A, I summarize some 16 terms that are equivalent to the term "serenity" that is so frequently heard and wondered about in self help groups and recovery oriented literature. While serenity is our natural state, it has also been described as being a mystical or a peak experience. William James called alcoholics "frustrated mystics". A mystic is a person who wants to experience everything in life,

Table IIA. Similar Terms & Descriptions of Highest States of Human Consciousness (compiled in part from Alcoholics Anonymous 1975; The Bible Bucke 1969; Course 1975; DiLeo 1985; Free John 1982; Jampolsky 1983; Morrison 1977; Stanford 1970; Maslow 1970; and Suzuki 1962).

Serenity A comfortable life and sobriety. Inner peace through being aware of and honoring all levels consciousness, flowing with and accepting what is, without trying to control it. Being a co-creator of our life's process with Higher Power. A life characterized by a progressivlely expanding process of genuineness, spontaneity, humor, openness to growth, living in the now, creativity, forgiveness, humility, surrender and intuitive understanding.

Enlightenment (Satori) Existential awakening to one's true Self. Entry into the life of non-duality. Union with life and with oneself. The enlightened person deals with all problems and with him or herself from within instead of from without. There is no final enlightenment, for life itself is not final.

Inner Peace Peace and equanimity that comes from handling and transcending one's suffering. This leads to sanity and total health.

Sanity A balance in one's life, an honoring of all levels of awareness. God's will for us.

Salvation Our natural condition, a secret kept from us by our ego. Salvation lies in teaching the exact opposite of everything the ego believes. God's will, which we have right now. Right-mindedness, forgivenss and peace.

Atonement (At-One-ment) Becoming aware that we are guiltless, sinless, and One. Our final lesson. Through forgiveness, giving up our ego's illusion of fear and suffering. The result of removing our blocks to love.

Cosmic consciousness Consciousness of the life and order of the universe. A new plane of existence. An indescribable feeling of elevation, elation and joyousness, and a quickening of the moral sense. A sense of eternal life.

Nirvana Extinction of self will; Self Realization. Healthily dealing with ego, suffering, birth, death and rebirth. Entry into the Transcendent realm of Unqualified Reality. God-Realization. Objects and states may arise, but they are simply recognized, or their binding power transcended in the Radiant Higher Power.

Samadhi Union with God. The mind becomes still and is transcended by a higher knowing, and duality of subject and object disappears. The last of the three stages of meditation. Spiritual consciousness, equanimity balance. Natural and native Realization of the Sublime Reality ultimate Bliss of Existence itself. Some of its several dimensions are Sahaj (natural Expression), Bhava (ultimate ecstatic expression), Nirvikalpa (the Void, beyond description), Ananda (bliss), and Savikapla Samadhi (earthly).

Sat-Chit-Ananda A state of infinite, positive being, consciousness and bliss.

Seeing/Realizing the Light Becoming enlightened. Realizing and experiencing that we are always, already enlightened. With eyes closed, at times we may see a warm, nurturing and loving light.

Self-Realization Individuation, integration; healed, whole.

God-Realization Our natural or native disposition, prior to all spiritual practices, wherein through all our existence we identify with the Radiant Higher Power or Transcendental Being. Sahaj & Bhava Samadhi

Mystical Experience (Peak experience) Direct unitive experience with Higher Power or God manifested, in part, by a feeling of peace and natural knowing. Transcendence of paradox. (see also table 11-B)

Kingdom of Heaven That unity consciousness which is within us. Inner peace from a uniting of opposites. A mysterious feeling of completion and contentment. Here, attack is impossible. A state of complete healing of body, mind and spirit.

Unity Consciousness A state which includes all of the above. Surrender to the Divine Mystery of the Universe.

Table 11 B. Some Characteristics of the Mystical or Peak Experience (compiled from Pahnke 1967, Maslow 1970, and DiLeo 1985)

Unity Feeling unifed internally and externally with the universe; feeling of completion, wholeness, serenity, enlightenment, rebirth, etc. (see Table 11-A).

Objectivity & Reality Feeling of accuracy and truth that transcends the ordinary; a non-analytical grasp that feels authoritative.

Deeply Felt Positivity Experience of any and all positive feelings, ranging from infinite freedom and safety to unconditional love.

Transcendence of Time & Space Experience of everlasting, infinite existence that is boundless; the eternal Now.

Sense of specialness Sacredness, awe, profoundness, not reducible to anything else; discovery that we are an important part of this specialness.

Ineffableness Alleged inability to describe the experience in concrete terms. Indescribable, beyond words.

Paradoxicality Opposites co-exist or unite comfortably; eg love and hate, pain and pleasure, death and rebirth.

Transiency Related to its energy, power and ectasy.

Positive Attitude/Behavior Change - Toward self, others and the universe; a flowing with and acceptance, combined with an increase in taking responsibility for one's life.

and especially Higher Power (Bancroft 1976; Deikman 1982). Some further characteristics of this "mystical" state of serenity are shown in Table 11-B.

However, serenity does not mean constant inner peace. Rather, it is a creative state through being fully aware of one's life - with all its pain and its ever increasing joy, as we come closer to God. As Tielhard de Chardin said

> The longer I live, the more I feel that true repose consists in "renouncing" one's own self, by which I mean making up one's mind to admit that there is no importance whatever in being "happy" or "unhappy" in the usual meaning of the words. Personal success or personal satisfaction are not worth another thought if one does achieve them, not worth worrying about it they evade one or are slow in coming. All that is really worthwhile is action — faithful action, for the world, and in God. Before one can see that and live by it, there is a sort of threshold to cross, or a reversal to be made in what appears to be man's general habit of thought, but once that gesture has been made, what freedom is yours, freedom to work and love.

Many people seek happiness, which is a part of serenity. Frankl (1985) said

> Primarily and normally man does not seek pleasure; instead, pleasure-or, for that matter, happiness-is the side effect of living out the self-transcendence of existence. Once one has served a cause or is involved in loving another human being, happiness occurs by itself. The will to pleasure, however, contradicts the self-transcendent quality of the human reality. And it also defeats itself. For pleasure and happiness are by-products. Happiness must ensue. It cannot be pursued. It is the very pursuit of happiness that thwarts happiness. The more one makes happiness an aim, the more he misses the aim.

Regarding serenity, we can now begin to summarize some of the approaches and connections that have been made throughout this book and that others have made elsewhere. These are as follows.

Some Possible Paths to Serenity

1. We are ignorant of our Journey, we are limited (humility): we can study universal laws, approximate them, and surrender to our lack of ultimate knowledge. Given these limitations, sages over the centuries describe something like the following.

2. Higher Power is in each of us, and we are in Higher Power.

3. We can view our reality as a hierarchy of levels of awareness, consciousness or being.

4. We are going Home (we <u>are</u> Home, already and always). Home on this earth is being all levels of our awareness or consciousness in our own unique fashion.

5. There will be conflict going Home (melodrama, cosmic drama). This conflict or creative tension is useful to us in some way, probably as a way home.

6. We have a choice. We can use our bodies, ego/minds, our relationships and this earth to reinforce our separation and our suffering. Or we can use them as vehicles for our Soul, Spirit or Higher Self to return Home and to celebrate that return.

7. Higher Power (Home) is Love (Love is perhaps the most useful way we know Higher Power).

8. We can remove the blocks to realizing our Higher Power by experiencing (including living in the Now), remembering, forgiving, and surrendering (these five realizations can be viewed as being ultimately the same). Regular spiritual practices help us with this realization.

9. Separation, suffering and evil are the absence of realizing Love, and are therefore ultimately illusions. They are also manifestations of our searching for Love, wholeness, and Home.

10. We create our own story by our thoughts and actions. What we think and feel in our mind and heart we will produce in our experience and our life. What we give, we get. As within, so without.

11. Life is a Process, Force or Flow that lives us. We do not live it. When we surrender to It, i.e. flow with its Process, and take responsibility for our participation in It, we become co-creators. We can then become free of our suffering that comes with our attachment to resisting flowing with our Life.

12. Inner peace or serenity is knowing, practicing, and being all of the above. We ultimately discover that we are already and always Serenity and Home.

(Some sources: Perennial philosophy, Christ, Tao, Muktananda, Fox, Wilber, Free John, Smith, Huxley, Schuon, and many other thinkers and sages.)

Chapter 24. Love and the Human Unconscious

Many alcoholics/CD's and co-dependents who are well into a solid recovery notice that they often repeat the same mistakes, whether they be in intimate or in less intimate relationships or in the way they perceive or feel about themselves. We may go out with or marry the same type person, or we may get into the same kinds of trouble, or we might feel that we are unworthy, over and over. Often, such repeated mistakes are indications of unresolved internal conflicts that have their roots in our unconscious and/or in our conscious mind.

We have been aware of our unconscious mind for thousands of years. Our imaginations and creativity - through the work of artists, poets, philosophers, mystics and others - gave us some of our most beautiful and useful expressions of and connections with our unconscious. But it was not until the past five centuries, perhaps starting with Paracelsus, Shakespeare, Spinoza and others, and especially over the past two centuries, with thinkers and intuiters such as Liebniz, the Romantic poets, Freud, Jung and Erickson, that our current knowledge of the unconscious unfolded (Mora 1980). And even with our knowledge of it, it remains a mystery. Some of what we do know can be summarized briefly as follows.

In its simplest definition, our unconscious is that in our life which we are not conscious (Oxford Engl Dict 1982). A part of us usually screens out its energies and experiential possibilities. Indeed, there is so much going on within us and around us, that to keep from being overwhelmed, our mind-brain screens or filters out that vast amount of information. Like the obverser self and the personal or object self (see "Watching the Dance . . ." in part II), when our conscious mind is most operative, our uncounscious mind tends to become less operative. And vice versa. For mental health, we appear to need a balance between the time that we spend in our conscious state and in a state in which we are in touch with our unconscious. We sleep and dream up to one third of our time, and we often go into a normal trance, whether it be in daydreaming, working a 12 Step recovery program, or in meditation or prayer.

The limited knowledge that we have of our unconsious can be described, mapped or diagrammed in many ways (realizing, again, that the map is not the territory). A few of these are as follows.

The first is Topographic which developed throughout the early period of Freud and others (Stewart 1980). Herein is described the conscious, the preconscious (or "subconscious"), which is easier to access than the unconscious, and the unconscious, which is more difficult to access. Later, Assagioli, and others called the unconscious the "superconscious" to avoid the perjorative connotations of the prefix "un-". This aspect of our psyche or our soul is related to high spiritual issues rather than to the dark, animal instincts of the Freudian conceived unconscious. DiLeo and others do not find this distinction necessary, because if we pursue the most dispicable aspects of our unconscious mind to its very depth, we move right into the highest level of the superconscious. This illustrates the psychologial and spiritual principle of complimentarity (DiLeo 1983-84).

The next model is the Evolutionary-Developmental, which includes the oral, anal, and gental (phallic, Oedipal) phases of human development in relation to the unconscious. While the implications of the early descriptions of the Oedipal phase have not proved to be strong, this model is nonetheless useful. A third model is the Structural i.e. the it (id), I (ego) and over I (superego). The it (id) is described as the common matrix of the drives of the unconscious from which we each, from birth on, gradually develop our own I (ego), progressively substituting the reality principle for the pleasure principle. That substitution is said to take place under the influence of the over I (supergo), which consists largely of unconscious parental and social mores and rules. Ultimately, the function of the I (ego) is to harmonize the needs of our drives (instincts) without external expectations (Mora 1980; Stewart 1980).

There is also the Dynamic model, which is concerned with the primary process (e.g. symbols and otherwise illogical associations), condensations and displacement within the unconscious. Fifth is the Economic model, which is concerned with the energy of the unconscious. Here the unconscious can be seen as a vast area of the mind that is full of psychic energies and experiential gestalts that exist in a form akin to electromagnetic waves.

A sixth and final model is a more comprehensive one. It views the unconscious as all of the above, plus a more expansive entity: one that encompasses a Spiritual view, as described by parts of Freud's writings (Bettelheim 1983), by Jung, Grof, and others (Welwood 1977; Peck 1978, DiLeo 1983-84; Taub-Bynum 1984).
Throughout this book I have made several references to the transpersonal or spiritual nature of the unconsious (e.g. Chaps. 5, 9, 11, 22 and Figures 5, 7, 8, and 12). These include the personal, the perinatal and the transpersonal or collective unconscious.

Most of the above models of the unconscious are derived from a strict methodological technique in studying dreams and by an introspective study of the self. Indeed, we can each even conduct our own study on the unconscious aspects of our life and its unfolding, its sorrows and its joys, its resentments and its serenity. This becomes an experiential and a sharing kind of study in its most evolved form. What we notice - if we are more and more conscious or aware - is that a Mysterious part of us, of which we were heretofore perhaps uncertain, plays an increasingly important and even powerful role. Among others, it has been given the name the "unconscious".

Our unconscious is a repository of unfinished business. This "business" includes both given and collective, and individual and created material and experiences. Parts and dynamic components of our unconscious have been given numerous names. Some of these include (DiLeo 1983-84): 1) the above Freudian and dynamic models, including unconscious childhood fantasies, screened memories, phylogenetic memories, and fixation of libido, 2) engrams, primitive ego nuclei (Volkan), unconscious psychic conflicts (Brenner) and traumatic memories, 3) complexes, archetypes, and synchronicities (Jung), 4) self and object representation (British School), ideal self and ideal objects, 5) system of condensed experiences ("COEX"), basic perinatal matrices, transpersonal configurations and experiences (Grof), 6) identifications, charged images, and inner psychic lenses or filters (DiLeo), 7) levels of development (Piaget, Eri kson, etc.), 8) chakras or energy systems, samsaric impressions, and morphic resonance fields (Sheldrake). These names are so numerous and often seemingly disparate that they represent at the same time our knowledge and our lack of knowledge of our unconscious mind.

We can simplify our unconscious by constructing a map that illustrates its repository nature, as a container of unfinished business (Figure 12-A). In this illustration, we notice that our ordinary awareness or our conscious is separated from our unconscious by some mechanism, which we can postulate as being our ego/mind. But our ego/mind can be "opened" to access or communicate with our unconscious, much like the valves on a wind instrument or like the starting gates at a racetrack. Within the unconscious there are energies, complexes or experiences that are perhaps waiting to be completed. While each of these seems to be different, we can simplify them as being various bundles of unfinished pain or of joy (Figure 12-A). Each time that our unconscious is "activated", which occurs many times each day and night, whatever of our business is unfinished, incomplete, or necessary for us comes into our conscious mind in some form or other. It then becomes our task to deal with it, or not.

Figure 12A - A Scheme of the Human Unconscious, Showing it's Activation or Accessment to Our Conscious Mind by Low Activation and by High Activation Activity or Techniques.

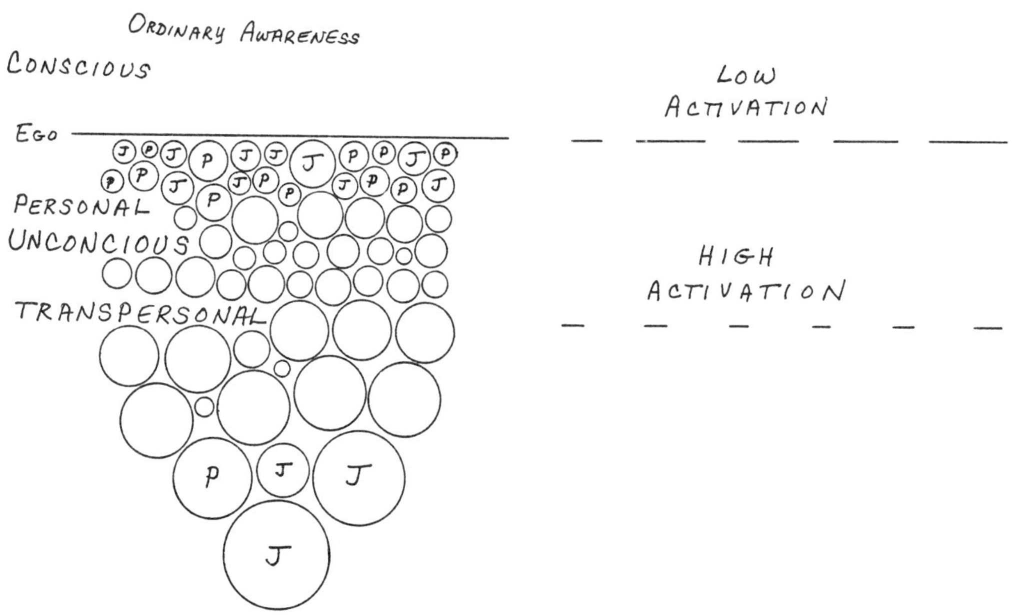

Some representations of experiencing this pain and joy are listed in Table 11-A. We usually want to run away from, to avoid the pain, and to embrace the joy. However, often related to a low self-esteem, many alcoholics/CD's and co-dependents may reverse this tendency, and prefer to stay in the pain, and become uneasy when joy appears, as if they are somehow unworthy of it. Getting free of this painful dynamic is part of a healthy recovery process, and can be facilitated by working the 12 Steps and in group therapy. While many recovering people and many others resist experiencing the joy within them, it can be helpful to reflect upon what A Course In Miracles says about joy, "There is no difference between love and joy. Joy is unified purpose. Sorrow can be turned to joy, for time gives way to the eternal. Joy does not return to sorrow, for the eternal cannot change. Joy is unlimited, because each shining thought of love extends its being and creates more of itself. What you seek is a source of joy as you conceive it. What is joyful to you is painful to the ego, and as long as you are in doubt about what you are you will be confused about joy and pain. Whenever you are not wholly joyous, it is because you have reacted with a lack of love to one of God's creations".

Table 11-A. Some Representations of Experiencing Pain and Joy (compiled & modified from DiLeo 1985).

Pain	Joy
Fear (anxiety to panic)	Unconditional Love
Death	Eternal and infinite existence
Shame, guilt and anger	Self-esteem, peace and serenity
Insanity	Ultimate understanding & peace of mind
Sadness and grief	Reasurance and contentment
Emptiness	Fulfillment
Suffering and anguish	Bliss and ecstasy
Sacrifice	Redemption and acceptance
Dread, horror and terror	Comfort, courage and peace
Ultimate failure	Ultimate victory
Blasphemy	Respect and adoration
Disgust	Heavenly delights
Hell	Paradise
Vipers and evil creatures	Angels and heavenly beings
Fire	Divine purity
Suffocation	Eternal breath and expansion
Eternal damnation	Ultimate and permanent salvation
Ignorance	Everlasting knowledge
Chaos and darkness	Harmony and Inner Light
Killing, hate, violence and destruction	Rebirth, love, peace and creation
Unbridled sexuality	Spiritual embrace

What activates or opens the gates to the unconscious appears to be a series of at least thirty normal, healthy functions and techniques, as well as some human-contrived ones (Table 11-B). Perhaps the most powerful of these functions and techniques are shown from the bottom-up of this list. For example, it appears that having a near-death experience is the most powerful opener of our unconscious. Since alcoholics, CD's and co-dependents get into repeated trouble using alcohol or other psychoactive drugs, using drugs to acess the unconscious is too dangerous, and there are so many other effective ways to do so. An increasingly popular technique among recovering people and others is that of holonomic integration, which is described in Chapter 10. Meditation and prayer are also powerful ways to open ourselves to our unconscious, especially to the joyous parts. Working a 12-Step program or equivalent self-help program, including telling our story, is also a very useful way of opening our unconscious. And there are numerous other ways, as listed in the remainder of Table 11-B.

Table 11-B. Some Techniques for Activating and Accessing the Unconscious: Rough Estimations According to Time Duration and Effectiveness (compiled in part from Jung, Assagioli, Freud, Muktananda, Erickson, and DiLeo)

Time Duration		Effectiveness (per time)
Longer		Less
	Daydreaming	
	Some biofeedback	
	Free association	
	Physical exercise and fasting	
	Deep muscle relaxation	
	Certain psychoactive drugs, low dose	
	Relaxation techniques	
	Paradox and reversal	
	Dreaming and dream analysis	
	Using affirmations	
	Guided imagery	
	Working a 12 Step Program	
	Storytelling and metaphor	
	Psychosynthesis	
	Art, movement, psychodrama and play therapy	
	Transference	
	Using intuition	
	Therapeutic bodywork	
	Active Imagination	
	Hypnosis	
	Meditation, prayer	
	Certain breathing techniques	
	Psychedelic drugs with appropriate psychotherapy	
	Near death experience	
Shorter		More

When we open the gates of our unconscious, whatever is there, comes up. Whatever is below the surface is what we experience, whether it may be joy or pain. For example, many alcoholics/CD's and co-dependents have used a psychedelic drug, but when they did, they did not consciously use it for the specific purpose of "opening their unconscious." If they had a "bad trip," they may have blamed it on the drug. With what we now know about this phenomenon, the most likely reason for their unpleasant experience was not the drug, but the fact that what was there, in their unconscious, is what came up. Also, their "set and setting" (i.e. mind set and environmental setting) may have influenced the experience.

Some of what we have learned from people's experiences in accessing the unconscious are the following. First, the more we practice communicating with our unconscious, the easier it becomes to access it and to know it. This allows us to get more and more in touch with the totality (e.g. sanity, from Step Two) of our being. And as we do so, our life tends to get gradually better. Also, we discover that we can begin to "program" our unconscious, and thus our life, by such techniques as using affirmations, meditating, praying, or working the 12 Steps. We thus become a co-creator of our life, in concert with Life or Process (which are descriptive words for Higher Power). While all of this is not "easy" in the strict sense of the word, as we are now becoming and taking more and more co-responsibility for making our lives work, and we experience many growing pains, nonethleless, our life tends to get better over the long run.

The more that we work with our unconscious, the more we discover that we have - within us - a rich repository of memories and skills that we can call upon, even after many years (Erickson and Rosen 1982). Indeed, we can trust our unconscious mind to produce appropriate responses at the right time, when we need them.

The deeper that we go, i.e. surrender, into our unconscious, the closer we come to what we can call its farthest reaches. While our unconscious remains a mystery, it may be, at its "end", pure joy, pure serenity. When we have worked through all of our stories or unfinished business, what may well remain is pure unconditional Love. Since our most simple and accurate description of Higher Power may be that of Unconditional Love, we can now postulate that our unconscious, at its depth, is Higher Power. Put another way, a road to realizing Higher Power, and to serenity, is through our unconscious. To repeat Peck's (1978) quote from chapter 5, "If you desire wisdom greater than your own, you can find it inside you. What this suggests is that the interface between God and man is at least in part an interface between our unconscious and our conscious. To put it plainly, our unconscious is God. God within us. We were part of God all the time".

If a part of God is our unconscious, then it may follow that a part of each of our levels of consciousness has an unconscious dimension to it. As we continue to learn more and more about ourselves, we become more in touch with this otherwise hidden dimension. If health is inner peace, through being our higher levels of awareness, then continued inner peace and health may also be being in frequent touch and harmony with our unconscious.

What Freud and many other depth psychologists have learned and would offer to us is that we become more aware of our unconscious. When we then find ourselves at a crossroad, in a dilemma or repeating the same unwanted pattern, not knowing which way to turn, and feeling blocked, we will not act out inappropriately or in an unhealthy way. We will not, in moments of great stress, be pushed by our unconscious to act in ways that will destroy us (Bettelheim 1984). In short, we will not be the victim of our unconscious and as we grow, we learn that we can become a co-creater with our unconscious, which appears to be a part or extension of Higher Power.

We learn that what we previously thought of as something alien that we need to deny, resist or parry is really a very important and useful part of us, and that it is to our advantage to recognize what it is and to integrate it into our personality and our being. We also learn that we can create both wanted and unwanted patterns or dynamics that we then deposit into our unconscious. We can create either good or bad, positive or negative, creative or destructive, joy or pain, death or rebirth and then plant it into our unconscious. In addition to this created material, we also seem to inherit or are given material for us to work upon, both individual and collective in nature. It is in part the struggle within us to resolve these materials and issues that make for our physical, mental, emotional and spiritual richness and growth, and which gives our life its deepest meaning. When we learn to balance and then to healthily resolve our conflicts in the ever changing process of co-creation, we realize that we were and are, always and already, serenity itself.

Chapter 25. Family, Children and Other Relationships

Throughout this book I have described the importance of spirituality in families and in other intimate relationships. Family, children and other intimate relationships are involved in a crucial way in one of the key definitions of spirituality described above: that spirituality is concerned with our relationships in three life areas: 1) self, 2) others, and 3) universe. When viewed in this way, interacting and participating with others then becomes a major spiritual practice.

The recovery of the person who is close to the alcoholic/CD, sometimes called co-alcoholic or co-dependent, follows many, if not most of the same dynamics and problems as the alcoholic/CD person. The resulting damage is as important to address and to heal as that of the chemical dependent. Their recovery process also progresses in the same manner as that of the chemical dependent, i.e. through physical, mental and spiritual processes.

The principles that I discuss about love and unconditional love apply equally in the family members. While most are seeking unconditional acceptance and love, during active illness and early recovery they tend to be stuck, addicted or attached to the lower levels of love (see Table 11). Paradoxically, that which they are so desperately seeking, they are so often desperately pushing away. This is in part due to the fact that active co-dependents usually need to use all of their resources to survive. To do so can keep them stuck at the lowest level of consciousness, Survival. They also frequently function on the Passion and lower part of the Ego/mind level, but seldom seem to get higher.

Clinicians working with this illness describe active alcoholic/CD/co-alcoholic families and other relationships by several characteristics: they are unpredictable, arbitrary, inconsistent, and chaotic, and most of all painful. These are part of the "crazy-making" disease of alcoholism/CD. They emphasize that it was not a question of whether your close relationships loved you, because most likely they did. But because of their illness, they could not express their love to you in a consistent, healthy, and loving way. "And if your parents (or other close people) sometimes accused you of causing the problems, it was only because they themselves were at a loss to understand why everything was falling apart, why they were behaving the way they were and why they were drinking the way they were drinking (or using drugs). By beginning to gradually acknowledge your early painful experiences, you will be able, perhaps for the first time, to find the meaning of all those feelings. And you can begin to forgive yourself, knowing that you were not resposible for what happended " (Gravitz & Bowden 1984).

Children of Alcoholics & Co-alcoholics

I mentioned above the parallels of the Twelve Step Al-Anon program to our life's journey through our levels of consciousness. Gravitz and Bowden (1984) have described six stages through which adult children of alcoholics tend to go during their recovery. These also parallel the seven levels of consciousness and the Al-Anon Program. They include the following stages: 1) survival, 2) emergent awareness, 3) core issues, 4) transformation, 5) integration, and 6) genesis. In describing the emergent awareness stage, they use the term "awakening" in which they describe a process that is similar, if not identical, to the spiritual awakening described above. The term emergent awareness addresses the person's changing level of consciousness.

The core issues with which the person tends to have the most problems, and with which they need to grapple during their recovery, pervade the fundamental issues of spiritual and transpersonal psychology. As they and others describe, among these issues are those of control, willpower, trust, responsibility, self-nurture, self-esteem, giving and receiving love, and recognizing and handling feelings (Cermak and Brown 1982; Gravitz and Bowden 1984). The struggle of working with these issues is analogous to the struggle of the hero/heroine's spiritual journey through life. Later, during the transformation and integration stages, the person continues to be tested upon these key issues, and during the genesis stage they continue to become more and more free of their attachments to their resentments about their families and their pasts.

Many children of alcoholics receive a double test, in that they also eventually become alcoholic or chemical dependent themselves. Although we would never wish such suffering upon them, it is possible that there is another important lesson for them to learn during their life's journey.

Those who work closely with adult children of alcoholics believe that they are a primary target for the prevention of alcoholism and chemical dependence. A potential problem is that many prevention workers conceive of prevention in a somewhat limited view. For example, law enforcement officials view prevention as making things illegal and intervening through penalties and punishment. Thus, they understand prevention as a problem of environment or availability. If one were to make an analogy of this view with our seven levels of consciousness, it would correspond to the Survival level. Others view prevention as a social, cultural or behavioral phenomenon (similar to level two, Passion). Still others view it as an interpersonal, an intrapsychic, or a self-esteem problem (level three, Ego/mind).

It may be useful to expand this lower self - oriented model of prevention. For example, at level four, Acceptance, one could view prevention through a commitment to growth of self and relationships, which happens often through working through conflicts and nurturing self and others. At the upper portion of this level, prevention is forgiving others and especially ourself. At level five, Understanding, prevention is being creative, through using our imagination and our other creative faculties. At level six, Compassion, prevention is unconditional love. And at level seven, Unity Consciousness, it is pure Being.

Whether alcohol-related or not, being in a family pushes us into relating intimately with others. Since it is fairly difficult to maintain a self image as being totally different from others when we are forced to be at least somewhat intimate with them, we are constantly reminded of our Oneness. Also, by knowing our children, parents and grandparents, and our brothers and sisters, we come to experience and to know deeply other dimensions of our own continuity (Rhead 1984). It is possible that even through alcoholism and other difficult times within a family, we each learn to become whole. To do so, we may need to encounter and experience our struggles. And then we can begin to transcend them. The fellowships of Al-Anon and Alateen are helpful to us in doing so. Also, couples group therapy and family therapy can be helpful.

Relationships also test our illusions about our ability to control things in our lives. Through them we come face to face with our own limitations (McKeon 1983). We are thereby continually encouraged to surrender to a power that is greater than we are, and by so doing we become more fulfilled, complete and whole.

In a couples relationship there is another spiritual dimension, that of sexual union. Here the experience of giving and receiving pleasure gets so blended that in our most ecstatic moments we lose our boundaries and have a unitive experience (Rhead 1984). The most sublime sexual union can be a reminder and a manifestation of our Oneness.

Vissell and Vissell (1984) write, "What we really see in our loved one - what we are really attracted to - is what we have not yet opened to in ourself. The beauty and wholeness which has always been within us we first project onto our beloved. Then we yearn to be with our beloved and enter full swing into the cosmic dance of relationships. Finally, the dance awakens us to the remembrance of our wholeness and holiness. However, unless we enter fully this dance of love, we might remain on the sidelines yearning for that which we already have." A Course in Miracles expands this statement to our global family of humankind: "When you meet anyone, remember it is a Holy encounter. As you see him you will see yourself. As you treat him you will treat yourself. As you think of him you will think of yourself. Never forget this,for in him you will find yourself or lose yourself."

The denial that we see as characteristic of the alcoholic, chemical dependent and co-alcoholic represents a powerful and complex process (Whitfield 1984). This denial is analagous to our "forgetting" our Higher Self, that we are connected to and are a part of a Higher Power. The denial by society, including many helping professionals, that these illnesses are primary problems and are highly treatable, tends to perpetuate the suffering. Fortunately, many of them are becoming more sophisticated about these problems and many professional schools are beginning to teach about this illness and how it affects the family.

As I have discussed throughout this book, each of us has several important issues with which to deal throughout our lives. Some of these are: control, trust, dependence/independence, self-esteem, difficulty with intimate relationships, spontaneity, and feelings (e.g. anger and resentment, sadness and emptiness, shame and guilt) and the inability to enjoy life and feel good. Alcoholics/CD's and co-dependents have all of these issues, though they tend often to have them in an exaggerated fashion. We deal with these issues 1) on all levels of our being, 2) with our self and with others, and we do so 3) repeatedly. Through a spiritual program of recovery, we begin to discover that every issue that we have with our family and other intimate relationships, we also have with Higher Power. In various ways we work on and work out our conflicts with God as we understand It.

Our conflicts with God generally center around two major areas, both which are related to our ego/mind's difficulty giving up "control". One is the univeral question or conflict of good versus evil, and how a loving God could allow so much evil and suffering. I have discussed this dilemma throughout this book, and especially under "Thinking Positively" in part II. This is also discussed in numerous books and articles, e.g. Kushner 1981 and Peck 1983. Our second area of conflict with God centers around our guilt over our having left It. We work through this guilt throughout our lives, with pain and suffering of all sorts, from feeling numb, angry, sad, empty and alone, until we discover that this conflict was all an illusion. We never left God, and God did not leave us. God was in us and we were in God all along. Only by our being attached to our ego/mind did we suffer. Yet, this process seems to be necessary, so that we can better know God. Each time that we "remember", whether it be through meditation, working the Steps, or working on a relationship, we get - gradually - closer to our Higher Power, to Universal Consciousness. Our conflicts with God are our ways of separaing from and then returning to God and to discovering the serenity that is already and always within us.

Unconditional Love

Kubler-Ross said that our greatest grief is over our never having experienced unconditional love (KR 1982). Unconditional love is not only available to each of us, but it is within us. We can remove the blocks to love's presence, and by so shifting our perception we create a miracle - we are Love (Jampolsky 1982). There is but one major block to being love: our ego, and paradoxically, it can be a major path to being love. Our ego generates attachments and expectations, which build a wall around us so that we cannot experience our Self. It also tries to convince us of our ultimate greatest illusion: that we are separate from the Whole (Free John 1983). This is why meditating and other spiritual practices lead us to our Self, which is Love, because by practicing them we transcend our ego. Each of us can listen to two voices. If we listen to our Self or our Higher Power, we will always find peace, whether now or eventually. If at the same time we listen to our mind, we may be hearing two voices in conflict. When we listen only to our ego/mind, we do not hear the voice of reality, which is forgiveness, love, and peace, and instead we are hurt and stressed, and we can become ill (Steinberg & Martin 1981).

We often hear that before we can love another we have to love ourself. While this is true in part - i.e. we have to have a healthy self-esteem, to be " somebody special ", before we can let go into being Nobody Special - waiting is not necessary. The way we get love, i.e. become love, is to give it away, to love someone - not conditionally - but unconditionally. People who are controlling and manipulating, such as actively drinking alcoholics and their close familiy members - and many other people - often have great difficulty surrendering into loving unconditionally. They are stuck at the lower levels of love, in their lower selves. Indeed, they may be in a dependent or an addicted relationship (Table 12), which may ocur in any relationship, although they occur commonly in alcoholic/CD families and their other relationships. If we cannot give unconditional love, we can ask our Higher Power that we can be a channel of unconditional love.

Table 12. Some Contrasts between Authentic Love and an Addicted Relationship (adapted and modified from Peck 1978, Branden 1979, and Capell-Sowder, 1984)

Authentic Love	Addicted Relationship
Open system	Closed system
Higher Self oriented	Lower self (ego/mind) oriented
Commit ment to other's physical - mental - spiritual growth	Lack of committment
Based on trust and acceptance through conflict	Based on neediness, security comfort, infatuation, jealousy, possession ("protects supply") and worship
Separate friends and interests	Same or limited friends and interests
High self-esteem	Low self-esteem. Seeks others for identity approval and self-esteem
Mutual integrity and respect	One partner's needs suspended for the other's self-deprivation
Willingness to risk and be authentic	Unwillingness to risk and be authentic
Encourages exploring feelings in and out of relationship	Discourages exploring feelings ; reassurance through repeated ritualized activity
Enjoys being alone	Uncomfortable being alone, can be severe ("withdrawal")
Fulfilling	Unfulfilling
Highest form is unconditional	Conditional
Accepts breakups without loss of own integrity and self-esteem	Loss of self-esteem and integrity at breakup
Can become friends after breakup	Cannot become friends ; may manipulate to get back ("craving")

Seeking happiness is less important than becoming free by expanding our consciousness. Although we usually feel happy or content when we love unconditionally, love's purpose is not to make us feel safe and secure. Rather, it is to invite us to reach deeper into our experience of life. We don't have to love someone outside of ourselves for us to receive love, i.e. to be love. We already have it in our Acceptance/heart level and in our Self. Here, we are alive, vibrant and non-judgemental, and through it we lift ourselves and our loved ones to higher levels of consciousness (Moss 1981). Love is thus not only what we are at our core, but is also a vehicle to expand our awareness to our Self and to others. We can thereby view its dynamics as our ultimate positive, nurturing, and unending cycle.

The way that love expands our consciousness and helps us grow is in the power of its energy (Kundalini, Chi, etc.). When love is absent, the opposite of growth occurs: stagnation and entropy (Peck 1978). We thus experience the down swing of non-growth, as shown below.

↓	↑
Fear	Love
Stagnation	Growth (positive transformation)
Projection	Extension
Laziness	Work
Evil (ultimate laziness)	Awareness
Death	Rebirth
Illusion	Reality
Defense mechanisms	Accepting reality
Entropy	Negentropy
Natural law	Universal law

Our mind's natural inclination is to fear, to react with its ego defense mechanisms, including projection and blaming the world, and to be lazy, to stagnate, and to wither away. This is part of our mind's natural law, part of the "human condition". And alcoholism, co-alcoholism and other states feed and exaggerate this natural law. But our mind is connected to our Self (Figs 5 and 7, in parts I & II). It is not only connected to our Self, but it can be viewed as being our contracted Self, i.e. it is contracted Consciousness (Muktananda 1981). Our mind can thus help us to reverse and to balance our natural law by transmuting it into our universal law of loving, extending, working, being aware, accepting reality, and growing (Small 1982). We each thus have and are pure Love, and when it is absent, i.e. blocked, we experience fear. This is how love is letting go of fear. When we grow, it is because we are working at it (working here includes surrendering), and we are working at it because we love ourselves (Peck 1978). Universal Consciousness wants us to become and return to Itself through our evolution, and the energy or force that provides our evolution is Love. We are thus the paradox of both being Love and using it to Be, i.e. it is a vehicle to reach itself. We are our own vehicle to reach our Self.

We also use our absence of love - which may be manifested by fear - to re-discover our love, to re-discover our Self, to reach and to be Universal Consciousness. And while alcoholism and other controlling behaviors can be viewed as being a manifestation of the absence of love, we can view these conditions in us as being at the same time a manifestation of our seeking love. They are both our curse and our gift. This sense is conveyed in the following verse.

Emptiness,
The feeling that something is missing
The stalker in the night,
The lonely wanderer, the void,
The goader to attachment and addiction,
No color, all colors, formless and form,
The healer, the necessary doorway,
The vessel for Universal Energy.

(Modified from Aarons 1983)

Love includes surrender and trust. When we face the challange of a major disease such as alcoholism and co-alcoholism, if we can surrender and trust, we can begin to move toward an experience of love to a degree that we probably never had. We may even wonder if the emptiness we feel, the feeling that something is missing in our lives, all along has been love : love in the deepest and most unconditional sense, and love as a new energy that unifies our psyche with a feeling of wholeness (Moss 1981).

Love is another paradox: it is both selfish and unselfish. Love is not simply giving. It is judicious giving, praising and comforting, and judicious withholding, arguing and confronting as well. Love's aim is always spiritual growth (Peck 1978) and celebration. It is a daily celebration of our aliveness and our permission to go deeper into our aliveness.

Having an awakening of our consciousness eventually includes an awakening of our love. We can be either led or forced to it by realizing that the quality of our love that we formerly knew has been narrow, self-serving, and limiting to us and to our relationships (Moss 1981). This new level of awareness - unconditional love - is surrendering all our thoughts and emotions that separate us from harmony and serenity. However, another paradox may present itself: when we experience it and become it, we can begin to think that love is in all ways " better " than some other experience, (although it feels so good). Thinking that way, we can become unhealthily attached to love in ourselves and in others, so that we may become unaccepting of where another is in our relationship with them, or unaccepting of our own uncomfortable emotions.

Whether it be alcoholism, co-alcoholism, or some other illness, we can view disease as either a defense or a barrier against the truth or as an external searching for love, or both. Disease is both a barrier and a way out. From the view of our Higher Self, we can thus view sickness as an illusion, when in reality it is a problem given to us to help us experience the truth, and our love. And our truth is that we are God's children, whole, on all our levels of consciousness, with the capacity to be loving and forgiving (Steinberg & Martin 1981). To maintain our love, we must both experience and forgive. Maintaining our love means living in and being our Self, and forgiving means forgiving everyone, including our loved ones, our self and even our enemies (King 1963). Even if loving, experiencing and forgiving are themselves an illusion, they are pleasant and growth-inducing ones.

We can begin to view the word "sin" as its original Greek meaning "off the mark" or "off center", rather than through a right/wrong or moral view, which some organized religions have taught us. In whatever path we chose to travel, we can view our separation from our wholeness from a number of somewhat different, yet mostly similar, perspectives. These are shown in Table 13. The result is our suffering. And we can use our suffering to re-discover our connectedness to the universe, to the One. All we need do is remember and forgive. What is left is who we in essence are - Unconditional Love.

Love is the most healing and therapeutic remedy, medicine or energy known to humankind. The helping professional who cares for his patient/client, and who demonstrates it, will likely help in the person's getting well. The therapist loves the patient at the higher levels of consciousness, and not in a sexual, romantic or possessive way. Appendix H shows several characteristics of an effective therapist. About half of these represent supportive characteristics and the other half confrontive ones, or " Tough love " (York & Wachtel 1983). An ultimate expression of love by a therapist is, while at the same time working with the patient, also working on him- or herself. For the optimal growth of the patient, the physical, mental and spiritual development and awareness of the therapist are equally as important as that of the patient. This does not mean that the therapist does not need to have strong basic skills in helping people get well and grow. A firm foundation of such clinical skills is indeed necessary. The complete therapist remains aware of all of his or her own levels of consciousness (Appendix I). On another level, the relationship of helper and helped, clinician and patient/client, and teacher and student - and these principles - are applicable in a broader sense in every aspect of our lives and in every one of our relationships.

Appendix H. Some Characteristics of an Effective Alcoholism and Chemical Dependence Therapist (from Truax & Carkhuff 1969, Wolf 1972, Peck 1978, Small 1981, Whitfield 1983)

Empathy	Ability to perceive another's experience and then communicate that perception back to the person. Said in " I " statements, feelings and here-and-now.
Genuineness	Ability of therapist to be freely himself - non-phoniness, non-role playing, non-defensiveness. His outer words and behavior match his inner feelings.
Respect	Ability to communicate to the patient/client the sincere belief that every person possesses the inherent strength to make it in life, and that each person has the right to chose his own alternatives and make his own decisions.
Self-disclosure	Sharing and exposing the therapist's own feelings, attitudes and experiences with a client for the sake of the client. Never used for the therapist's own need to confess or ventillate, it is used in an accurate context, content, and timing so as to be therapeutic.
Warmth	Non-verbal behaviors, such as smiles, voice inflection, touching (non-sexual), and at times even tears shed with a person suffering a loss or experiencing great joy.
Immediacy	Dealing with feelings between therapist and patient in the here-and-now through open sharing.
Concreteness	Keeping person talking about himself and his own feelings, including what, when, where and how of relevant concerns of the now.
Confrontation	Bringing the person face to face with his reality as you perceive him or her as a whole person. Used only appropriately (see text).
Potency	Being in command of self and communicating a dynamic, involved attitude.
Self-actualization	Therapist flows with the patient and the process, self accepting and able to learn and grow from the patient. Therapist is non-judgmental, flexible and spontaneious. Uses all of above characteristics.
Creativity	From both content and process, using all faculties, including intuition, therapist discovers, formulates, and institutes new and useful approaches and changes for growth of both patient and therapist.
Ego-transcendence	Therapist transcends own ego, allowing for a grater therapeutic range and degree of creativity, intuitive understanding, compassion and caring.
Caring	Extending oneself to nurture the patient's growth. Willingness to risk and to struggle with patient and with self. Related to warmth, above. Love at the higher levels of consciousness.
Responsibility	Taking time and extending oneself to respond constructively to transcend the patient's denial and acting out to guide the patient to recovery, e.g. calling patient at missed appointments.
Detachment	After doing and being all of the above, remaining unattached to the therapeutic outcome. Helps prevent therapist burn-out.

Appendix I

Some Principles and Assumptions of Transpersonal Psychotherapy

(compiled from Sutich 1969, 1973, 1976; Meadow et al 1979; Ram Dass 1974-83; Vaughan 1982; Whitfield 1984 & Morrison 1984)

1) We have a strong base of clinical skills in any of a number of disciplines (Principle)

   a Our helping requires a foundation of effective skills. (Assumptions)

   b Our approach is eclectic, cross cultural & multidisciplinary.

   c We use an extensive body of knowledge that has accumulated through the ages.

   d We honor the importance of the individual's having a strong ego or personal self.

   e While we use our skills functionally, we do not identify with them.

2) We help people with their problems and their lives on all levels of consciousness.

   a We know that people can attain levels of psychological health that surpass what is commonly accepted as normal.

   b We address blocks or "being stuck" within the lower self and the Higher Self.

   c We are concerned with people's belief systems, their true identity, their relationship with self, others and universe, and with their growth of and through consciousness.

   d Thus, our consciousness itself is both the object and the instrument of change.

   e We are students of the process of transformation.

3) We work "from our heart" as well as our head.

   a We recognize that there are other ways of knowing than our senses and intellect. We keep our imagination open.

   b When appropriate, we can view symptoms and illness as part of a creative process.

   c We can thus view aberrent behavior as not necessarily pathological, but possibly that our patients or clients know something that we don't know.

   d We know that individual differences are manifestations of form, and not of Essence or Self.

   e We do not see motives, cognitive structures and attitudes as a person's identity, but merely as their forms of expression.

4) We regard the therapeutic relationship as an honor and a privilege.

   a Our patients and clients are providing us with a new and important opportunity for psychological and spiritual growth.

   b They are our teachers, as we are theirs.

   c Their therapeutic issues and their lives bear directly upon our own.

   d Our meeting is not accidental. It is purposeful.

5) Unconditional acceptance of the patient or client is essential.

   a The essence of our beings is love.

   b The essential Self is universal.

   c When we unconditionally accept the client, we accept ourselves.

   d We can interpret all behaviors as expressions of love or as reaching out for love.

   e When appropriate, "tough love" and limit setting are a strong and healing energy.

6) Through our own giving, we transform.

   a We cannot change the patient or client, only our own attitudes and actions.

   b Loving is giving.

   c We heal ourselves by giving love.

   d Our own healing process is a transformative force.

7) We welcome conflict as an opportunity for growth and transcendence.

   a Conflict is a necessary vehicle for spiritual growth.

   b Life is ultimately fair.

   c While we treat conflict with reverence, we hold empathy for the burdens of pain and suffering.

   d We view accepting paradox as a way to inner peace.

8) We engage in Transpersonal Psychotherapy in part for our own continuing self-healing. We must work on ourselves if therapy is to succeed.

   a We are not gurus or self-realized spiritual teachers.

   b We can neither control nor change our clients, only ourselves.

   c Our issues are mutually interdependent. Therefore, progress in therapy demands that we work too.

   d We work on ourselves by not just filling our minds with constructs, but rather in simultaneously learning to empty our minds into quietness.

9) Although we are engaged in self-healing, we address the person's needs, not our own.

   a Healing is giving.

   b We can neither define nor enforce the process of spiritual growth for another person.

   c All issues and conflicts, no matter how mundane, are vehicles for spiritual growth.

   d Ego strengthening (individuation) is prerequisite to transcendence.

10) By giving-up control of the psychotherapeutic process, we gain control.

   a We are not in ultimate control.

   b In Transpersonal Psychotherapy, we actively participate in surrendering control to the Self within.

11) We always view the patient or client as an equal.

   a The Self within is universal.

   b Perceptions of inequality, by ourselves or the client, signal needs for transpersonal growth and healing.

12) Transpersonal Psychotherapy is free.

   a The patient or client fee pays for our time, our training, and skills we have acquired.

   b The fee does not pay for the opportunity for spiritual growth and self-healing the patient gives us.

   c It does not pay for the struggles and joys we encounter enroute to our self-healing.

13) Therapy is not limited to the therapy hour.

   Our relationships, personal struggles, dreams, meditations and prayers all bear upon the therapeutic relationship.

14) Our relationship with the client is a lasting one — beyond the limits of the therapeutic contract.

   We forge a transpersonal kinship with our patient or client via our own committment to a spiritual therapeutic relationship.

Regarding people who are doubters, Moss (1981) wrote " Sometimes a person will approach me and say ' Well I guess you're another one of those poeple who says that all there is is love '. I get the feeling that this person thinks he has got me and love all figured out. I smile at how the mind, because it can say the words, beguiles itself into thinking it knows. The mind is a coward, and most of our approaches to life are cowardly. But to approach the process of health and disease from the perspective of conscious transformation and unconditional love is certainly not the experiment of cowards. One is no longer in the realm of simple answers, burying one's head in the sand, projecting magic powers on healers, or hiding behind spiritual dogma. One is in the cauldron through which the heart is opened, wisdom is learned and a whole new level of Beingness may be attained".

Table 13. Similarities among Terms for Separation from Wholeness, the Resulting Suffering, and the Solution or Way Out.

	Organized Christian	Buddhist/Hindu/ Tao	Perennial Philosophy	Course in Miracles (revised Christian)
Terms for Separation from Wholeness	Sin	Ignorance, Ego-attachment	Fragmented consciousness	Forgetting, "distorted lens," dream, illusion, mistake
Result	Eternity separated from God	Suffering	Suffering	Fear, separation, suffering (guilt + shame)
Way Out	Faith in Christ Repentence & Community	Understanding, Insight, Compassion	Realizing God within, Wholeness	Remember Forgive Love

Muktananda (1975) said, " Love is the sole reason for living and the sole purpose of life. We are able to live only if there is love. If we think love has left us, we become desperate. When we experience real love, we get into a state that is beyond words. We are filled with a joy that goes beyond all emtoions. We are searching for love because we do not go inside. . . . To attain love you have to become love. When you meet a friend after a long time and embrace him, you close your eyes and go within and for a fraction of a second you feel joy within yourself. That joy is nothing but a shadow of the inner love - the love of the Self. . . . Everything is inside you. The one you are looking for is you. The one you want to attain is you. "

Chapter 26. Conclusion

We can now see that alcoholism, co-alcoholism, and other attachments are multi-dimensional conditions among our levels of consciousness. At level one, Survival, alcoholism and co-alcoholism are a toxicity. They destroy our tissues and can destroy our lives. At level two, Passion, they are painful, controlling, and very bothersome. At level three, Mind or ego, they are a stigma, an embarassment and a curse. Level four, Acceptance, presents a turning point: While we experience ambivalence about being alcoholic or co-alcoholic, part of that ambivalence is that we might be able to recover, learn something about ourselves, and grow. At level five, Understanding, we know that having the disease of alcoholism or of co-alcoholism is a gift. At level six, Compassion, we hope others don't fall victim to them and yet we accept it in them when it occurs, and we help them when we can. Finally, at level seven, Unity Consciousness, we are pure Being, pure Serenity. We forgive others and ourselves.

The subject of spirituality is so vast, whether in recovery from alcoholism/CD, or in any other area, that such a discussion as this is but the briefest of introductions. It is clear that spirituality plays a major role in recovery. Indeed, I and many others believe that a person cannot recover to complete mental and physical health, to wholeness, without it. In short, recovery is spirituality.

The ultimately aware spiritual person lives and is all seven levels of consciousness at the same time, accepting the ups and the downs as they come, and experiencing every second of it all. To do so takes risking, which can bring great benefits. The whole spiritual person uses everything that comes as a teaching and as a learning experience, and thus goes through a lifelong series of transformations and personal growth. The person is not only fully awake, but fully conscious of everything that is happening, both outside and inside him or herself. And at the same time he or she is no " better " than the person who is not so aware, only more conscious of life.

The more fully conscious and aware we become, the more often life becomes interesting and exciting, and the better we are able to handle our difficulties. Even so, entering and living on a spiritual path is not easy. Indeed, because of our increased awareness, at times doing so seems more difficult.

Regarding his own spirituality and personal transformations, Prather (1980) said, " I had long since been through my night of crisis and therefore had already seen that I had no personal way of being certain of anything. And yet I was continuing to act on a set of new assumptions : that one could trust the events of his life; that each person would be provided whatever he needed to do the work he had been given; that the nature of that work was not known or knowable to his ego; that everything he did, every act, thought, fantasy, dream and feeling contributed helpfully and precisely to the overall purpose of his life; that ultimately there were no mistakes in any of this and therefore no grounds for judging himself or others; and that on some level he did not yet understand, everything was his decision and responsibility. "

We can now see that there is only one disease - being separate. And there is only one cure - Unity. And from such a vantage point we can know, through our Understanding level, that a spiritual approach to healing is compatible with any approach. Indeed, it generally re-enforces, supports and encourages that approach. However, it may be difficult to find a friend or a helping professional to talk with who understands what we mean by experiences such as transformation and spirituality.

I and countless others far wiser than I believe that every aspect of our lives, every thing we do, can be viewed as and experienced as being spiritual. If we use it and are it, spirituality is thus one-hundred percent practical in our life. In the long run, it is the most efficient stress management. Our life has far more richness and joy than our minds would lead us to believe.

It is all spiritual.

References

1. Aarons K: Emptiness and the Holy Spirit. Talk given at Common Boundary Conference, Washington, DC, 10 November 1983
2. Alcoholics Anonymous: The Story of How Many Thousands of Men and Women Have Recovered from Alcoholism. 3rd edition. AA World Services, Box 459, Grand Central Sta, NY, 10163, 1976
3. Al-Anon Pamphlet: Detachment. Al-Anon Family Group Headquarters, P.O. Box 182, Madison Sq Sta, NY 10159, 1981
4. Anonymous: Living Sober: some methods AA members have used for not drinking. AA World Services, NY, 1975
5. Alibrandi LA: The folk psychotherapy of Alcoholics Anonymous. in Zimberg S, Wallace J and Blume SB: Practical Approaches to Alcoholism Psychotherapy. Plenum Press, NY, 1978
6. Anderson MS, Savary LM: Passages: a guide for pilgrims of the mind. Collins/Harper & Row, NY, 1972
7. Armstrong T: Transpersnal experience in childhood. J Transpersonal Psychol 16:207-230 1984
8. Assagioli R: Psychosynthesis. Penguin Books, NY, 1976
9. Association for Humanistic Psychology. San Francisco, 1982
10. Ayse Whitney: Chap 9. The spiritual dimension. in Deliman & Smolowe (eds): Holistic Medicine: harmony of body, mind, spirit. Reston/Prentice-Hall, Reston, VA, 1982
11. Bach R: Illusions: The Adventures of a Reluctant Messiah. Dell, NY, 1977
12. Bancroft A: Twentieth Century Mystics and Sages. Henry Regnery Co, Chicago, 1976
13. Bandler R, Grinder J: Chapter 6. Reframing dissociated states: alcoholism, drug abuse, etc. in Reframing: neuro-linguistic programing and the transformation of meaning. Real People Press, Moab, Utah, 1982
14. Barry H III: Chapter 6 Alcohol. In Pradhan SN & Dutta SN: (eds) Drug Abuse: clinical & basic. Mosby, St. Louis, 1977
15. Baskin J: Humor & social change in 20th Century America. Boston Public Library, 1979
16. Bean M: Alcoholics Anonymous. Psychiatric Annals, Insight Publications, NY, Feb & Mar 1975
17. Bean M, Williams KH, Whitfield CL: Alcoholics Anonymous in Whitfield CL et al (ed): The Patient With Alcoholism and Other Drug Problems. in submission for publication, in press.
18. Becker E: The Denial of Death. Free Press/Macmillan, NY, 1973
19. Begental JFT: The existential crisis in intensive psychotherapy. Psychotherapy 2:16:20, 1965
20. Bell RA, Keeley KA, Clements RD et al: Alcoholism, life events and psychiatric impairment. Ann NY Acad Sci 273:467-480, 1976
21. Benson H, et al: Consciousness & healing: shifting currents in contemporary medicine. ReVision 7: 49-93, 1984
22. Bentov I, Bentov M: A Cosmic Book on the Mechanics of Creation. EP Dutton, NY, 1982
23. Bettelheim B: Freud and Man's Soul. Knopf, NY, 1983
24. Black C: Children of alcoholics workshop. Meadows Recovery Center, Gambrils, MD, March 1984
25. Blaike W: Seminar on stress and addictions, Olney, Md 1980
26. Blitz L: Giant molecular cloud complexes in the galaxy. Scientific American 246: 84-194, 1982
27. Boales GF: Toward a cognitive reconceptualization of meditation. J Transpersonal Psychology 10:143-169, 1978
28. Bonny HL, Tansill, RB: Chapter 9. Music Therapy: a legal high. in Waldrof G (ed): Counseling the Addictive Client. School of Scoial Work, U Md, Baltimore, 1977
29. Booth L: Spirituality is reality. Talk given at S E Conf Alc Drug Ab, Atlanta, Dec, 1982
30. Boskin J: Humor and Social Change in Twentieth-Century America. Boston Public Library, 1979
31. Boucouvalas M: Transpersonal psychology: a working outline of the field. J Transpersonal Psychology 12:37-46, 1980
32. Bozarth - Campbell A: Life is Goodbye, Life is Hello: grieving well through all lands of loss. Compcare Publications, Minneapolis, 1984

33. Brallier L: Successfully Managing Stress: transition & transformation. National Nursing Review, Los Altos, A, 1982
34. Branden N: Honoring the Self. Tarcher/Houghton Mifflin, Los Angeles and NY, 1983
35. Branden N: The Psychology of Romantic Love. JP Tarcher, Los Angeles, 1980
36. Branden N: The Disowned Self. Nash, Los Angeles, 1971
37. Brandon D: Zen in the Art of Helping. Delta/Seymour Lawrence/Dell, NY, 1976
38. Brenner C: The Mind in Conflict. Intl Universities Press, NY, 1982
39. Brown B: Between Health and Illness: New Notions on Stress and the Nature of Well Being. Houghton Mifflin, 1984
40. Bry A: Visualization: Directing the Movies of Your Mind. Barnes & Noble, NY, 1978
41. Boorstein S (ed): Transpersonal Psychotherapy. Science and Behavior, Palo Alto, CA 1980
42. Boorstein S: Lightheartedness in psychotherapy. J Transpersonal Psychol 12: 105-115, 1980
43. Bucke RM: Cosmic Consciousness. Dutton, NY, (available from ARE, Box 595, VA Beach, VA 23451) 1969
44. Burns J et al: The Answer to Addiction. Harper & Row, NY, 1975
45. Campbell J: The Hero with a Thousand Faces. Princeton Univ Press, 1949
46. Campbell J: Seven levels of consciousness. Psychology Today 9:76-78, 1975
47. Capra F: The Tao of Physics. Shambala, London, 1975
48. Castaneda C: Journey to Ixtlan. NY Simon & Schuster, 1972
49. Cell E: Learning to Learn from Experience. State Univ. NY Press, Albany, 1984
50. Cermak TL: A Primer on Adult Children of Alcoholics. Health Communictions, Pompano Beach, FL, 1985
51. Cermak TL, Brown S: Interactional group therapy with the adult children of alcoholics. Inernal J Group Psychother 32:375-389, 1982
52. Clinebell HJ: Philosophical - religious factors in the etiology and treatment of alcoholism. Q J Stud Alcohol 24:473-488, 1963
53. Colton H: The Gift of Touch: how physical contact improves communication and health. Seaview/Putnam, NY, 1983
54. Comfort A: Reality and Empathy: Physics, Mind & Science in the 21st Century. State Univ. NY Press, Albany, 1984
55. Coomaraswamy AK: Hinduism & Buddhism, Philosophical Library, NY, 1943
56. Course in Miracles, A. Foundation for Inner Peace, Box 635, 19 Main Street, Tiburon, CA, 94920, 1975
57. Cousins N: Anatomy of an Illness. Norton, NY, 1979
58. Cousins N: The Healing Heart: antidotes to panic & helplessness. Norton, NY, 1973.
59. Cox T: Stress. University Park Press, Baltimore, Md 1979
60. Davis B, Davis GW: The Heart of Healing. Inner Light Books, Fairfax, CA 94930
61. Davis JE, Bloom RL, Whitfield CL: Group therapy in the treatment of alcoholism & chemical dependence. in Whitfield CL et al (eds): The Patient with Alcoholism and Other Drug Problems. in submission for publication, 1985
62. de Caussade J: Abandonment to Divine Providence. (Transl J Beevers) Image Books, Garden City, NY, 1975
63. de la Pena AM: Psychobiology of Cancer: Automization and boredom in health and disease. Praeger Special Studies, NY, 1983
64. Dayringer R: Fair fight for change: a therapeutic use of aggressiveness in couple counseling. J Mar Fam Counseling, April, 1976
65. Deikman AJ: The Observing Self. Beacon Press, Boston, 1982
66. Delehantz EJ: The therapeutic value of the twelve steps of AA. Utah Alcoholism Foundation, Salt Lake City, date not listed
67. Derlega VJ, Chaikin AL: Sharing Intimacy: what we reveal to others and why. Prentice-Hall/Spectrum, Englewood Cliffs, NJ, 1975
68. Dick C: Spirituality in a twelve step program. Conference Corder Productions, Indianapolis, 1982
69. DiLeo FB: Nadir-experiences and transpersonal psychotherapy. presented at 7th An Conf Intl Transpersonal Assoc, Bombay, India, Feb 1982

70. DiLeo FB: Transpersonal Tapestries: excursions in the transpersonal realm (working title) of book in process. Baltimore, 1983-84
71. DiLeo FB: Personal communication, Baltimore, 1983
72. DiLeo FB: A theory of psychic self and object representational systems. J Relig and Psych Research 7: 17-25, 1984
73. Dorr D, Bonner, JW, Ayres, PR: Love and the addicted psysician. J Religion & Health 22: 92-97, 1983
74. Dossey L: Space, Time & Medicine. Shambhala, London, 1932
75. Easwaran E: Meditation: an eight point program. Nilgiri Press, Box 477, Petaluma, Co, 94953, 1977
76. Easwaran E: Dialogue with Death: the spiritual psychology of the Katha Upanishad. Nilgiri Press, Petaluma, Co, 1981
77. Edelwich J, Brodsky A: Burn-out: stages of disillusionment in the helping professions. Human Sciences Press, NY, 1980
78. Edinger E: The Ego and Archetype. Penguin, Baltimore, 1974
79. Elgin D: Voluntary Simplicity. Morrow, NY, 1981
80. Eliot RS, Breo DL: Is it worth dying for? Bantam Books, NY, 1984
81. Engel GL: The need for a new medical model: a challenge for biomedicine. Science 196:129-136, 1977
82. English Language Institute of America: The Living Webster Encyclopedic Dictionary of the English Language. Chicago, 1975
83. Erhard W: The forum sattelite event: a breakthrough in transformation. Washington, DC, February and March, 1984
84. Erickson MH, Rosen S: My Voice will go with you: the teaching tales of Milton H Erickson MD., WW Norton, NY, 1982
85. Fankhauser J: The Power of Affirmations. Coleman Graphics, NY, 1983
86. Ferguson M: The Aquarian Conspiracy: Personal & Social Transformation in the 1980's. St. Martins, NY, 1980
87. Ferguson M - 2: Here Ferguson uses the term "conspiracy", which fits better with the title of her book, referenced above. I have chosen the term "being" because it reflects closely her meaning while avoiding a possibly controversial term.
88. Ferrucci P: What We May Be: techniques for psychological and spiritual growth. Tarcher, Los Angeles, 1982
89. Fillmore C: The highest form of prayer. in A Guide to Spiritual Growth. Unity, Unity Village, MO, 64065, 1982
90. Fine R: A History of Psychoanalysis. Columbia Univ Press, 1979
91. Flores F: Working draft on computers and cognition. Hermenet Inc, San Francisco, 1984
92. Forest J: Interview - Confronting/Spirituality in medical practice. J Christian Healing 5: 26-29, 1983
93. Forer BR: The Therapeutic Value of Crisis. Psycho Rep 13:275-281, 1963
94. Fosdick HE: The Meaning of Prayer. (in The Three Meanings: Prayer, Faith, Service) Garden City Books, NY, 1951
95. Fox M: Original Blessing: a primer in creation spirituality. Bear & Co, Santa Fe, NM, 1983
96. Francuch PD: Principles of Spiritual Hypnosis. Spiritual Advisory Press, Santa Barbara, 1981
97. Francuch PD: Fundamentals of Human Spirituality. Spiritual Advisory Press, Santa Barbara, 1982
98. Friedman MAF: Grief reactions: Implications for treatment of alcoholic clients. Alcoholism Treatment Quarterly 1: 55-69, 1984
99. Friedman M, Thoresen CE, Gill JJ et al: Feasibility of altering type A behavior pattern after myocardial infarction: recurrent coronary prevention project study - methods, baseline results and preliminary findings. Circulation 66:83-92, 1982
100. Free John: The seven stages of life. Laughing Man 4(1): 4-6, 1983a
101. Free John: Diet is not the answer. Laughing Man issue on health, Spring, 1984a
102. Free John: The Paradox of Instruction. Dawn Horse Press, Clear Lake, CA, 1977
103. Free John: Do You Know What Anything Is? Dawn Horse Press, Clear Lake, CA, 1984
104. Free John: Easy Death. Dawn Horse Press, Clearlake, CA, 1983

105. Fremantle F, Trungpa C: Tibetan Book of the Dead. Shambala, Boulder & London, 1975
106. Friel PB: Death & dying. Ann Intern Med 97:767, 1982
107. Fromm E, Suzuki DT, DeMartino R: Zen Buddhism & Psychoanalysis. Harper Colophon Books, NY, 1960
108. Fromm E: Psychoanalysis and Religion. Bantam, NY, 1967
109. Frost R: in Chief Modern Poets of Britian and America. MacMillian, NY, 1970
110. Gabbard GO, Twemlow SW: Explanatory hypothesis for near-death experiences. ReVision 4:68-71, 1981
111. Galanter M: Religious influence & the etiology of sbustance abuse. in Gottheil E, Douley KA, Skoloda TE, et al (eds): Etiologic Aspects of Alcohol & Drug Abuse, Charles C Thomas, Springfield, 1983
112. Gallup G: Adventures in Immortality. McGraw-Hill, 1982
113. Garfield PL: Creative Dreaming. Simon & Schuster, NY, 1974
114. Gawain S: Creative Visualization. Whatever Publishing, Mill Valley, CA, 1978
115. Gendlin ET: Focusing. Everest House, NY, 1978
116. Gilchrist A: Life of William Blake. MacMillan, Lond, 1963
117. Gilman AG, Goodman LS, Gilman A: The Pharmacological Basis of Therapeutics, 6th Ed. Macmillan, NY, 1980
118. Girdano D, Everly G: Controlling Stress & Tension: a holistic approach. Prentice Hall, Englewood Cliffs, 1979
119. Gitlow S: Chap 1 in Gitlow SE & Peyser HS: Alcoholism: a Practical Treatment Guide. Grune & Stratton, NY, 1980
120. Gitlow SE, Peyser HS: Alcoholism: a Practical Treatment Guide. Grune & Stratton, NY, 1980
121. Glasser W: Stations of the Mind. Harper & Row, NY, 1981
122. Glasser W: Positive Addiction. Harper & Row, NY, 1976
123. Glasser W: The basic concepts of reality therapy (the "blue chart"). Wm Glasser Institute for Reality Therapy, Los Angeles, revised Jan 1980
124. Goldberg P: The Intuitive Edge: Understanding and developing intuition. JP Tarcher, Los Angeles, 1984
125. Goldstein J: The Experience of Insight: a simple and direct guide to Buddhist meditation. Shambala, Boulder, 1976
126. Goleman D: The Varieties of the Meditative Experience. Dutton, NY, 1977
127. Goleman D: Meditation and consciousness. Amer J Psycho Ther 30:41-54, 1976
128. Gordon D: Therapeutic Metaphor: helping others through the looking glass. Meta Publications, Cupertino, CA, 1978
129. Gorsky TT, Miller M: Relapse: the family's involvement. Focus on Family Nov/Dec, Health Communications, Hollywood, Fla, 1983
130. Graham B: Prayer (pamphlet, radio message no 50, Box 779, Minneapolis, 55440) 1982
131. Grateful Members: The Twelve Steps for Everyone. Compcare Publications, Minneapolis, 1977
132. Gravitz H, Bowden JD: Guide to Recovery: a book for adult children f alcoholics. Learning Publications, Holmes Beach, FL, 1985
133. Green A: The integral yoga of Sri Aurobindo. Synthesis, San Francisco, 1978
134. Green EE, Green AM: On the meaning of transpersonal: some metaphysical perspectives. J Transpersonal Psychology 3:27-46, 1971
135. Green E, Green A: Beyond Biofeedback. Delacourte, NY, 1977
136. Groeschel BJ: Spiritual Passages: the psychology f spiritual development. Crossroad, NY, 1984
137. Grof S: Theoretical and empirical basis of transpersonal psychology & psychotherapy: observations from LSD research. J Tanspersonal Psychol 5:15-51, 1973
138. Grof S, Halifa J: The Human Encounter with Death. EP Dutton, NY, 1977
139. Grof S: Realms of the Human Unconscious: Observation from LSD Research. The Viking Press, NY, 1975
140. Grof S: East & West: ancient wisdom and modern science. J Transpersonal Psychology 15:1-36, 1983
141. Grof S: LSD Psychotherapy. Hunter House, Pomona, Ca, 1980-a
142. Grof S: Taped discussion on Cosmology. Esalen, Big Sur, Ca, 1980-b

143. Grof S, Grof C: Beyond Death. Thames and Hudson, London, 1980-c
144. Grof S (ed): Ancient Wisdom & Modern Science. SUNY Press, Albany, 1984
145. Guillaumont A et al (Transl): The gospel according to Thomas. Harper & Row, NY, 1959
146. Hall CS, Nordby VJ: A Primer of Jungian Psychology. Mentor, New American Library, NY, 1973
147. Hall MP: Visions and the Metaphysical Experience. cited in Ram Dass, 1974-83
148. Hall N: The Moon and the Virgin: reflections on the archytypal feminine. Harper Colophon, NY, 1980
149. Hallesby O: Prayer. Augsburg, Minneapolis, 1931 & 1975
150. Halpern HM: How to break your addiction to a person. McGraw-Hill, NY, 1982
151. Halpern S, Savatz L: Sound Health: the music and sounds that make us whole. Harper & Row, San Francisco, 1985
152. Hampden-Turner C: Maps of the Mind: charts & concepts of the mind and its labyrinths. Collier-Macmillan, NY, 1982
153. Happold FC: Mysticism: a study and an anthology. Penguin, NY, 1970
154. Harding ME: The i and the not i: a study in the development of consciousness. Bollingen, Princeton, 1965
155. Hazelden pamphlet: Tough Love. Hazelden, Center City, Minn, 1983
156 Hazelden: Christian Education Materials for Youth & Families: Alcohol & Drugs. Hazelden, Center City, Minn, 1983
157. Henderson B: Self-help books emphasizing transpersonal psychology: are they ethical? J Transpersonal Psychology 15: 169-171, 1983
158. Hesse H: Siddhartha. New Directions & Bantam, NY, 1951
159. Hillman J: A note on story. Parabola: the Journal of Myth & Meaning 4:43-45, 1979
160. Hillman J: Puer's wounds & Ulysse's scar. Dromenon 3:13-27, 1981
161. Holmes A: Listening to God - effective answer to prayer. Talk given at Koinonia, Baltimore, 19 May, 1984
162. Hora T: Existential Metapsychiatry. Seabury Press, NY, 1977
163. Houston J: Life-Force: the Psycho-Historical Recovery of the Self. Delacourte Press, NY, 1980
164. Huxley A: The Perennial Philosophy. Harper & Row, NY, 1945 & 1971
165. International Assoc of Near-Death Studies (IANDS), Storrs, Conn (publishe journal Anabiosis)
166. Jaffe DT, Bresler DE: The use of guided imagery as an adjunct to medical diagnosis and treatment. J Humanistic Psychol 20:45-59, 1980
167. James W: The Varieties of Religious Experience. Penguin, NY, 1982
168 Jampolsky GG: Love is Letting Go of Fear. Bantam Books, NY, 1981
169. Jampolsky GG: Symposium on "Love is letting go of fear." Johns Hopkins Univ, Baltimore, Fall, 1982
170. Jampolsky GG: Article on his life and beliefs, Success Magazine, Sept, 1982
171. Jampolsky GG: Teach Only Love: the seven principles of attitudinal healing. Bantam, NY, 1983
172. Johari H: Leela: Game of Knowledge. Routledge & Kegan Paul, London, 1980
173. John M: The Tip of the Iceberg. Beach Hill Publ, Dublin, NH, 1983
174. Johnson D: Spiral of Growth. Quest, Wheaton, 1980
175. Jourard SM: The Transparent Self. Revised edition. Van Nostrand, NY, 1971
176. Joy WB: Joy's Way: A Map for the Transformational Journey: an introduction to the potentials for healing with body energies. Tarcher, Los Angeles, 1979
177. Jung CG: The Bill W Carl Jung letters. AA Grapevine, Jan 1968, Reprinted Nov 1974
178. Jung CG: The Undiscovered Self. Mentor, NY, 1957
179. Jung CG: Memories, Dreams & Reflections. (A Jaffe ed, Transl Winston) Vintage, Random House, NY, 1965
180. Jung CG: Psychological Commentary on "The Tibetan Book of the Great Liberation." Vol. 11 (2nd ed) pp 475-526, of Collected words, Bollingen series XX, 1969
181. Kadowaki JK: Zen and the Bible: a priests experience. Routledge & Kegan Paul, London & Boston, 1980

182. Kalf M: The negation of ego in Tibetan Buddhism & Jungian psychology. J. Transpersonal Psychology 15: 103-124, 1983
183. Kapleau P (ed): The Three Pillars of Zen. Beacon Press, Boston, 1965
184. Kaufman BN: To Love is To Be Happy With. Fawcett/Crest Ballantine, NY, 1977
185. Kaufman G: Shame - the Power of Caring. Schenkman Publishing Co, Cambridge, MA 1980
186. Kaufman G, Raphael L: The Dynamics of Power: building a competent self. Schenkman Publishing Co, Cambridge, MA 1983
187. Keen S: The Passionate Life: Stages of Loving. Harper & Row, NY, 1983
188. Kellerman J: Grief: a basic reaction to alcoholism. Hazelden pamphlet, Center City, Minn
189. Kernberg OF: The self, ego, affects and drives. J Amer Psychoanalytic Assoc 30: 893-917, 1982
190. Keyes K: Handbook to Higher Consciousness. DeVorss, Marina del Rey, Ca, 1975
191. Khalsa GS, Briggs G: Stress Away: the way to relax. Gage, Toronto, 1979
192. King ML: Strength to Love. Fortress Press, 1963
193. King TM, Salmon, JF (eds): Teilhard and the Unity of Knowledge: the Georgetown University Centennial Symposium. Paulist Press, NY, 1983
194. Kohut H: The Analysis of the Self: a systematic approach to the psychoanalytic treatment of narcissistic personality disorders. Int Univ Press, NY, 1981
195. Korzybski A: Science & Sanity. Country Life Press, Garden City, NY, 1948
196. Kritsberg W: Gifts: advanced skills for alcoholism counselors. Health Communications Inc, Hollywood, Florida, 1983
197. Krishnamurti J: Krishnamurti's Notebook. Harper & Row, NY, 1976
198. Kubler-Ross E: Death - The Final Stage of Growth. Prentice-Hall, Englewood Cliffs, 1975
199. Kubler-Ross E: from notes taken at her talk "Life, death and transition", Healing in Our Time: a Symposium on the Dynamics of Healing, Washington DC, 22 Oct 1982
200. Kung H: Does God Exist? Doubleday, Garden City, NY 1978
201. Kurtz E: Not-God: A History of Alcoholics Anonymous. Hazelden Educational Services, Center City, Minn, 1979
202. Kurtz E: The spirituality of Alcoholics Anonymous. Talk given at the American Medical Society on Alcoholism meeting, Houston, April, 1983-a
203. Kurtz E: Alcoholics Anonymous and the professional. Talk given at Rutgers Summer School on Alcohol Studies, (manuscript in process), June 1983-b
204. Kurtz E: Why AA Works: The intellectual significance of Alcoholic Anonymous. J Stud Alcohol 43: 38-80, 1982
205. Kushner HS: When Bad Things Happen to Good People. Schocken Books & Avon Books, NY, 1981 & 1983
206. Laski M: Ecstasy. Crescent Press, London, 1961
207. Lacoursiere R: The Life Cycle of Groups: Group developmental stage theory. Human Sciences Press, NY, 1980
208. Lavine TZ: From Socrates to Satre: the philosophic quest. Bantam, NY, 1984
209. LeBoeuf M: Imagineering: How to Profit from your Creative Powers. McGraw-Hill, NY, 1982
210. Leech K: YouthQuake: spirituality and the growth of a counter-culture. Sphere Books Ltd. London, 1976
211. Leite E: Detachment - the art of letting go while living with an alcoholic. Johnson Institute, Minneapolis, Minn, 1980
212. Leonard GB: The Transformation: a Guide to the Inevitable Changes in Humankind. Delacorte press, NY, 1972
213. LeShan L: The Medium, the Mystic and Physicist. An Esalen Book, Viking Press, NY, 1974
214. Levine S: Who Dies? An Investigation of Conscious Living & Conscious Dying. Anchor/Doubleday, NY, 1982
215. Levine S: Meeting at the Edge. Anchor Doubleday, Garden City, NY, 1984
216. Litman GK: Stress, affect and craving in alcoholics. Quart J Stud Alcohol 35: 131-146, 1974
217. Litvak S: Unstress yourself: strategies for effective stress control. Ross-Erikson, Santa Barbara, 1980
218. Locke SE and Hornig-Rohan M: Mind and Immunity: Behavioral Immunobiology. an annotated bibliography 1976-1982. Institute for Advancement of Health, NY, 1983

219. Loye D: The Sphinx and the Rainbow: brain, mind and future vision. New Science Library, Shambhala, Boulder, 1983
220. Mahler MS: The Psychological Birth of the Human Infant. Basic Books, NY, 1975
221. Mahler MS, McDevitt JB: Thoughts on the emergence of the sense of self, with particular emphasis on the body self. J Amer Psychonaly Assoc 30:827-847, 1982
222. Marsh C: A framework for describing subjective states of consciousness. in Zinberg NE (ed): Alternate States of Consciousness. Free Press/Macmillan, NY, 1977
223. Martin J: Lecture on alcoholism, Baltimore, 1982
224. Maslow AH: Toward a Psychology of Being. Van Nostrand, Princeton, NJ, 1962 (revised 1968)
225. Maslow AH: The Farther Reaches of Human Nature. Viking, NY, 1971
226. Maslow AH: Religions, Values, and Peak-Experiences. Ohio State Univ Press, Columbus, 1964
227. Materi M: Assertiveness training: a catalyst for behavior change. Alcohol Health & Research World 1: 23-26, 1977
228. May G: Simply Sane: stop fixing yourself and start really living. Paulist Press, NY
229. McKeon B: Spirituality of Recovery. Conference Corder Productions, Indianapolis, 1983
230. Meadow MJ, Ajaya S, Bregman L et al: Spiritual and transpersonal aspects of altered states of consciousness: a symposium report. J Transpersonal Psychology, 11:141-160, 1979
231. Meher Baba: God Speaks. (2nd ed) Dodd, Mean & Co., NY, 1973
232. Metzner R: Ten classical metaphors of self-transformation. J Transpersonal Psychology 12:47-62, 1980
233. Miller MS: Child Stress, Understanding and Answering Stress Signals of Infants, Children and Teenagers. Doubleday, NY, 1981
234. Mills JW: Coping with stress: a guide to living. John Wiley, NY, 1982
235. Mitchell Joni: Song "Amelia" from her album Hejira, Asylum, 1976
236. Mogar RE: Current status and future trends in psychedelic research. J Humanistic Psychol, Fall p. 147-166, 1965
237. Moody RA: Life after Life. Bantam, NY, 1976
238. Moody RA: Laugh After Laugh: the healing power of humor. Headwaters Press, Staunton, Va, 1978
239. Montague A: Touching. 2nd ed, Harper, NY, 1978
240. Mora G: Chap 1 Historical & theoretical trends in psychiatry. in Comprehensive Textbook of Psyhciatry/III. Kaplan HJ, Freedman AM, Sadock BJ (eds), Baltimore, Williams & Wilkins, 1980
241. Morrison D: A Glossary of Sanscrit from the Spiritual Tradition of India. Nilgiri Press, Box 477, Petaluma, Ca, 94953, 1970
242. Morrison R: Principles of transpersonal psychology. Talk given at workshop "Spirituality in Our Time", Koinonia, Baltimore, February 11, 1984
243. Moss R: The I that is We. Celestial Arts, Millbrae, Ca 1981
244. Motoyama H: Theories of the Chakras: Bridge to Higher Consciousness. Quest, Wheaton IL, 1981
245. Motoyama H, Brown R: Science and the Evolution of Consciousness. Autumn Press, Brookline, MA & Random House, 1978
246. Moustakas CE: Loneliness. Spectrum/Prentice Hall, Englewood Cliffs, 1961
247. Muktananda S: Where Are You Going? a guide to the spiritual journey. Gurndev Siddah Peethm, Ganeshpuri, India; Box 600 So Fallsburg, NY 12779, 1981
248. Muktananda S: A book for the mind. (above address) 1976
249. Muktananda S: I love you. (above address) 1975
250. Muktananda S: Brochure on meditation. (above address) 1980
251. Murphy M, Donovan, S: A bibliography of meditation theory and research, 1931 - 1983
252. Murphy LR: Handling Stress: Current National Institute for Occupation Safety & Health Research. Occupational Health & Safety. Nov - Dec 1983, p 14-17
253. Naisbitt J: Megatrends. Warner Books, 1982
254. Narcotics Anonymous. CARENA Publishing (no city listed), 1982
255. Needleman J: Psychiatry and the sacred. Dromenon 3:3-11, 1981
256. Neumann E: The Origins and History of Consciousness. (2nd ed) Bollingen Series XLII, Princeton University Press, 1971
257. Newton C: The soul voice. Talk given in Baltimore, 1981

258. Nuernberger P: Freedom from stress: a holistic approach. Himalyan Intnl Institute, Honesdale, PA, 1981
259. O'Connell WE: Freudian humor: the eupsychia of everyday life. in Chapman A, Foot H (eds): Humor & Laughter: Theory, Research & Applications. Wiley, London, 1976
260. Olsouk: The Art of Hanging Loose in an Uptight World. Fawcet Crest, Greenwich, 1974
261. Orman M: Course on Stress Management, Mercy Hospital, Baltimore, June 1982
262. Orman M: Personal communication, Baltimore, 1984
263. Ornish D, Scherwitz LW, Doody RS, et al: Effects of stress management training and dietary changes in treating ischemic heart disease. JAMA 249: 54-59, 1983
264. Ornstein RE (ed): The Nature of Human Consciousness: a book of readings. Freeman, San Francisco, 1973
265. Ornstein RE: The Psychology of Consciousness. Freeman, San Francisco, 1972
266. Pachuta DM: The Mastery of Health & Well Being. Course given in Baltimore, April-June, 1982
267. Pagels E: The Gnostic Gospels. Random House, NY, 1979
268. Pattison M, Kaufman E: Encyclopedic Handbook of Alcoholism. Gardner Press, NY, 1982
269. Peck MS: The Road Less Traveled: a new psychology of love, traditional values & spiritual growth. Touchstone/Simon & Schuster, NY, 1978
270. Peck MS: People of the Lie: the hope for healing human evil. Simon & Schuster, NY, 1983
271. Perls F: Gestalt Therapy Verbatim. Bantam, NY, 1971
272. Pelletier KR: Mind as Healer, Mind as Slayer: a holistic approach to preventing stress disorders. Delta, NY, 1977
273. Peter LJ, Dana B: The Laughter Prescription. Ballantine, NY, 1982
274. Pittenger WN: The Word Incarnate. Jas Nisbet & Co, Digswell Place, 1959
275. Pitts E: Organizational Enlivenment. Talk given at workshop "Spirituality in Out Time", Koinonia, Baltimore, Feb. 11, 1984
276. Plato, in Happold, FC: Mysticism: a study and an anthology. Penguin, NY, 1970
277. Pohorecky LA: The interaction of alcohol and stress: a review. Neuroscience & Biobehav Rev 5: 209-229, 1981
278. Pohorecky LA, Brick J: Stress and Alcohol Use. Elsevier Biomedical, NY, 1983
279. Powell J: Unconditional Love. Argus Communications, Allen, TX, 1978
280. Prather H: There is a Place Where You Are Not Alone. Dolphin/Doubleday, Garden City, NY 1980
281. Prather H: Notes to Myself: my struggle to become a person. Bantam, NY, 1976
282. Prather H: A Book of Games: a course on spiritual play. Doubleday, NY, 1981
263. Progoff I: At a Journal Workshop. Dialogue House Library, NY, 1975
284. Progoff I: Process Meditation. Dialogue House Library, NY, 1980
285. Puryear HB, Thurston MA: Meditation and the Mind of Man. Revised Ed & ARE Press, VA Beach, 1982
286. Quell G, Stauffer, E: Love. in Coates JR (ed & transl) Bible Key Words (Vol 1), Harper, NY, 1951
287. Quinn W: Ananda K Coomaraswamy on the philosophia perennis. ReVision. Summer/Fall, 1979, p 18-27
288. Rahner K, Metz JB: The Courage to Pray. Crossroad, NY, 1981
289. Ram Dass, Gorman P: How Can I Help? Stories and reflections on service. A Knopf, NY, 1985
290. Ram Dass: Journey of Awakening: a meditator's guidebook. Bantam, NY, 1978
291. Ram Dass, Levine S: Grist for the Mill. Unity Press, Santa Cruz, CA, 1976
292. Ram Dass: Tape series of talks, 1974-83. Hanuman Foundation, Santa Cruz, Ca 95061
293. Ram Dass: The Only Dance There Is. Anchor/Doubleday, NY, 1974
294. Ram Dass, Gorman P, et al: Helping Out: Service, social action and spiritual growth. Seminar at Omega Institute, Box 571, Lebanon Springs, NY, 12114 June, 1983
295. Rangell L: The self in psychoanalytic theory. J Amer Psychoanalytic Assoc, 30: 863 - 891, 1982
296. Ray S: Loving Relationships. Celestial Arts. 231 Adrian Road, Millbrae, CA 94030, 1980
297. Reiser DE, Rosen DH: Medicine as a Human Experience. Univ Park Press, Baltimore, 1984

298. Rhead J: Spiritual dimensions of family therapy. Talk presented at Seventh Annual Family Therapy Network Symposium, Washington DC, March, 1984
299. Ring K: Life at Death: a scientific investigation of the near-death experience. Coward, McCann & Geoghenan Pub, NY, 1980
300. Roberts T: Beyond self-actualization. ReVision 1 : 42-46, 1978
301. Roessler SJ: The role of spiritual values in the recovery of alcoholics. Doctoral dissertation, Wesley Theological Seminary, Washington, DC, 1982
302. Romanyshyn RD: On the metaphorical characters of psychological life. ReVision p. 15-19, Spring 1981
303. Royce JE: Chapter 18. Spiritual aspects. in Royce JE: Alcohol Problems and Alcoholism. Free Press/Macmillan, NY, 1981
304. Ryan RS, Tavis JW: Wellness Workbook. Ten Speed Press, Berkeley, 1981
305. Sabom M: Recollections of Death. Harper & Row, NY, 1983
306. Sadava SW, Thistle R, Forsyth R: Stress, escapism & patterns of alcohol and drug use. J Stud Alcohol 39:725-736, 1978
307. Samuels M, Samuels N: Seeing with the Mind's Eye: the history, techniques & uses of visualization. Random House, NY, 1975
308. Sanford J: Dreams: God's Forgotten Language. Crossroads, NY, 1982
309. Sanford J: The Kingdom Within. Lippincott, NY, 1979
310. Sanford J: Evil - The Shadow Side of Reality. Crossroads, NY, 1981
311. Sannella L: Kundalini - Psychosis or Transcendence? HS Dakin Co, San Francisco, 1977
312. Schoun F: The Transcendent Unity of Religions. Harper & Row, NY, 1976
313. Schreder R: in a course on Stress Management & Spirituality during Recovery. Co-taught with Whitfield CL, Univ Md at Baltimore, Nov-Dec, 1982
314. Schwartz J: Letting Go of Stress. Pinnacle, NY, 1982
315. Search for spiritual experience. AA Grapevine, 2-16, April, AA Central Office, NY, 1978
316. Seashore C, Malcolm H: Learning to love your core of rot. Social Change (from NTL) 9: 8-10, 1979
317. Sehnert KW: Stress/unstress. Augsburg, Minneapolis, 1981
318. Seikh AA: Death before life. Talk given at conference on Power of Imagination: uses & imagery in the healing arts. Washington, DC, 12 May, 1983
319. Selye H: Stress without Distress. Lippincott, NY, 1974
320. Shaef AW: Women's Reality. Winston Press, Minneapolis, 1981
321. Shah I: Nasrudin: the pleasantries of the incredible mulla. EP Dutton, NY, 1971
322. Sharman JE: Exercise - the neglected medicine. Ala J Med Sci 16:56-58, 1979
323. Sherman H: How to Use the Power of Prayer. Crest Fawcett, Greenwhich, 1958
324. Sharpe R, Lewis D: Thrive on Stress. Warner, NY, 1978
325. Sheldrake R: A New Science of Life: the hypothesis of formative causation. Tarcher, Los Angeles, 1982
326. Shore JJ: Use of paradox in the treatment of alcoholism. Health and Social Work 6: 11-20, 1981
327. Siegel A: The problem of problems. ReVision 4:32 - 39, 1981
328. Silverman J: Eight lectures on a course in miracles. Dolphin Tapes, Box 11, Big Sur, CA 93920, 1980
329. Simonton OC, Matthews-Simonton S, Creighton J: Getting Well Again. JP Tarcher, Los Angeles, 1978
330. Simonton SM: The Healing Family. Bantam Books, NY, 1984
331 Sirota G: Love Food: gourmet recipes for holistic health. Living Loving Learning Center, Topanga, CA 1984
332. Siu RGH: The Tao of Science: an essay on Western Knowledge & Eastern wisdom. MIT Press, Cambridge, 1957
333. Siu RGH: Ch'i: A Neo-Taoist Approach to Life. MIT Press, Cambridge & London, 1974
334. Small J: Becoming Naturally Therapeutic. Eupsychian Press, 950 Roadrunner Rd, Austin, TX 78746, 1981
335. Small J: Healing the inner child through guided imagery. Taped talk, Access, Indianapolis, 1983

336. Small J: Transformers: the Therapists of the Future. Eupsychian Press, Austin, TX, 1982
337. Small AP: Mutiny on the Beagle (evolution & onsciousness). ReVision 7:18-34, 1984
338. Smith H: The Religious of Man. Harper & Row, NY, 1958
339. Smith H: Forgotten Truth. Harper & Row, NY, 1976
340. Sontag S: Illness as a Metaphor. Vintage, NY, 1979
341. Starratt AB: Your Self, My Self & The Self of the Universe. Stemmer House, Owings Mills, MD, 1979
342. St John of the Cross: Dark Night of the Soul. New York, Image Books, 1959
343. Steinberg P, Martin B: Workshop tapes on A Course in Miracles. Scottsdale, AZ, 1981
344. Sterling P, Eyer J: Biological basis of stress-related mortality. Soc Sci Med 15: 1-42, 1981
345. Stewart RL: Psychoanalysis and Psychoanalytic Psychotherapy. in Kaplan et al (eds): Comprehensive Textbook f Psychiatry, Williams & Wilkins, Baltimore, MD, 1980
346. Sun P: Lecture on spirituality given at the Institute for the Art & Science of Living, Atlanta, 1980
347. Sutich AJ: Some consideration regarding transpersonal psychology. J Transpersonal Psychology 1 : 11 - 20, 1969
348. Sutich AJ: Transpersonal therapy. J Transpersonal Psychology 5:1-6, 1973
349. Sutich AJ: The emergence of a transpersonal orientation: a personal account. J Transpersonal Psychology 8: 5 - 19, 1976
350. Suzuki DT: The Essentials of Zen Buddhism (ed by B. Phillips) E P Dutton, NY, 1962
351. Swedenborg E: Heaven and Hell. Swedenborg Found, NY, 1976
352. Tanner F: The Mystery Teachings in World Religions. Quest, Wheaton, IL, 1973
353. Tart CT: Transpersonal Psychologies. Harper & Row, NY, 1975
354. Tart CT: States of Consciousness. Dutton, NY, 1975
355. Taub-Bynum EB: The Family Unconscious. Quest, Wheaton, IL, 1984
356. Teresa of Avila: Vol 2 - The Collected Works of. (transl O Rodriguez & K Kavanangh) Institute of Carmetlite Studies, Washington, 1980
357. Teilhard de Chardin P: The Phenomenon of Man. Harper & Row, NY, 1945
358. Thera Nyanaponika: The Heart of Buddhist Meditation. Samuel Weiser, NY, 1962
359. Thiebout HM: Conversion as a psychological phenomenon. Pamphlet reprint from a 1944 talk, National Council on Alcoholism, 733 Park Avenue, NY 10017
360. Thiebout HM: The ego factors in surrender in alcoholism. Quart J Stud Alcohol 15:610-621, 1954 (Reprint available Hazelden, Center City, Minn)
361. Thompson C, Mazer M, Witenberg E: An Outline of Psychoanalysis. Revised ed, Modern Library, NY, 1955
362. Thurston M: Discovering your Soul's Purpose, ARE, VA Beach, 1984
363. Thurston MA: Experiments in Practical Spirituality. ARE Press, VA Beach, 1980
364. Thurston MA: Experiments in a Search for God. ARE Press, VA Beach, 1980
366. Toffler A: The Third Wave. Bantam, NY, 1980
367. Truax CB, Carkhuff RR: Toward Effective Counseling & Psychotherapy. Aldine, Chicago, 1967
368. Trungpa C: Cutting Through Spiritual Materialism. Shambhala, Boulder, 1973
369. Twelve Steps and Twelve Traditions. Alcoholics Anonymous World Services, NY 1953
Twenty-four Hours a Day. Hazelden, Center City, MN, 1975
370. Twerski AJ: Self-discovery in Recovery. Hazelden, Center City, MN, 1984
371. Unity, Unity Village, MO 64065
372. Vaillant GE: Adaptation to Life. Little, Brown, NY, 1977
373. Valle RS, von Eckartsberg R: The Metaphors of Consciousness. Plenum, NY, 1981
374. Vaughan F: Awakening Intuition. Anchor/Doubleday, NY, 1979
375. Vaughan F: Workshop on awakening intuition. Johns Hopkins U, Baltimore, April, 1983
376. Vaughan F: The transpersonal perspective: a personal overview. J Transpersonal Psychology 14:37-45, 1982
377. Vaughan F: Transpersonal dimensions of psychotherapy. ReVision 2:26-29, 1979
378. Vaughan F: The Transpersonal perspective. in Grof (ed): Ancient Wisdom & Modern Science. SUNY Press, Albany, 1984
379. Vissell B, Vissell J: The Shared Heart: relationship initiations & celebrations. Ramira

Publishing, Aptos, CA, 1984
380. Wallace J: Chapter 7 Behavioral - modification methods as adjuncts to psychotherapy. in Zimberg S Wallace J & Blume SB (eds): Practical Approaches to Alcoholism Psychotherapy. P 99-117, Plenum, NY, 1978
381. Walsh RN, Vaughan F: Beyond Ego: Transpersonal Dimensions in Psychology. Tarcher, Los Angeles, 1980
382. Walsh R: A model for viewing meditation research. J Transpersonal Psychology 14:69-84, 1982
383. Wapnick K: Forgiveness & Jesus. Coleman Publ Farmingdale NY 1983
384. Wapnick K: Glossary-Index for "A Course in Miracles." Foundation for A Course in Miracles, 30 Eastern Dr, Ardsley, NY, 10502, 1982
385. Ward M: The Brilliant Function of Pain. Optimus Books, NY, 1977
386. Washburn MC: Observations relevant to a unified theory of meditation. J Transpersonal Psychology 10:45-65, 1978
387. Watts AW: Beyond Theology: The Art of Godmanship. Vintage/Random House, NY, 1973
388. Watts AW: The Supreme Identity. Pantheon Books, NY 1965
389. Watts A: The Essence of Alan Watts. (Published posthumously) The Basic Philosophy in Nine Illustrated Volumes. Celestial Arts, Millbrae, Ca, 1975
390. Watts AW: Zen Buddhism and psychiatry. Talk given at U Maryland School of Medicine, Psychiatric Institute, 1973
391. Watts AW: Behold the Spirit. Vintage/Random House, NY, 1971
392. Weber R: On compassion: an interview with his holiness the Dalae Lama, ReVision, Fall/Winter 1981, p 49 - 54
393. Wegsheider S: Another Chance: Hope & Health for the Alcoholic Family. Science & Behavior Books, Palo Alto, Ca, 1981
394. Weil A: The Marriage of the Sun and Moon. Houghton Mifflin, Boston, 1980
395. Weil AT: The Natural Mind. Houghton Mifflin, Boston, 1973
396. Weil A: Health & Healing: Understanding Conventional and Alternative Medicine. Houghton Mifflin, NY 1984
397. Welwood J: Meditation and the Unconscious. J Transpersonal Psychology 9:1-26, 1977
398. Welwood J (ed): Awakening the Heart: East/West approaches to psychotherapy and the healing relationship. New Science Library, Shambhala, Boulder, 1983
399. Welwood J: Befriending emotion: self-knowledge and transformation. J Transpersonal Psychology 11:141-160, 1979
400. Wegsheider-Cruse S: Choice-Making: for co-dependents, adult children & spirituality seekers. Health Communications, Pompano Beach, FL, 1985
401. Westermeyer J, Walzer V: Drug usage: an alternative to religion? Dis Nerv System 36:492-495, 1975
402. White LW: Recovery from alcoholism: transpersonal dimensions. J Transpersonal Psychology 2:117-127, 1979
403. Whitfield CL: Alcoholism. in Conn HF(ed): Conn's Current Therapy, WB Saunders, Phila, 1981
404. Whitfield CL: Followup treatment of alcoholism. in Whitfield CL et al (eds) The Patient with Alcoholism & Other Drug Problems. in submission for publication, in press for 1984a
405. Whitfield CL: Unpublished survey of 20 recovering alcoholics. Baltimore, 1982
406. Whitfield CL: Co-alcoholism: recognizing a treatable illness. Family and Community Health Vol 7, Summer 1984
407. Whitfield CL: Outpatient management of the alcoholic patient. Psychiatric Annals 12:447-458, 1982
408. Whitfield CL et al: Detoxification of 1,024 alcoholics without psychoactive drugs. JAMA 239:1409-1410, 1978 and letter response 241:2597-2598, 1979
409. Whitfield CL: Treatment of alcohol withdrawal without drugs in Masserman J (ed): Current Psychiatric Therapies, Grune & Stratton, 1980a
410. Whitfield CL: Non-drug detoxification in Fann WE et al (eds) Phenomenology and Treatment of Alcoholism, Spectrum Medical & Scientific, NY, 1980b
411. Whitfield CL, Liepman MR, Williams KH: The Patient with Alcoholism and Other Drug Problems. in submission for publication, in press for 1984b

412. Whitfield CL, Schreder R: Course on Stress Management & Spirituality during Recovery. University of Maryland at Baltimore, Nov - Dec, 1982
413. Whitfield CL: Alcoholism, Other Drug Misuse & Violence: an overview. in Hertzberg L, Ostrum G, Field J (eds): Handbook of Violence, Vol 1, Spectrum, NY, 1985
414. Whitfield CL: Denial in Alcoholism & Chemical Dependence: Recognition and Management. in preparation for publication, 1985b
415. Whitfield CL, Davis JE, Barker RL: Chap 21. Alcoholism in Barker, Burron & Zieve (eds) Principles of Ambulatory Medicine. 2nd ed, Williams & Wilkins, Baltimore, 1985
416. Wilber K: The Holographic Paradigm & Other Paradoxes: exploring the leading edge of science. Shambhala, London, 1982
417. Wilber K: Up from Eden. Anchor Press/Doubleday, Garden City, NY, 1981
418. Wilber K: No Boundary. Shambhala, London, 1979
419. Wilber K: Ontogenetic development: two fundamental patterns. J Transpersonal Psychol 13:33-58, 1981
420. Wilber K: Eye to eye. ReVision 2:3-25, 1979-b
421. Wilber K: Psychology perennis: the spectrum of consciousness. J Transpersonal Psychol 7:105-133, 1975
422. Wilber K: The Spectrum of Consciousness. Quest/Theosophical Publ, Wheaton, IL, 1977
423. Wilber K: The Atman Project: a transpersonal view of human development. Quest/Theosophical Publ, Wheaton, Il, 1980
424. Wilber K: The pre/trans fallacy: an essay distringuishing transcendence from regression. ReVision Fall 1980-a, p 51-72
425. Wilber K: The developmental spectrum and psychopathology: Part I, stages & types of pathology. J Transpersonal Psycho 16:75-118, 1984
426. Wilber K: The developmental spectrum and psychopathology: Part II, Treatment modalities. J. Transpersonal Psychol 16:137-166, 1984
427. Wilber K: A developmental view of consciousness, J Transpersonal Psychol 2:1-21, 1979-c
428. Wilber K: A Sociable God: a brief introduction to a transcendental sociology. New Press/McGraw-Hill, NY, 1983-a
429 Wilber K: Eye to Eye: the quest for the new paradigm. Anchor/Doubleday, Garden City, NY, 1983-b
430. Wilber K (ed): Quantium Questions: mystcal writings of the grest physicists. Shambhala, Boulder, 1984
431. Williams SK: Jungian-Senoi Dreamwork Manual. New revised expanded edition. Journey Press, Berkeley, 1980
432. Wolfe S: Reference cited in talk on alcoholism counseling. Baltimore, 1975
433. Yogananda P: How You Can Talk with God. Self-Relization Fellowship, Los Angeles, 1957
434. York D, Wachtel, T: ToughLove. Bantam Books, NY, 1983
435. Zinberg NE (ed): Alternate States of Consciousness. Free Press/Macmillan, NY 1977
436. Zink M: Recovery: turning negatives into positives. CompCare pamphlet, date unknown
437. Zukav G: The Dancing Wu Li Masters: an overview of the new physics. Bantam, NY, 1979

The journey to God is merely the reawakening of the knowledge of where you are always, and what you are forever. It is a journey without distance to a goal that has never changed.

Teach only love, for that is what you are.

A Course In Miracles

One day at a time.

Twelve Step Programs